The Principal's Playbook:

Tackling School Improvement

Nancy Protheroe

ERS

Because research and information make the difference.

Educational Research Service
1001 North Fairfax Street, Suite 500 • Alexandria, VA 22314
Phone: 703-243-2100 • Toll Free: 800-791-9308
Fax: 703-243-1985 • Toll Free: 800-791-9309
Email: ers@ers.org • Web site: www.ers.org

Because research and information make the difference.

Educational Research Service

1001 North Fairfax Street, Suite 500, Alexandria, VA 22314
Tel: 703-243-2100 or 800-791-9308
Fax: 703-243-1985 or 800-791-9309
Email: ers@ers.org • Web site: www.ers.org

Educational Research Service is *the* nonprofit organization providing school leaders with essential research for effective decisions. Founded by the national school management associations, ERS is the school leader's best source for resources and data to build more successful schools. Since 1973, education leaders have utilized the ERS advantage to make the most effective school decisions in both day-to-day operations and long-range planning. Refer to the last page of this publication to learn how you can benefit from the services and resources available through an annual ERS subscription. Or visit us online at www.ers.org for a more complete picture of the wealth of preK-12 research information and tools available through ERS subscriptions and resources.

ERS Founding Organizations:
American Association of School Administrators
American Association of School Personnel Administrators
Association of School Business Officials International
National Association of Elementary School Principals
National Association of Secondary School Principals
National School Public Relations Association

ERS Executive Staff:
John C. Draper, Ed.D., Chief Executive Officer
Katherine A. Behrens, Chief Operating Officer

Author: Nancy Protheroe
Editor: Tracy Pastian
Editorial Assistant: Alyssa Howell
Layout & Design: Susie McKinley and Libby McNulty

The observations and opinions expressed in this monograph are solely those of the authors and do not necessarily represent those of Educational Research Service or any of its founding organizations.

Ordering information: Additional copies of *The Principal's Playbook: Tackling School Improvement* can be purchased at the list price of $30.00 each. ERS School District Subscriber price: $15.00; ERS Individual Subscriber price: $22.50. Quantity discounts available. Add the greater of $4.50 or 10% of total purchase price for shipping and handling. Phone orders accepted with Visa, MasterCard, or American Express. Stock No. 0784. ISBN 978-1-931762-88-5.

Table of Contents

Preparing Your Faculty for Success

by Dr. John Draper

My school was under a severe thunderstorm watch and the weather was turning nasty. It was the kind of day that made every principal nervous. This was no exception. The local fire chief and I were standing in the middle of the high school cafeteria surrounded by several hundred students eating lunch. We both smelled smoke—but the fire alarm hadn't gone off. His men were beginning a hunt for the source of the burning smell. The chief was taking charge.

"You've got to evacuate the building now!" he said with authority. "You need to evacuate until we find the fire." I knew that meant putting over 1,000 students on the football practice field behind the building—with two metal goalposts in their midst to serve as lightning rods.

"Chief, if you say evacuate, we will, but just remember that we are under a severe thunderstorm watch. It's starting to rain, and the wind is picking up. If students get killed in a lightning strike, I just want it to be clear that you ordered us out there."

He paused and I could tell he was wrestling with the situation. After a few moments he looked at me and said, "You're the principal. It's your decision." And it was.

Decisions, decisions, decisions! Principals *are* their decisions. Countless decisions ranging from the trivial to the traumatic confront principals every day. Sometimes we make those decisions with forethought and planning. Sometimes we must act quickly using only our instincts and judgment. Sometimes we fail to make a decision and that lack of action becomes our choice—often an undesired one. We are defined by our decisions.

Sometimes it is a matter of student safety and the priority is clear. But other times it is a tug-of-war involving the different demands of superintendents, school board members, parents, teachers, and students. These groups constantly weigh in a principal's decision process. Several years ago I conducted a study with 100 principals to see if there was a correlation between the priority given these different groups and student achievement. When a principal had to make a really tough decision, with no clear right or wrong answer, would one specific priority result in higher student achievement?

I assumed that principals who put students at the top of their priority list would be associated with the highest-achieving schools. I collected the responses, eliminating those who had been principals at their respective schools for less than 3 years. Of the over 70 principals remaining, two-thirds chose students as their first priority, a fourth put the superintendent as their first priority, and only a tenth of the principals ranked teachers as their first priority. (Not one principal put school board members or parents as the first priority.)

Then came the interesting part—I analyzed the school student achievement data disaggregated by the principals' professed priority. Those principals who ranked the superintendent as their first priority had the lowest student achievement. That came as no surprise to me. Those principals, when interviewed, showed a marked tendency to defer to the superintendent's authority in decision making. They were hard-working, manager-focused principals who respected the chain of command.

> *Principals are their decisions.*

Next I looked at the largest group of principals, the student-priority principals. I was nodding my head in agreement as their schools amassed student achievement scores that were almost 10 points higher than the superintendent-priority principals! When interviewed, these principals prided themselves on being student-centered, caring, engaged principals. Several used such phrases as, "it's the right thing to do," "it's why we are here," and "it's my role to be an advocate for the students." When pressed to give examples of how they put students as their first priority, most of these principals had a difficult time describing specific actions, but were confident in their priority.

Finally, I looked at the smallest group of responding principals—the ones who named teachers as their first priority. When I computed the student achievement scores for their schools, I was surprised. The achievement scores at the schools of teacher-priority principals were the highest of all three groups! I expected them to be higher than the superintendent-priority schools, but not the student-first principals. When interviewed, these principals appeared to feel strongly about the importance of supporting teachers and placing them as the first priority. They expressed a clear understanding that the work of the principal was accomplished through the teachers. They articulated that building a team mentality when it came to the success of the school and its students was critical to student achievement. Though all indicated that students were the most important, they expressed a belief that the best way to care for the students was to care for teachers, motivate teachers, and provide for teachers. Said one with a chuckle, "If you don't feed the teachers, they'll eat the students."

They were in agreement that teachers represented the best source of information and advice when making difficult decisions. These principals indicated that supporting teachers *who put students first* would always be their first priority.

As I pondered the responses and data, it became clear that these principals were on the right track. As long as a teacher put the needs of students first, the principal's job was to put that teacher's needs first. Engaging and improving our teachers is the best way to care for our students. That is the basis for this book. To use a sports analogy, you need a wide variety of good plays in your playbook. You don't use the same play all the time. Different situations call for different plays. Sometimes you try a new play and it doesn't work well, so you regroup and try another. Some of the most important decisions you make are how to best use the limited amount of time available to engage your faculty in improving teaching and learning. What plays do you use with your team?

As a former principal, I know that you have too little time and too much information. That is why we at ERS have assembled the 20 research-based—and practical—chapters included in this playbook for engaging your faculty in powerful conversations that could benefit students and teachers. There are thousands of articles and books that you could choose for staff discussion and study—many would be excellent. But the truth is that you have a limited amount of time, and there are many other demands clamoring for your attention. So my best advice is to assess the learning needs of your students, consider the composition of your faculty, weigh the unique blend of your community, and then review each chapter in this book for the right "fit." The point isn't to have your faculty read every chapter at once; instead, select the topics most applicable to your school and team and use them to focus your school's work and create your own plays.

As principal, you are the head coach of your teaching team, which means you get to call the plays. Talk with other school leaders, get advice from your central office team, but always remember that your success as a school administrator hinges on the effectiveness of those you lead. Every good decision is based on a good diagnosis. The more you know about your school, students, teachers, district, and community, the more effective your prescription will be. But regardless of what prescription you choose, there are some basic designs that will prove helpful.

Understand that your teachers usually reflect a wide range of abilities and motivation levels. You will have some who are self-motivated to do a great job and need you primarily to support them and stay out of their way. As the principal, you know that if one of these great teachers chooses to leave, you will have a difficult time finding another teacher who will do the job as well.

> *Your success as a school administrator hinges on the effectiveness of those you lead.*

Next is a larger group of good teachers. These teachers do a relatively good job, especially when they are in an encouraging, supportive environment. They care about children but if one of them chooses to leave, you are likely to find another teacher of equal caliber. This group can be swayed by an effective leader to much greater success and diligence, or they can be negatively influenced by the third group of teachers.

This third group of teachers is the most difficult for the principal to motivate. They can be negative with students, parents, and fellow teachers. Since they are frequently complainers, we try to avoid confronting them. Many of these difficult teachers have been behaving the way they do for years without anyone really addressing it. But good and great teachers need their principals to address concerns with the difficult teachers—in a respectful manner. Just like in a classroom, good students will support teachers when they correct unruly students, as long as it is done in a professional manner. The success of a teacher is contingent on maintaining the support of the good and great students. Similarly, the success of a principal is contingent on maintaining and growing the support from good and great teachers.

Avoid the trap of making decisions based on the difficult teachers. Sometimes principals fail to implement a potentially beneficial change because of a concern that a small group of teachers will react negatively by complaining, bad-mouthing the change, or simply dragging their feet. For example, I once decided that my school would benefit from teachers visiting other teachers' classrooms. I set up a plan that called for each teacher to visit two other classrooms each semester during planning time. I had a couple of teachers complain about how this was inconvenient and a waste of time, which I had expected. I listened to them, disagreed politely with their complaints, and went on with the program. At faculty meetings, I began to invite teachers who were visiting in other classrooms to share something they liked about another teacher's class. It became a time of positive faculty reinforcement. The complainers had no effect on the program, and it eventually became a source of pride to be visited by other faculty members. I admit that I encouraged a couple of my great teachers to start sharing the compliments. After the first two shared, other teachers began to step up and it was self-propelled from that point.

The message is—treat all of your teachers as if they want to be great teachers. Involve your great teachers first because they will approach a project with positive enthusiasm and a willing spirit—especially if it helps other teachers or students to be more successful. By worrying too much about your difficult teachers, you give them too much influence and power. Teachers who are ineffective often don't know they are, don't know how to change, or don't have the skills to change. Your job is to make difficult teachers want to change and then help them do it—or move on. The best way to do this is to focus on designing situations that support and reinforce great teachers. In so doing, you make difficult teachers uncomfortable, reduce their influence on others, and increase the pressure to work positively.

Involving Teachers in School Improvement

Using Professional Learning Communities (PLCs) is a popular and effective way of engaging teachers in school and instructional improvement. Very few teachers alter the way they teach or are willing to try a new technique because they listened to a lecture. Participating in authentic, peer-to-peer conversations about how to better teach students is a far more effective motivator—and the purpose of PLCs. For a PLC to work, however, teachers must be fully involved in the process and invested in the result. Without involvement there will be no improvement.

PLCs also require access to the best research available on the topics impacting today's schools. *The Principals' Playbook* brings together much of that research and thinking on successful schools and classrooms. It is designed to provide you, the principal, with multiple strategies and approaches to actively engage your teachers in their own improvement. You can't mandate improvement, but, as a school leader, you should use the greatest power you have—the power to frame the conversation.

Change comes slowly in our schools. We still have mostly self-contained classrooms in elementary schools, departments in secondary schools, and too little time in the school year for teachers to interact and improve. Even with the connectivity in today's world, teaching is still, for the most part, one adult leading the learning for a specific group of students. The difference between the great teacher and the poor one is not the content—it's the manner in which the content is presented and the students are engaged. Those skills develop as teachers interact with one another by sharing successes, challenges, and solutions.

Trying to improve the quality of your teachers without facilitating their interaction is like running a basketball practice with five players in five separate gymnasiums. They might all learn to shoot free-throws, but they won't ever develop the knowledge, skills, and team spirit essential for a winning season. Teachers are the same. Like players on an athletic team, teachers will improve their own performance, learn more quickly, and enjoy it more when they are part of a team. That makes you not only the principal, but also the team captain. Make good decisions—your team time is precious and limited.

Speaking of decisions, you may be wondering what happened with the fire chief, the tornado watch, and the smoke in the lunchroom. It was an important decision and, as the principal, I decided that we would put all the students in the gym while the firemen hunted for the source of the fire. The students stayed dry and we soon found the smoky culprit—a burned-out exhaust fan in the boys' bathroom. It was a good decision.

How to Use This Book

To get the most out of this book, choose the topic (or topics) that will most positively affect your faculty and align with your school improvement plan. Engage a few of your excellent teachers in the discussion and selection. If you can, provide them with copies of this book to review. You know that real change won't occur just because of one teacher professional development day or one motivational speaker. Real change comes slowly, over time and with care and attention.

One way to do this is to create faculty teams. You can call them any unique name you choose (e.g., Growth Teams or Insight Squads). Take some time to think this through. You want to choose your teams carefully. Dilute your difficult teachers by putting them on different teams as much as possible. Be sure that you consider personalities and put your excellent teachers where they will have the most influence and support them with several of your good teachers. Mix teachers by grade level, gender, experience level, and subject as much as possible. You want diversity on every team. You might intentionally split teachers who are close friends just to build some new relationships. I recommend no fewer than five teachers on a team and no more than eight. In my experience, too few teachers have a hard time keeping the conversation going and too many will allow some teachers to lose interest or carry on side conversations. I found six or seven teachers on a team to be the best.

Once you set up your teams, structure the first team meeting thoughtfully. Provide refreshments and introduce each team's work in a positive manner. Explain that teachers often meet within grade levels or departments, but that you want these teams to be focused on helping each teacher to be more effective with less work. Share that some of the best ideas for better teaching that you ever had came from fellow teachers and that you think everyone will benefit from connecting with other faculty members. Explain that you will provide topics for the conversations and resources to help with the discussions.

For the first meeting, help your teachers get to know one another. Principals assume that since teachers work together in the same building, often next door to one another, that they know one another well. That is not always the case, especially with newer teachers. You won't have the open, meaningful conversation that is needed without a strong level of trust among the team members. I recommend beginning the initial meeting with an exercise such as the following:

1. Organize the teachers into their teams.

2. Have the teachers pair up (if you have an odd number of teachers on a table you will have one group of 3).

3. Ask each team member to interview his or her partner to gather the following information (be sure to display the list of interview questions so that they have a handy reference):
    a. Name
    b. Birthplace and hometown
    c. Family (parents, siblings, spouse, children, grandchildren)
    d. Favorite food
    e. Hobbies (not related to school)
    f. Something people would be surprised to know about me

4. Allow about 4 minutes for the interviews, and then give teachers a 2-minute warning to be sure they finish gathering the requested information.

5. After everyone has completed the interview with their buddy, have each teacher introduce her buddy to the team.

This entire exercise should be easy to do. Allow 2 minutes to introduce the exercise, about 6 minutes for partners to interview, and about 2 minutes per table member for table introductions. With seven teachers at a table, this will take about 22 minutes.

After teachers have completed table introductions, tell them to point one finger toward the sky and, without talking to anyone, think about the most unusual "you would be surprised to know" story from their table. Tell them that you are going to count to three, at which time they should all point at the same time to the best "you would be surprised to know" story at their table. Most of the time they will point to one or maybe two individuals. Then you invite the chosen teacher(s) from each table to share his or her story with the entire group. This can be great fun and your entire faculty will enjoy finding out some unusual information about fellow teachers. You can do it in 45 minutes or less, even with a faculty of 80 teachers.

For all future team meetings, set aside at least 15 minutes during a faculty meeting or even an entire faculty meeting for team discussions. Don't do the team meeting last because the teachers will cut the conversation short to get out early. Also, don't do the team meeting at every faculty meeting or it will get old. Let faculty know in advance when you will have team meetings and remind them to sit at their original tables with their team members for those meetings.

Assign an article or section of an article for each team meeting session. Select (in advance) a facilitator to do a 3-minute summary of the assignment for the entire faculty, then ask them to discuss the reading with their teams. The conversation should focus on application by individual teachers in your own school. Train your teachers to ask one another three questions:

1. How would this change the way you teach?

2. How would this change the way students learn?

3. Specifically, what would you do differently in your classroom?

The most important tool we as school leaders have is the power to control the conversation. Take some time and make deliberate decisions about the conversations in which your faculty will engage. Be intentional about feeding your professional learning community. It will be one of the best decisions you can make as a principal.

Dr. John Draper
Chief Executive Officer
Educational Research Service

Section

I

Increasing
Student
Engagement

Chapter 1

Learning and the Teacher-Student Connection

Teacher efforts to provide a safe and caring environment for students pay off in higher levels of student learning.

Any educator knows a teacher's knowledge of content and classroom management skills is only part of what is needed to encourage high levels of student learning. Establishing positive connections with students is important—even critical—to effective teaching.

Mendler recognizes that relationship building takes time, which is a scarce resource for teachers:

> The challenge for educators to *achieve high standards* in a *differentiated classroom* while addressing *multiple intelligences* in an *inclusive* environment is enormous…. All these factors and demands lead many educators to believe that they simply do not have the time it takes to "connect" with kids, because of the time taken from academics. (2001, pp. 5-6)

However, he goes on to stress the need for positive teacher-student relationships:

> We know that the need to belong is as essential to learning as the need for food is to survival. A wise philosophical maxim suggests that students will only care what we think when they think that we care…. For us to truly succeed with our students, we must create schools and classrooms that are rich with warmth and nourishment for the mind and for the spirit. (2001, pp. 6-7)

Such warm and caring classrooms can have an especially strong impact on students who are considered to be at risk by providing essential support for students who are having difficulty meeting standards. Research has repeatedly demonstrated that a close, long-term relationship with an adult significantly increases the likelihood of success in school and life for at-risk youth. For many students who "beat the odds" and succeed even though their home environments provide little support, a teacher fills this role.

Wolin and Wolin found that teachers working with these resilient students often embed the following three key elements in their relationships:

- provide students with opportunities to experience success and build a sense of personal competence;

- acknowledge both the students' strengths and the difficulties they are facing; and,

- "understand and communicate to these children that they can prevail" (1996, p. 68).

> *"A wise philosophical maxim suggests that students will only care what we think when they think that we care." (Mendler, 2001, p. 6)*

Benard also discusses the importance of those teachers who help at-risk students develop resilience:

> Repeatedly, these turnaround teachers are characterized, first and foremost, as caring individuals who develop relationships with their students. They convey the message that they are "there for" a youth…. Being interested in, actively listening to, and validating the feelings of struggling young people, as well as getting to know their strengths and gifts, conveys the message, "You matter." (1998, p. 32)

Impact of Positive Relationships on Motivation

A link between student motivation and teacher caring makes intuitive sense—when students feel a strong connection with their teachers, they are more easily motivated to learn. Further, studies consistently indicate that highly motivated students reach higher levels of academic achievement (Fisher, 2003).

Research also identifies some classroom techniques and strategies that help motivate all types of learners in all types of classrooms. Central to many of these strategies is a student's "sense of relatedness to others"—including teachers (Fisher, 2003). In an interview with John O'Neil (2004), Jere Brophy identifies some particularly important lessons concerning student motivation that are relevant to this discussion of teacher-student relationships:

- *Climate Is Key.* Students—especially those who don't have a great track record of school success—are more motivated and perform better when they believe the classroom is safe and supportive. A child who feels intimidated or fears being picked on for "not knowing" something is less likely to get engaged in the classwork.

- *Ya Gotta Think You Can.* "The student has to believe that he can succeed at an acceptable level if he invests reasonable effort," says Brophy. "For many students, that's not a reasonable expectation because they're so far behind." For teachers, that means finding ways to get them extra help and reassuring them that if they put in steady effort, they can learn it. "You have to build the kid's trust and confidence," says Brophy. "The teachers who tend to be particularly successful with struggling students convey that they're willing to work with them if the student meets them halfway. They communicate to these students, I know some things about how to help students like you."

- *When to Praise or Reward?* It's one of the most controversial aspects of motivating students—one that has divided researchers and practitioners alike. Critics of the overuse of praise and rewards argue that it undermines a student's own intrinsic motivation to perform in school. In other words, giving students free pizza or tokens for getting good grades or reading a certain number of books makes kids focus on the reward and be less likely to do these things when a reward isn't attached. Successful teachers praise kids individually and privately, focusing on their progress, giving feedback. "Those sorts of comments are rewarding, but rewarding in ways that are motivating. Those support greater efficacy. That's much more powerful than: You got a 97 so you get a candy bar." Brophy cautions against giving rewards in ultra-competitive classroom situations. "That makes a few kids temporarily happy. For the other 20, it's just more depressing news about school." His advice: focus on the class as a whole. Congratulate the whole class for doing well on the test. Have an unannounced surprise treat for everyone. Save individual things for private comments. And don't publicly praise or criticize students or compare them. (Excerpted from Brophy, in O'Neil, 2004, p. 33.)

High Expectations as an Element in Teacher-Student Relationships

Research suggests that teachers' high expectations for their students' success can have a direct impact on academic achievement. Such findings have led Wasley, Hampel, and Clark to suggest that "high expectations are part of caring—that teachers cannot be caring without expecting a good deal from students" (1997, p. 74). Noddings (1992) points out that true caring involves a continuous search for competence and a desire to help those we care about flourish.

In a study of the impact of school reform on students, students stressed the importance of teacher caring and teacher-student relationships. In their view, they worked harder for teachers who cared about them. At the same time, it was important to the students that their teachers "pushed" them to succeed and showed by their actions that they believed the students could achieve. Unfortunately, not all teachers fuse caring with high expectations. Wasley, Hampel, and Clark (1997) found many of the teachers they observed exhibited caring—but not high expectations.

Teachers' high expectations for their students should extend to student behavior as well. In classrooms characterized as caring, supportive communities, students are held to high "standards of citizenship," including kindness to and respect for peers and adults. It must also be made clear that teachers and other adults in the school hold themselves to the same high standards (Wagner, 1999).

> *"While there may be many definitions of what constitutes 'good teaching,' the students' view of good teaching [is] related to caring." (Adler & Moulton, 1998, p. 52)*

The Student Perspective

In their study of student opinions about good teaching, Corbett and Wilson found student comments focused on a central theme—that of teacher caring:

> Most important to students was that a teacher's willingness and ability to help them with their work and with other problems showed them how much a teacher cared about them…. Caring meant that a student was worth worrying about and had a chance to be successful in school and life. (2000, p. 22)

Bosworth discusses data collected from a year-long study of students in two middle schools. The researchers found "helping with schoolwork was the most frequently mentioned characteristic of a caring teacher" (1995, p. 692):

> When asked to describe what they would see in the classroom of a caring teacher, most students gave descriptions similar to this one from an eighth-grade male: "Everyone would be in their seats, doing work. The teacher would go around the room talking to everyone to see how they were doing [and] to answer questions. Sometimes she'd just say, 'Good job.'" In this scenario, the teacher is involved with each student, meeting the needs of each student for specific help with an academic problem, or offering positive reinforcement and encouragement. (1995, p. 690)

Student opinions about teacher behaviors that support learning are typically both clear and concrete. In their view, good teachers:

- "Made sure that everyone understood what was being talked about before moving on to the next topic or assignment. Repetition and questions seemed to be indicative to students of the extent of a teacher's supportiveness."

- "Not only checked to make sure everyone understood what was going on in class but also explained material over and over [and] explained in a variety of ways."

- "Always seemed to find time to talk with students about their work and in ways that were most comfortable to the students."

- "Tried to establish real relationships with them. This implied that the topics of interactions went beyond the academic and that students highly valued teachers' sensitivity to their situations."

- "Were strict…. [Students] rolled their eyes when we asked whether this quality seemed a lot like nagging to them and nodded slowly when we inquired whether the behavior made them angry at times. They countered, however, that they wanted teachers to be like this."

- "Had an edge to them. Rather than pandering to students' habitual complaining about how much work they had to do or ignoring students who refused to work, the teachers basically would not excuse anyone from doing an assignment or getting a passing grade."

- "Gave them second chances to redo missed or poorly executed work and to retake tests....
  [To students,] this meant that teachers wanted them to learn and understand the material"
  (Corbett & Wilson, 2000, pp. 19-21).

The most striking finding from these and other studies in which students were asked to describe caring teachers is the emphasis students place on academic support. Alder and Moulton conducted a year-long study of eighth-grade students to identify teacher behaviors that demonstrated caring and also found it was linked to key instructional elements. In the students' view,

> caring teachers thoroughly explained material to students.... Caring teachers not only took time to help students but also made learning fun and interesting.... Students agreed that when teachers reminded students of homework and nagged to get it turned in, it was a sign of caring.... Students interpreted teaching to understanding, respecting academic confidentiality, encouragement, urging the completion of assignments, and making assignments fun, interesting, and adaptable to the style of the learner as caring. (1998, p. 52)

On a less positive note, Bosworth talks about what she characterizes "missed opportunities"—many of them easy to implement behaviors—for teachers to make caring connections with students that "need not detract from the pursuit of academic goals" (1995, p. 693). For example, the researchers "observed too many classes in which teachers rarely smiled, said anything positive to a student, or used a student's name other than for a reprimand" (1995, p. 693).

Making Personal Connections

Although comments from students make clear the importance of teaching in ways that demonstrate caring, teachers can also build personal connections with their students. These connections typically are most important for students having difficulty in their personal or academic lifes. Simply knowing a respected adult cares about his or her interests and concerns may provide such students with the emotional support needed to focus on learning.

However, this does not need to translate into being a "buddy." McLeod, Fisher, and Hoover remind us that "students need and want teachers to be firm. The ability to blend firmness with warmth and caring is difficult, but certainly possible; firmness, warmth, and caring are not mutually exclusive. In fact, effective teaching involves blending these three ingredients together" (2003, p. 63). In other words, the relationship can demonstrate caring and still clearly be one involving an adult who is "in charge" and a child or adolescent.

Mendes talks about other simple ways in which teachers can build connections with students:

> Knowing students' interests and concerns is one sure way to build rapport. Being physically on the same level when talking with students—matching their rate of speech and their tone when it is positive—can help build rapport. Using students' names during lectures and acknowledging all responses in some way during class discussions are also part of building rapport. (2003)

Strategies for Developing Personal Connections

- *Greet students in the hallways in the mornings.* Making eye contact, greeting students with a "good morning" or addressing them by name is a very simple way to connect on an everyday, personal level with students (Trudeau, 2002).

- *Collect personal index cards.* Generic questions such as a student's favorite color or number of siblings can be addressed on these cards. However, more creative or thought-provoking questions might help you to get to know your students even better. For example, ask your students about current events, local school issues, or even sports experiences that you think interest them.

- *Keep pictures of your family and friends posted in the classroom.* One teacher uses this approach to spark conversation and feels it "helps to humanize him in the eyes of students" (in O'Neil, 2004a, p. 28).

- *Do the "2 x 10."* Mendler recommends this technique for those really "hard to like students" and describes the approach this way:

  Make a commitment to invest two uninterrupted, undivided minutes a day for 10 consecutive days to "relationship build." If it is impossible to follow this guideline, then try to get as close to meeting it as possible. During these two minutes, you cannot do or say anything related to correcting the student's behavior or telling the student what he must do differently to be successful in class. Anything else that is within proper moral and ethical guidelines is allowed. Expect awkwardness and abrupt communication during the first few days: most students will be wary of your intentions, and you are unlikely to feel comfortable about knowing what to say or do. By the 10th day, most teachers report improved communication with the student, as well as evidence of better behavior (2001, pp. 25-26).

- *Catch them being good.* This is especially effective with your more difficult students. O'Neil acknowledges, "[i]t's easy to fall into the trap of correcting negative behavior—again and again" (2004a, p. 28). Throw them a curve ball and write them a little note of acknowledgment to encourage a positive behavior or attribute.

- *Acknowledge absenteeism (phone, email, or note).* Often, kids who feel disconnected think their absence can easily go unnoticed. Be sure your students know that they are missed when they are not in class through a one-on-one discussion, phone call home, or a personal note.

- *Attend a student event.* Being involved in more than one facet of your students' lives can help show that you care. Attending a school sporting event or a school play in which one or many of your students participates is a simple way to demonstrate this. Or write them a congratulatory note acknowledging their participation or accomplishments.

- *Eat lunch with a student who seems disconnected.* The National Mental Health and Education Center offers this as a "weekly rewards" suggestion (Brock, 1998).

Developing Academic Connections

In addition to general types of behaviors identified by students as characteristics of caring teachers, there are some additional instructional strategies that any teacher can employ—and that will help to send the message that every student is valued.

- *Respond nonevaluatively at least three times per class.* It is important that students feel comfortable participating in class and asking questions—particularly the quieter, harder-to-reach students. Mendler offers this easy strategy:

  > When students answer questions with something other than what you consider the "right" answer, make your next response nonjudgmental at least three times each class. Offer comments like "good try," "that's an interesting way of looking at it," or "that's unique but different from what I was actually looking for" (2001, p. 48).

- *Connect academic content with real-life meaning.* Your students will have a better grasp of each lesson if they somehow feel a real-life connection to the topic of the day. Challenge yourself to connect your lessons to something that is of *authentic* interest to them. This could be through a career day with guest speakers or a newspaper clipping highlighting a current event.

- *Plan a lesson from the perspective of your least capable student.* Reflect on the skills of your academically weakest students. Consider aspects of the lesson they might have trouble with— might there be too much reading required, is the material too abstract or do some students need a more hands-on approach?

- *"Look at your class as a collection of individuals with different needs, experiences, and goals"* (Algozzine & Algozzine, 2001, p. 6). It's common sense—every student makes connections through his or her own unique learning styles and experiences. Thus, be sure to employ a wide range of teaching techniques that capitalize on student strengths. For example,

  > some students benefit from a daily outline of the most important concepts to be learned. Others feel more academically connected when they can express their knowledge in less conventional ways, such as drawing, dramatizing, singing, or rapping. Students with writing difficulties can be allowed to explain an answer to you before putting it on paper. (Mendler, 2001, p. 55)

- *Learn from them.* Put your students in charge of teaching the class occasionally. You might assign components of a unit to different groups (Mendler, 2001).

- *Fill the room with student work.* "It's good for self-concept, egos, and morale" (Algozzine & Algozzine, 2001, p. 15).

- *Follow-up.* "When you ask your students to do something, don't follow it with 'Okay?' Instead, ask if they understand, and then say, 'Tell me what you are going to do'" (Algozzine & Algozzine, 2001, p. 45).

- *Consult your colleagues.* Share ideas and ask for suggestions from fellow teachers who are also looking for better ways to reach their students. Inquire specifically about some of your more "difficult" students. Other teachers may be able to offer suggestions or techniques that proved successful for these students in the past.

Working With Challenging Students

While much of this sounds like common sense, there will be times when more special skills and lots of energy are needed to build connections—especially with difficult or hard-to-reach students. Mendler (2001) talks about some special strategies that may be helpful in such situations:

- See your challenging students as having something to teach you: It is difficult for students to stay disconnected when caring, persistent adults reach out to them in ways that convey an eagerness to learn.

- Stay optimistic and be persistent: An emotionally distant student who believes that anonymity will keep him or her safe from high expectations is unlikely to respond quickly to a teacher's efforts to connect.

- Build on strengths instead of trying to fix deficits.

The Role of the Principal

A key role for principals is helping teachers understand how important their connections with students can be for maximizing possibilities for learning. In addition, principals should understand how important their own behaviors are to demonstrating that school is a caring place.

Reitzug and Patterson (1998) shadowed Debbie Pressley, who was considered by other educators to be an excellent principal. Pressley's interactions with students contained five components also relevant for teachers:

- *Establishing/developing a personal connection*—behaviors included calling students by their first names and focusing on each student as a person rather than on the student as a problem;

- *Honoring voice*—soliciting the perspectives of others and "accepting their problems, concerns, and wishes as significant," (p. 169) as well as using gentleness to combat verbal violence or disrespect;

- *Showing concern for the individual well-being of students via his or her expectations of them*—communicating expectations (especially academic expectations) for individual students;

- *Connecting individuals to their communities*—demonstrating that "caring does not mean that 'anything goes,' or that those caring always have to be 'nice' or 'easy'…. [and that students need to be aware] that they are part of a broader community whose well-being they affect through their actions" (p. 173); and,

- *Seeing alternative possibilities*—helping students leave problem situations "with a way of proceeding that had potential to resolve the situation" (p. 174).

In Summary

This brief overview of the teacher-student connection makes two points clear. First, much of what both students and educators define as caring behaviors—those that help to create caring connections between teachers and students—are also simply good teaching. Second, many behaviors—such as calling students by name when they provide a correct answer or contribute to a class discussion—are "small" in terms of the effort required but not in the impact they have on students.

While the focus in today's schools is rightfully on ensuring students achieve academically, it is important not to lose sight of their need to feel their teachers care about them as individuals. By developing trusting relationships with their students, educators provide a key ingredient of the teaching-learning connection.

References

Adler, N. I., & Moulton, M. R. (1998, January/February). The eye of the beholder: Middle schoolers talk about caring. *Schools in the Middle*, 7(3), 6-7, 52-53.

Algozzine, B., & Algozzine, K. (2001). *Every teacher's little book of wisdom: Ideas, insights, and inspirations*. Arlington, VA: Council for Exceptional Children.

Benard, B. (1998). *How to be a turnaround teacher/mentor*. Retrieved from http://www.resiliency. com/htm/turnaround.htm

Bosworth, K. (1995, May). Caring for others and being cared for: Students talk caring in school. *Phi Delta Kappan*, 76(9), 686-693.

Brock, S. E. (1998). Time on task: Strategies for teachers. In A. S. Canter & S. A. Carroll, (Eds.), *Helping children at home and school*. Bethesda, MD: National Mental Health and Education Center.

Corbett, H. D., & Wilson, B. L. (2000). *Students' perspectives on the Ninth Grade Academy of the Talent Development High Schools in Philadelphia: 1999-2000*. Philadelphia: Philadelphia Education Fund. Retrieved from http://philaedfund.org/pdfs/wilsoncorbett.pdf

Fisher, H. (2003, Spring). Motivational strategies in the elementary school setting. *Kappa Delta Pi Record*. Retrieved from http://findarticles.com/p/articles/mi_qa4009/is_200304/ai_n9210174/

McLeod, J., Fisher, J., & Hoover, G. (2003). *The key elements of classroom management: Managing time and space, student behavior, and instructional strategies*. Alexandria, VA: Association for Supervision and Curriculum Development.

Mendes, E. (2003, September). What empathy can do. *Educational Leadership*, 56-59.

Mendler, A. N. (2001). *Connecting with students*. Alexandria, VA: Association for Supervision and Curriculum Development.

Noddings, N. (1992). *The challenge to care in schools: An alternative approach to education.* New York: Teachers College Press.

O'Neill, J. (2004). Motivation 101. *NEA Today*, 33.

Reitzug, U. C., & Patterson, J. (1998, May). "I'm not going to lose you!" Empowerment through caring in an urban principal's practice with students. *Urban Education, 33*(2), 150-181.

Trudeau, M. (2002, May 23). School 'bonding' effort shows lasting results: Seattle's project SOAR credited with drop in risky teen behavior. *National Public Radio Online.* Retrieved from http://www.npr.org/programs/morning/features/2002/may/teens/index.html

Wagner, T. (1999, May 12). Standards for the heart? *Education Week, 48*, 33.

Wasley, P. A., Hampel, R. L., & Clark, R. W. (1997). *Kids and school reform.* San Francisco: Jossey-Bass.

Wolin, S., & Wolin, S. J. (1996, August). Beating the odds. *Learning*, 66-68.

Implications for Our School: Questions for Discussion and Reflection

- Would our students say most teachers in the school demonstrate caring attitudes? How might we ask them about this?

- Has the stress of high standards and high-stakes testing negatively affected the way we relate to our students? If so, how can we turn this around?

- Are there students in the school that we think might especially benefit from some of the resilience factors identified by Wolin and Wolin? How can we ensure they get the extra support they might need?

- Generate and discuss additional ideas like those mentioned in "Strategies for Developing Personal Connections."

Follow-up and Action Items

_____

_____

_____

_____

_____

_____

_____

_____

_____

_____

_____

_____

Chapter 2

Enhancing Students' Beliefs in Their Ability to Learn

*Some students' beliefs that they
can't learn presents a formidable barrier to learning.
Teachers can help to turn these beliefs around.*

Among teachers' most daunting challenges is the need to have all students engaged in and motivated by learning. Obviously, skilled teachers look to instructional strategies such as differentiation and hands-on learning as ways to increase student engagement. But what about students who have the potential to do well but seem satisfied to just get by? Such students often don't complete tasks or avoid challenges. Although they may sit quietly and pose no discipline problem, they are also shortchanging their own ability to learn.

While there may be a variety of reasons for such behavior, one possibility may be a student's lack of confidence in his or her own ability to learn—low self-efficacy. Margolis and McCabe talk about this:

> Low self-efficacy beliefs, unfortunately, impede academic achievement and, in the long run, create self-fulfilling prophecies of failure and learned helplessness. . . . For example, if struggling learners believe that composition writing is impossible for them, that whatever they write will earn a failing grade because they lack and can never develop the ability to write, they may resist writing by feigning illness, creating diversionary behavior problems, writing no more than a carelessly created sentence, or completing the assignment in a thoughtless, slipshod fashion. (2006, p. 219)

Siegle (2000) characterizes self-efficacy as "a student's 'I can' or 'I cannot' belief." This belief about personal capability to accomplish meaningful tasks—known as self-efficacy—can directly affect a student's motivation to learn. Students with high self-efficacy willingly approach learning activities, expend effort to achieve goals, persist in the face of challenge, and use strategies effectively, while learners with low self-efficacy more typically avoid challenge, expend little effort and then give up, and believe they are not in control of their learning (DiCintio & Gee, 1999; Lucking & Manning, 1996).

Orstein's (1994) description of two characteristics of highly engaged learners highlights the possibly strong connection between self-efficacy and engagement. They are more likely to have feelings of:

- *Confidence*. Highly engaged learners have gained a positive perception of their own efficacy through repeated experiences of success. Those who believe they can achieve will try harder and concentrate on difficult tasks longer than those who believe they cannot.

- *Control*. Highly engaged learners believe that outcomes are related to their own actions. People are more likely to work hard when they believe that they, rather than outside forces, control the results.

Looking at one of these factors—confidence—from a commonsense point of view clarifies the impact it can have on a student's belief in his or her own ability. A confident student is more likely to "anticipate successful outcomes… [while] those who lack confidence in their academic skills envision a low grade" (Pajares, 2005, p. 342) even before beginning an assignment. The less confident student may avoid a sense of failure by simply avoiding the task. In essence, "if I haven't tried, I haven't failed."

From an educator's point of view, it is also important to understand that a student who seems generally self-confident may still feel less than capable in a school setting. Researchers call this subset academic self-efficacy and have found that it can impact effort, persistence, and perseverance (Pajares, 2002), all traits important to a student's engagement in the learning process.

> *"A strong sense of efficacy enhances human accomplishment and well-being in countless ways. Confident individuals approach difficult tasks as challenges to be mastered rather than as threats to be avoided. They have greater interest and deep engrossment in activities, set themselves challenging goals and maintain strong commitment to them, and heighten and sustain their efforts in the face of failure. They more quickly recover their confidence after failures or setbacks, and attribute failure to insufficient effort or deficient knowledge and skills which are acquirable. High self-efficacy helps create feelings of serenity in approaching difficult tasks and activities. Conversely, people who doubt their capabilities may believe that things are tougher than they really are, a belief that fosters stress, depression, and a narrow vision of how best to solve a problem. Not surprisingly, confidence in one's academic capability is a critical component of school success." (Pajares & Schunk, 2001)*

How Do Students Develop a Sense of Self-Efficacy?

Pajares stresses that self-efficacy is a learned trait. It is "not so much about learning how to succeed as it is about learning *how to persevere when one does not succeed*" (2005, p. 345). Bandura, a researcher with a long-time interest in self-efficacy points to three "sources of influence" that affect the characteristic:

> The most effective way of creating a strong sense of efficacy is through mastery experiences. Successes build a robust belief in one's personal efficacy. Failures undermine it, especially if failures occur before a sense of efficacy is firmly established…. The second way of creating and strengthening self-beliefs of efficacy is through the vicarious experiences provided by social models. Seeing people similar to oneself succeed by sustained effort raises observers' beliefs that they too possess the capabilities to master comparable activities required to succeed…. Social persuasion is a third way of strengthening people's beliefs that they have what it takes to succeed. People who are persuaded verbally that they possess the capabilities to master given activities are likely to mobilize greater effort and sustain it than if they harbor self-doubts and dwell on personal deficiencies when problems arise. To the extent that persuasive boosts in perceived self-efficacy lead people to try hard enough to succeed, they promote development of skills and a sense of personal efficacy. (1998)

> *"By focusing on self-efficacy,…teachers can help struggling learners develop a more accurate, optimistic, "can-do" attitude." (Margolis & McCabe, 2006, p. 226)*

Impacting Students' Sense of Self-Efficacy

Since prior experiences obviously have a significant impact on the development of a sense of self-efficacy, it is clear that teachers can make a difference through the ways they provide instruction to students. Knowing about approaches to impact self-efficacy can also provide a roadmap for teachers who want to build confidence and a sense of control in a student whose low assessment of his own ability is creating a barrier to his learning.

First, empty praise for doing well on "easy" tasks is not the answer. Instead, the key linkage is between an authentic mastery experience and the student's understanding that his competence, engagement, and persistence led to that mastery (Pajares & Schunk, 2001). So, for a student with a misplaced understanding of this linkage, high-quality teacher feedback focused on the role of student effort in success is critical. While working to "repair" a student's sense of self-efficacy that may be impairing effort, it is especially important to provide feedback that is frequent, focused, and task-specific (Margolis &

McCabe, 2006). "Praise and encouragement should be delivered honestly and in their proper measure when they are deserved…. [while, in contrast] knee-jerk praise sends the quite peculiar message that putting forth minimal effort is praiseworthy" (Pajares, 2005, p. 349). In addition, "adults who provide such [knee-jerk] praise soon lose credibility" (p. 350).

Pajares provides additional suggestions in regard to providing feedback and, specifically, praise to students. In his view, it is important to "praise effort and persistence, not ability." He elaborates on this:

> Foster the belief that competence or *ability* is a changeable, controllable aspect of development, and encourage effort, perseverance, and persistence as ways to overcome obstacles. Praising with statements such as "You are so smart!" or "How bright you are!" can often have the opposite effect intended. Praising for "smarts" tells young people that success is a matter of intellectual ability (which one either has or doesn't have). How can young people develop confidence in an ability they believe is beyond their control? Praising for effort tells people that the harder you work the more you accomplish and the smarter you get. Whether at home or at school, rather than praising for ability, make it a habit to praise the *genuine* effort and persistence the young person puts forth. (2005, p. 350)

This assessment is in line with research findings of Carol Dweck (2006) who sees many people, including students, as having either a "fixed mindset" or "growth mindset." Parents and teachers can influence which of these mindsets a child develops by the messages they send. For example, a parent might praise a child by saying, "You learned that so quickly! You're so smart!" However, the intent of this message—with its emphasis on ability over effort—can boomerang if a previously successful student suddenly comes up against a difficult problem and, looking at it from a fixed mindset point of view, feels powerless to address the problem. By reinforcing students' sense that their effort makes a difference, parents and teachers can help them develop a growth mindset and so encourage them to take on challenges.

Bandura provides a second overarching theme for strategies teachers can use to support the development of strong student sense of self efficacy:

> Successful efficacy builders do more than convey positive appraisals. In addition to raising people's beliefs in their capabilities, they structure situations for them in ways that bring success and avoid placing people in situations prematurely where they are likely to fail often. (1998)

Pajares puts this relationship in commonsense terms: "success raises self-efficacy; failure lowers it" (2005, p. 344). Margolis and McCabe (2006) talk about strategies that help to build the potential for success. These include careful attention to matching instructional tasks to a student's skills and prior knowledge, with a moderate challenge as the goal. Another approach may be to intentionally offer choices in how a student might complete an assignment, since a higher level of interest may encourage more engagement and increase the likelihood of success.

What Are the Effects of Self-Efficacy Beliefs?

- First, students' confidence influences the *choices* they make and the courses of action they pursue. Students engage in tasks in which they feel competent and tend to avoid those in which they do not.

- Efficacy beliefs also help determine how much effort students will expend on an activity, how long they will persevere when confronting obstacles, and how resilient they will be in the face of adverse situations. The higher the sense of efficacy, the greater the *effort, persistence, and resilience*.

- Of course, our confidence influences the amount of *stress and anxiety* we experience as we engage in a task.

A strong sense of efficacy enhances human accomplishment and personal well-being in countless ways:

- Confident students approach difficult tasks as challenges to be mastered rather than as threats to be avoided.

- They have greater intrinsic interest and deep engrossment in activities, set challenging goals for themselves and maintain strong commitment to those goals, and heighten and sustain their efforts in the face of failure.

- Moreover, they more quickly recover their confidence after failures or setbacks, and they attribute failure to insufficient effort or deficiencies in knowledge and skills that they can acquire. For confident students, failure is a healthy reminder that they need to work harder.

- Conversely, students with low self-efficacy may believe that things are tougher than they really are, a belief that fosters stress, depression, and a narrow vision of how best to solve a problem. When students lack confidence in their capabilities, they are likely to attribute their failure to low ability that they perceive as inborn, permanent, and not acquirable. For them, failure is just another reminder that they are incapable.

- Students who doubt their academic ability typically envision low grades often before they even begin an examination.

Source: Pajares, 2000

Helping students, especially students who seem to be inefficient learners, develop more productive learning strategies and learn how to generalize these across tasks may also help them to experience success. The strategy may be something as simple as learning how to set stepping stone goals for a large project so that the task seems more manageable. In addition, completion of each element can be checked off as a success. When a student correctly applies a strategy, teachers should use the opportunity for the type of reinforcement—honest, on target, and in proportion to the task—already described. If incorrect use of a strategy is the problem, verbalizing that "failure is not due to permanent limitations" is important for the student (Margolis & McCabe, 2006, p. 225). For example: "Kelly, you did not outline the essay before writing it. That is why you did poorly…. Let us do an outline together" (Margolis & McCabe, 2006, p. 225).

Of course, the teacher in the above example must take care not to provide too much support since this can contribute to learned helplessness—an easy trap into which students with a low sense of self-efficacy can fall. The assistance provided should help the student develop a capacity for independently applying knowledge and skills as well as a more accurate appreciation of these.

Helping students become more self-aware of how their sense of self-efficacy may be affecting their performance is another strategy that teachers can employ. Pajares (2005) talks about two approaches aligned with this:

- Challenge underconfidence by providing concrete examples of students' inaccurate perceptions of their own abilities; and,

- Help students develop a more adaptive sense of self-efficacy, for example, by helping them to more accurately assess their own capabilities in regard to specific tasks.

Teachers can also help individual students by maximizing the collective efficacy of the classroom as a whole (Pajares, 2005). Projecting a can-do attitude that signals belief in both the teacher's and the class's abilities to take on challenges sets the stage for focusing on effort, not lack of ability.

A final category of teacher strategies focuses on teaching students that all "mistakes" are not failures. Instead, sometimes taking the wrong path is a natural part of learning. Pajares suggests that teachers help students understand this by modeling appropriate behaviors:

> Adults who . . . good-naturedly admit their errors when they are pointed out ("Oops, I was a little careless. Thanks for pointing that out.") help youngsters to understand that missteps are inevitable, that they can be overcome, and that even authority figures can make them. (2005, p. 346)

In Summary

By taking students' sense of self-efficacy into account, schools can impact student engagement, effort, and perseverance—and, ultimately, student learning. These efforts may be especially important for struggling students whose past experiences with failure sometimes act as significant barriers to their future success. In addition, helping students gain a sense of confidence and control can provide them with a life skill that goes far beyond the classroom.

References

Bandura, A. (1998). *Self-efficacy.* Retrieved from http://www.des.emory.edu/mfp/BanEncy.html

DiCintio, M. J., & Gee, S. (1999, July). Control is the key: Unlocking the motivation of at-risk students. *Psychology in the Schools, 36*(3), 231-237.

Dweck, C. (2006). *Mindset: The new psychology of success.* New York: Random House.

Lucking, R., & Manning, M. L. (1996, Winter). Instruction for low-achieving young adolescents: Addressing the challenge of a generation imperiled. *Preventing School Failure, 40*(2), 82-87.

Margolis, H., & McCabe, P. P. (2006, March). Improving self-efficacy and motivation: What to do, what to say. *Intervention in School and Clinic, 41*(4), 218-227.

Ornstein, A. C. (1994, July). Yearning to learn. *The Executive Educator, 16*(7), 27-30.

Pajares, F. (2000). *Schooling in America: Myths, mixed messages, and good intentions.* Retrieved from http://www.des.emory.edu/mfp/pajaresgtl.html

Pajares, F. (2002). *Self-efficacy beliefs in academic contexts: An outline.* Retrieved from http://des.emory.edu/mfp/efftalk.html

Pajares, F. (2005). *Self-efficacy beliefs of adolescents.* Charlotte, NC: Information Age Publishing.

Pajares, F., & Schunk, D. H. (2001). Self-beliefs and school success: Self-efficacy, self-concept, and school achievement. In R. Riding & S. Rayner (Eds.), *Perception* (pp. 239-266). London: Ablex Publishing. Retrieved from http://www.des.emory.edu/mfp/PajaresSchunk2001.html

Siegle, D. (2000). *An introduction to self-efficacy.* Retrieved from http://www.gifted.uconn.edu/siegle/SelfEfficacy/section1.html

Implications for Our School: Questions for Discussion and Reflection

- Do any of us have students in our classes that the descriptions of low self-efficacy provided here describe?

- What are some ways we could diagnose whether students' beliefs that they aren't capable of learning are acting as barriers to their learning?

- What are some strategies we could use to help students—especially struggling students—feel more capable?

- Will teachers need any resources or development opportunities to help them effectively address this problem?

Follow-up and Action Items

_____

_____

_____

_____

_____

_____

_____

_____

_____

_____

_____

_____

Chapter 3
Learning Strategies as a Key to Student Success

Teaching metacognitive skills to students, especially struggling students, can improve their academic performance.

In schools and classrooms across the country, educators are working to raise the achievement of all students to ever-higher levels. Yet, often missing in discussions about how to raise academic performance is the *way* in which individual students go about learning. One aspect of a student's approach to learning is his or her use of learning strategies.

Schumaker and Deshler define a learning strategy as "an individual's approach to a task. It includes how a person thinks and acts when planning, executing, and evaluating performance on a task and its outcomes" (2006, p. 122). Much of this thinking about learning is done unconsciously. For example, most of us automatically slow down when reading content that is difficult for us to understand. We also make use of a variety of strategies for helping us organize and remember—both key elements of the learning process.

As with many characteristics about people, however, there is wide variation in terms of the number of learning strategies we know and how well we use them. Think, for example, of a student you have known who approached new types of tasks with enthusiasm and who was typically able to "figure out" how to apply what he or she already knew to tackling a new problem. Now think about another student who reads a textbook but, when asked to summarize the main points in the chapter, can present only a disjointed list of thoughts with little sense of how they fit together. In math, this child might use only one strategy when approaching a problem—even when that method repeatedly fails.

Often, the difference between these two students is neither cognitive ability nor content knowledge. Instead, the second student lacks metacognitive skills. Activities such as planning, monitoring comprehension, and evaluating progress toward completion of a learning task are metacognitive in nature. Students with better-developed metacognitive skills typically have a better sense of their own strengths and needs related to the learning process. They have a larger repertoire of learning strategies and they use many of them almost unconsciously. And, perhaps most importantly, they are likely to select and use the learning strategy that is most effective in helping them address a particular learning task.

> *"A student's capacity to plan, monitor, and, if necessary, re-plan learning strategies had the most powerful effect on his or her learning." (Wang, Haertel, & Walberg, 1993/94, p. 75)*

Researchers Wang, Haertel, and Walberg can help us understand just how important such metacognitive skills are to student learning. They created a knowledge base of 11,000 statistical findings from a wide range of studies on student learning. Their intent was to identify the relative strength of the contribution of several major factors. They found that "student aptitude was the most influential of the six broad types of influences. Among the categories of student aptitude, a student's metacognitive processes—that is, a student's capacity to plan, monitor, and, if necessary, re-plan learning strategies—had the most powerful effect on his or her learning" (1993/94, p. 75).

An increasingly strong research base points to the potential of strategy instruction to help support struggling learners, including students with learning disabilities (Protheroe, 2002; Protheroe, Shellard, & Turner, 2004; Riggs & Gil-Garcia, 2001). Specifically, teaching students how to use learning strategies by helping them choose and implement them effectively helps to strengthen their metacognitive abilities. This, in turn, translates to improved student learning. Good strategy instruction can help:

- Improve student performance, especially of students who have not previously developed effective metacognitive skills;

- Increase student independence and engagement with learning; and,

- Help students realize that it is sometimes the use of ineffective strategies—not lack of ability—that hinders performance.

This last factor is especially important because it may help increase motivation. Students who have repeatedly experienced failure in school due to a lack of "tools" that can help them approach learning efficiently are likely to become less persistent in addressing school tasks. Acquiring some additional tools—learning strategies—increases their likelihood of success, and so may also increase their willingness to take on new challenges.

How to Teach Learning Strategies

"Researchers and practitioners who have studied and applied learning strategy instruction in the classroom generally agree on the *how* of instruction" (Clarke, 2008, p. 5). Three components of this skill are considered essential: knowledge of what the strategy is, how to apply it, and when and where to use it (Jones, Palincsar, Ogle, & Carr, 1987). Effective instruction must address all three components.

First, learning skills are most effectively taught in the context of content-area instruction. Perkins-Gough discusses some related findings of the RAND Reading Study Group, specifically,

Teachers foster comprehension development when they connect comprehension strategy instruction with in-depth learning of content in such disciplines as history and science. If students learn that these strategies are tools for understanding the ideas in texts, then the strategies become purposeful and integral reading activities. (2002, p. 92)

> *Learning skills are most effectively taught in the context of content-area instruction.*

When students are encouraged to develop learning strategies in the context of learning about content, they:

- Receive more opportunities for teacher support than they would if the instruction was provided only during pullout classes or special sessions focusing on study skills instruction; and,

- Have more—and more meaningful—opportunities to practice the skills.

However, there are three caveats to meshing strategy and content-area instruction. The first is that only one new element should be presented at a time. Thus, instruction on a new strategy should be presented in the context of familiar content. Otherwise, struggling students are likely to overload and find it difficult to learn either the strategy or the content.

Second, the skills taught—and the approaches used to teach them—should be age- and grade-appropriate. For example, the metacognitive skill of summarizing might be addressed with children in primary grades by small-group discussions about a story, with the teacher writing down student comments. The teacher might then read the comments aloud and ask, "What were the two big things this story was about?" Students would be taught different ways to summarize and to "report" their summaries as they advanced through the grades.

Third, instruction about strategies should be explicit. It should begin with the teacher modeling the skill or strategy, followed by structured opportunities for students to practice and apply the skills—with teacher feedback provided to reinforce appropriate use of the strategy and correction or reteaching if the strategy is incorrectly applied. The instruction should also include elements that help students learn how to appropriately use a strategy to complete other tasks and in other classes (Kiewra, 2002). According to Kiewra, good strategy instructors:

- Introduce the strategy by modeling it and describing it;

- Sell the strategy by telling why it works;

- Generalize the strategy by telling where else it is useful; and,

- Help students perfect the strategy by providing practice opportunities.

Rafoth, Leal, and DeFabo developed a mnemonic—MIRRORS—to assist teachers in remembering the elements of effective strategy instruction:

- Model the strategy; explain how to carry it out;

- Inform the students about when and how to use it;

- Remind them to use the strategy;

- Repeat the strategy: practice, practice, practice;

- Outline the strategy's usefulness via constant feedback;

- Reassess the student's performance as a result of using the strategy; and,

- Stress strategy generalization (excerpted from 1993, p. 71).

Teacher modeling is an especially important component of strategy instruction. Students who have demonstrated an inability to use strategies—or to generalize a strategy they have used successfully to another task—need more than simply hearing a description. They need to see it in action and, even better, see it applied to a few slightly different tasks. Protheroe (2003) adds another element to modeling by suggesting that teachers consistently "think out loud" and encourage their students to do the same. To use this technique, teachers talk through use of the strategy while they use it. This helps students understand learning strategies and how to use them "because they can see how a mind actively responds to thinking through trouble spots and constructing meaning" (Vacca & Vacca, 2005, p. 83).

Protheroe provides another reason to apply the "thinking-out-loud" approach to help students use learning strategies. The teacher:

who encourages it on the part of students also has an excellent diagnostic tool available. Strengths and weaknesses of individual students in the area of metacognitive skills and strategy use are immediately apparent. The teacher can use the information collected to begin addressing inappropriate use of strategies by some students, pinpoint the type of both classwide and individualized instruction needed, and use effective learners' techniques as an example for those with weaknesses in the area. (Protheroe, 2003, p. 7)

The goal of strategy instruction should not be rote memorization of a particular approach but instead the development of a repertoire of tools a student can access as needed.

The last of the elements suggested by Kiewra—opportunities for practice—is also critically important. Students who do not develop their own strategies naturally need to be able to take a learned strategy from the abstract to the concrete. Although teacher modeling helps with this, practice with the strategy—accompanied by feedback from the teacher and help in correcting use of the strategy if there is a problem—will help to make the strategy a potentially useful habit.

Finally, the goal of strategy instruction should not be rote memorization of a particular approach but instead the development of a repertoire of tools a student can access as needed. Thus, teachers should build in opportunities for students to generalize use of a strategy to a new type of task. This is another skill that most highly effective learners have. They mentally—often subconsciously—select from among a variety of strategies. In contrast, less effective learners may fixate on the skill learned most recently or one that worked well for them in the past—although in regard to a very different type of task.

The Importance of Schoolwide Implementation

According to McEwan, developing teachers who are effective in learning strategy instruction "requires considerable investment" (2007, p. 78) and may take several years. "Strategies are used situationally. Teaching students how and when to use them is a completely different enterprise than drilling students on a discrete skill or serving up a smorgasbord of content and expecting students to help themselves" (McEwan, 2007, p. 78).

A coordinated schoolwide effort greatly increases the likelihood that teachers will become competent in strategy instruction and successfully embed the instruction in the content areas (Lenz, 2006; Riggs & Gil-Garcia, 2001). Strategy instruction should not be presented as an ad hoc fix taught at one grade level or in a particular class, but rather should follow an established scope and sequence that involves teachers from all grade levels and all content areas (Riggs & Gil-Garcia, 2001). As students enter fifth grade, for example, all fifth-grade teachers will know what learning strategies have been taught in third and fourth grade and they can remind students to use appropriate ones. In addition, a strategy taught in a math class can be identified by a science teacher as one that would be helpful for a specific science task.

Teachers should meet regularly with one another to discuss successes and challenges and to learn new strategies (Clark, 1993). "The optimum situation occurs when a school staff as a collaborative group determine the strategies to be emphasized and agree to integrate strategies consistently" (Switlick, 1997, p. 264). The importance of these opportunities has been demonstrated. For example, Chamot, Barnhardt, El-Dinary, and Robbins conducted a 3-year study that investigated how foreign language teachers could be supported to teach language learning strategies. They concluded that, while workshops were motivational, follow-up support, such as model lessons, one-to-one coaching, and peer discussions, were "invaluable to their integrating learning strategies into language instruction" (1999, p. 175).

In Summary

The research summarized here identifies three important links between learning strategies and academic achievement. First, effective use of learning strategies can enhance a student's ability to achieve academically. Second, while some students independently understand and apply a wide repertoire of learning strategies, others do not. Finally, these strategies can effectively be taught as part of content-area instruction.

References

Chamot, A. U., Barnhardt, S., El-Dinary, P. B., & Robbins, J. (1999). *The learning strategies handbook*. White Plains, NY: Pearson Education.

Clark, F. L. (1993). Preparing teachers to implement strategy instruction. *Preventing School Failure, 38*(1), 50-52.

Clarke, S. (2008). *ERS focus on: Learning strategies*. Alexandria, VA: Educational Research Service.

Jones, B. F., Palincsar, A. S., Ogle, D. S., & Carr, E. G. (1987). *Strategic teaching and learning: Cognitive instruction in the content areas*. Alexandria, VA: Association for Supervision and Curriculum Development, in cooperation with North Central Regional Educational Laboratory.

Kiewra, K. A. (2002, Spring). How classroom teachers can help students learn and teach them how to learn. *Theory into Practice, 41*(2), 71-80.

Lenz, B. K. (2006). Creating school-wide conditions for high-quality learning strategy classroom instruction. *Intervention in School and Clinic, 41*(5), 261-266.

McEwan, E. K. (2007). *Raising reading achievement in middle and high schools: 5 simple-to-follow strategies* (2nd ed.). Thousand Oaks, CA: Corwin Press.

Perkins-Gough, D. (2002, November). RAND report on reading comprehension [Special report]. *Educational Leadership*, 92.

Protheroe, N. (2002). Teaching students to be efficient learners. *Principal, 82*(2), 48-51.

Protheroe, N. (2003). *ERS focus on: Helping students develop the skills of highly effective learners*. Arlington, VA: Educational Research Service.

Protheroe, N., Shellard, E., & Turner, J. (2004). *What we know about: Helping struggling learners in the elementary and middle grades*. Arlington, VA: Educational Research Service.

Rafoth, M. A., Leal, L., & DeFabo, L. (1993). *Strategies for learning and remembering: Study skills across the curriculum*. Washington, DC: National Education Association.

Riggs, E. G., & Gil-Garcia, A. (2001). *What we know about: Helping middle and high school readers*. Arlington, VA: Educational Research Service.

Schumaker, J. B., & Deshler, D. D. (2006). Teaching adolescents to be strategic learners. In D. D. Deshler & J. B. Schumaker (Eds.), *Teaching adolescents with disabilities: Accessing the general education curriculum* (pp. 121-156). Thousand Oaks, CA: Corwin Press.

Switlick, D. M. (1997). Integrating specialized curricula. In D. F. Bradley, M. E. King-Sears, & D. M. Tessier-Switlick, *Teaching students in inclusive settings: From theory to practice* (pp. 252-282). Boston: Allyn and Bacon.

Vacca, R. T., & Vacca, J. A. L. (2005). *Content area reading: Literacy and learning across the curriculum*. Boston: Pearson.

Wang, M. C., Haertel, G. D., & Walberg, H. J. (1993/94, December/January). Synthesis of research: What helps students learn? *Educational Leadership*, 74-79.

Implications for Our School: Questions for Discussion and Reflection

- Is explicit learning strategy instruction a routine part of our content-area learning? If not, where and how can we incorporate learning strategy instruction into content-area learning schoolwide?

- When we develop supports for individual students who are struggling, do we consider what learning strategies the student may lack and have a process in place to strengthen these areas?

- Do teachers in our school have a strong repertoire of learning strategies to share with students? If not, how can we build this repertoire?

- How can we begin to develop a carefully sequenced, grade-to-grade plan for strategy instruction?

Follow-up and Action Items

_____

_____

_____

_____

_____

_____

_____

_____

_____

_____

_____

_____

Chapter 4

Motivating Reluctant Learners

"Reluctant learners" pose a challenge teachers must actively address to remove this barrier from student learning.

They are the students who avoid challenges, who don't complete tasks, and who are satisfied to "just get by" in class. They are "reluctant learners," and their lack of motivation can have a profound effect on their school experience. The Center on Innovation & Improvement talks about aspects of motivation critically important to a student's willingness to engage with learning:

> Motivation is measured by: 1) willingness to attempt and 2) persistence. When we are presented with a challenge, how willing are we to attempt it? How persistent are we in sticking with it to the end? (Center on Innovation & Improvement, 2008, p. 11)

Identifying the reasons behind these students' reluctance to learn is integral to piquing their interest in schoolwork and helping them to acquire the knowledge they need to succeed. For example, some reluctant students have been told or have received the message over time that they are poor students, and, as a result, they may feel frustrated, inadequate, confused, or even ashamed (Hebb, 2000). This effect can lead to a downward spiral. As they receive negative feedback from teachers and parents, there is often even less motivation to engage. Sullo talks about student behaviors such as habitually failing to complete work:

> All behavior, even behavior we don't understand, is purposeful. That doesn't mean it is responsible or effective. It simply means that behavior serves a function. The purpose of behavior is to feel better. (Sullo, 2007, p. 13)

The "purpose" of this unwillingness to engage could come from a fear of failure or simply from not seeing the value in doing the work. However, from the perspective of the adults involved, this failure to apply oneself is both unproductive and irrational. Thus, all parties—students, teachers, and parents—are likely to become increasingly frustrated, with the potential for even more student disengagement from academic tasks.

Why Are Some Students Reluctant to Learn?

The National Research Council (2003) identifies three categories of "internal" student factors that can impact the school-engagement connection:

- "Student perceptions of competence and control (I can)—Students will not exert effort in academic work if they are convinced they lack the capacity to succeed or have no control over outcomes. . . . They need to know what it takes to succeed and to believe they can succeed." (pp. 34-35)

- "Student values and goals (I want to)—Even if students believe they can succeed in school, they won't exert effort unless they see some reason to do so." (p. 37)

- "Social connectedness (I belong)—Although feeling psychologically connected to school is not sufficient for meaningful engagement in academic work, it is probably necessary for many students." (p. 42)

Shore provides some additional details on factors that can contribute to low motivation:

- *Lack of relevance.* A student may believe that schoolwork is unimportant and does not relate to his or her life or interests.

- *Peer concern.* A student may opt for appearing "cool" rather than to try and risk embarrassment.

- *Learning problems.* The student who struggles to keep pace with peers in the classroom may simply give up in frustration.

- *Lack of challenge.* Apathy toward schoolwork may stem from assignments that are below a student's ability.

- *Desire for attention.* A student may try to gain the teacher's attention and support by appearing helpless.

- *Emotional distress.* Lack of interest in schoolwork or ability to focus may actually be an indication of anxiety, distress, or depression.

- *Expression of anger.* A student may perform poorly in school as an act of rebellion against parental pressure to excel academically (2001, p. 17).

Motivation to Learn: Eight Research-Based Principles

Motivational beliefs act as favorable contexts for learning. Knowledge about your students' motivational beliefs will allow you to plan learning activities that make good use of their favorable motivational beliefs and prompt them to reconsider unfavorable beliefs.

Students are not motivated to learn in the face of failure. Students who state that they will never be able to complete the task successfully signal to you that they no longer perceive a link between their actions and a positive outcome. You can help them to re-establish the link by creating learning situations where they can experience success. However, it is not sufficient that they get the correct solution. They also need to understand why the solution plan was correct and what they can do (actions) to improve their skill further.

Students who value the learning activity are less dependent on encouragement, incentives, and reward. Unfortunately, not all students are intrinsically motivated and you also have to cater to those students who are less motivated to learn. It is important to realize that classroom climate and the way you interact with your students facilitates or impedes their motivation. Try to make tasks and activities meaningful for your students by referring to the intrinsic value of the task and to potential applications in other subject areas and outside school. How can you help your students to develop favorable motivational beliefs? Translate the curriculum in terms of the skills that your students find relevant and interesting.

Students who are mastery-oriented learn more than students who are ego-oriented. The extent to which you succeed in creating a mastery-oriented learning setting is an indication of your professional competence. You can play down ego-orientation by explaining to your students that you are not interested in seeing one correct outcome, but that you focus instead on their attempts to come up with a solution strategy. Students will only believe this "trying is more important than the product" statement when you act according to what you preach.

Students expect value for effort. In general, students' theory of effort is underdeveloped. They need assignments to build up domain-specific effort beliefs and to be encouraged to update these beliefs as their skill develops. When you encourage and value effort, your students will begin to view themselves as responsible for their own learning. It is essential, however, that you provide your students with adequate feedback. A good way to start is by providing assignments that require students to predict the effort needed to do a task. After finishing the task, students could be asked to reflect on the invested effort. Was it sufficient or superfluous, and why? Once students get into the habit of reflecting on their effort, they are better equipped to self-regulate their own learning.

Students need encouragement and feedback on how to develop motivational strategies. What can be done to encourage your students to develop motivation strategies? The goal-setting process can be facilitated by asking students to stop and think about why a particular learning task is important, relevant, fun, boring, challenging, difficult, or easy. Why are they confident (or doubtful) about their own skills to do a task, and what triggers their doubt or confidence? When students have completed a task they can reflect on their original appraisal of the task again. Ask them to formulate in their own words whether their appraisal of the task has changed and why.

Students need encouragement and feedback on how to develop willpower. In order to be able to interpret student initiative, persistence, and disengagement meaningfully, you need to have a good idea of the way your students perceive the learning goal and also of how much effort they need to invest to reach it. Students should be given plenty of opportunities to practice striving for goals. You can coach this process by reminding them to set a series of sub-goals and to compose a checklist that will help them to monitor, assess, and reflect on the quality of their engagement and commitment during the solution process.

Students are more committed to learning if the objectives are compatible with their own goals. Students bring their own goals into the classroom and want to negotiate with you about how, when, and with whom they want to reach the learning goals…. For example, Sandra may ask: "Can I hand in my homework tomorrow because I did not have enough resource material to make a good job of it?"… If you grant these requests, your students will experience self-determination. The positive cognitions and feelings that are part of that experience will further the learning process.

Excerpted from Boekaerts, 2002.

In the Classroom

Although there are definitely student-specific factors that contribute to low motivation, no discussion about motivating reluctant students is complete without attention to the classroom as context. However, taking all the relevant elements is a complex task. Consider some of the variables:

> The teacher contributes to a student's desire to learn by modeling an enthusiasm for learning and for the specific topic; presenting material clearly, interactively, and directly; interacting socially and academically with students; and allowing students a degree of self-direction or self-management toward clear objectives. Students respond to the right blend of caring and expectation, the knowledge that the teacher "knows me and thinks there is something special about me," recognition for accomplishment derived from evidence of effort and mastery, the opportunity to manage work tasks and to be responsible for them, and content that is challenging and interestingly presented. (Center on Innovation & Improvement, 2008, p. 11)

It is also important to understand that "motivation is not a character trait but rather a state that manifests itself differently in diverse settings" (Gehlbach & Roeser, 2002, p. 41). Rahal (2010) talks about this:

> The challenge . . . is to find the individual key that unlocks a child's motivation to succeed, and build on that foundation. One thing is certain: teachers cannot expect to use a one-size-fits-all technique to motivate all students. Instead, they must ask and answer the question, "What makes *this* student tick?"(p. 1)

Brewster and Fager (2000) agree with Rahal's assessment and also point to the research base about motivation:

> Research has shown that teachers can influence student motivation; that certain practices do work to increase time spent on task; and that there are ways to make assigned work more engaging and more effective for students at all levels. (p. 4)

They go on to provide details about ways in which teachers can impact a student's level of motivation:

> Research tells us that the teachers who are most successful in engaging students develop activities with students' basic psychological and intellectual needs in mind. In general, students need work that develops their sense of competency, allows them to develop connections with others, gives them some degree of autonomy, and provides opportunities for originality and self-expression. The challenge teachers face, then, is to create a learning environment that attends to all or most of these needs. (p. 13)

Finally, Good and Brophy (2008) suggest that teachers can build motivation by ensuring that students view the classroom as a community that supports learning and is a safe place in which to take risks.

Offer Students Choices

"The more that students perceive autonomy, the more engaged they become in learning," say Gehlbach and Roeser (2002, p. 42). In one study, students indicated that having control over their learning makes them feel more involved and competent (DiCintio & Gee, 1999). Teachers can strengthen students' feelings of self-determination by allowing them reasonable choices in their assigned activities—for example, by sometimes allowing students to choose whether they will work in a group or individually on a particular project (Gehlbach & Roeser, 2002).

Other specific techniques for motivating students through involvement include:

- *Allowing flexible sequencing and due dates.* This technique enables students to determine the order for independent practice activities. A complete social studies unit, for example, may require a product map, a written summary, and an oral report within a particular time period. However, teacher reminders may be required until students acquire necessary time management skills.

- *Incorporating self-scoring and self-correction.* For example, select seatwork assignments that fall within students' independence level (i.e., above an 80% accuracy level) so that the need for assistance will be minimized. Provide answer keys and instruct students to self-score their work and to make necessary corrections independently or with the assistance of a "study buddy," the teacher, an aide, or taped study guides.

- *Varying assignment length.* For example, construct assignments so that the most critical problems are contained within the initial section of the exercise or worksheet and instruct students to self-correct when they reach a certain point within the assignment. Set a target level (e.g., 90% correct) and students who reach that level are exempt from the remainder of the assignment and can move on to alternative activities (Fulk & Montgomery-Grymes, 1994).

Help Students Set Goals

Goal setting also can help students develop an internal sense of control and responsibility for their learning. The goals should be:

- *Specific and measurable in quantity of achievement.* For example, students can count how many assignments were finished on time or how many points in a week they earned in a particular class to stay on pace for a "B" grade.

- *Something the student wants to improve on.* The goals can be negotiated with a teacher, but are established primarily by the student.

- *Attainable and practical for a specific time period or for a term of school.* Goals should have starting and finishing dates.

- *In writing.* For discipline and clarity, goals should be written down. They then become concrete and allow students to plan, organize, and develop responsibility and pride in effort.

- *Stated in terms of expected results.* Focusing on clear expectations helps create a "road map" by which students can form a mental image of each goal. Once the students can "see" a particular goal, they are better able to find ways to accomplish their objectives.

- *Displayed on a "scoresheet."* Students can employ personal scorecards to count their "wins" (progress), both small and large (Martino, 1993).

Classroom Practices That Undermine Motivation

Dolezal, Welsh, Pressley, and Vincent (2003) report on practices they observed that actually undermine student motivation:

- ability attributions (teacher comments tie success to ability, not effort)
- competitive environment in which "winning" is stressed over working together and improving
- few displays of student work and accomplishments
- lack of scaffolding for students who are struggling
- ineffective/negative feedback
- lack of connection of new material to students' prior knowledge
- lack of monitoring of students' behavior, level of attentiveness, and so on
- lack of established routines and procedures
- low task difficulty
- negative classroom atmosphere
- negative approach to classroom management
- overly difficult tasks
- poor/incomplete planning
- public punishment
- slow pacing
- sparse classroom environment
- task completion emphasized over learning
- uninspiring instructional practices

Make Learning "Attractive"

Students need to understand the "significance" of the material being presented. For example, teachers might make explicit efforts to connect content or skills to real world settings or capture students' interest by activating their prior knowledge of specific topics (Fulk & Montgomery-Grymes, 1994). Appealing to what students like or consider fun can motivate reluctant learners (Herzog, 2002). Even simply being aware of which students react positively to specific instructional strategies and which students have difficulty with certain approaches—for example, knowing that a particular student is more comfortable sharing information in a small group than with the whole class—can increase some learners' educational participation (Educational Research Service, 1998).

Educator Mike Muir suggests asking a group of underachieving students the following questions about how they think they learn best, and then using the information when planning instruction:

- Think of a good learning experience. What made it good?

- Describe a good class or teacher that you have now or have had in the past. What made them good?

- Imagine that the state department of education came to you and asked you how to design courses and units so that you could really learn well. What would you tell them?

- What one thing would you change about how your classes are taught or how your teachers teach that would help you to learn better? (2001, p. 38)

> *"A common theme among effective practices is that they address underlying psychological variables related to motivation, such as competence and control, beliefs about the value of education, and a sense of belonging. In brief, engaging schools and teachers promote students' confidence in their ability to learn and succeed in school by providing challenging instruction and support for meeting high standards, and they clearly convey their own high expectations for student success." (National Research Council, 2003, pp. 2-3)*

Teach Students About the Learning Process

Some reluctant learners may not know how to study effectively, which becomes a barrier that makes learning difficult and unattractive. Teachers can help by incorporating skill building in their instruction or by providing explicit cues to assist students. For example, they can:

- Ensure that they have students' attention before they present directions.

- Allow sufficient time between each step if lengthy directions are necessary.

- Monitor clarity by asking students to restate the directions in their own words.

- Provide demonstrations or modeling prior to students' independent work.

- Employ a system of "study buddies" from whom students can quietly request clarification prior to independent work (Fulk & Montgomery-Grymes, 1994, p. 32).

Finally, no matter how uncomfortable it might be, educators should speak honestly to students about their performance while also providing concrete suggestions for improvement. Doing the required grade-level standards that must be met can help motivate students to try harder—especially before it is too late. Teachers should explain the required grade-level standards that must be met to students at the beginning of the school year and periodically through the year. "If students don't know what standard they must meet and what progress they are making toward meeting the standard, how can they remain hopeful? Are we asking students to keep learning without telling them the target?" asks Tufly (2001, p. 39).

Recognizing the Importance of the Affective Environment

Mendler (2002) reminds us that teachers can do "small" things that can have a great impact on making the classroom a safe and encouraging place—a place in which it is easier for students to take risks. For example, he suggests that teachers:

- congratulate five students during each class on something they have achieved;

- respond nonevaluatively at least three times per class by offering comments such as, "That's an interesting way of looking at it;" or,

- have an "on-a-roll" program that acknowledges students for demonstrating improved effort or performance.

Finally, VanDeWeghe talks about the importance of teachers *modeling* engagement. He views this as going beyond the modeling more typically done by teachers:

For many teachers, modeling means showing students how to complete some task—for example, set up a lab experiment, write an introductory paragraph, or give a dramatic reading—that students are then expected to do themselves. Engaged modeling goes much further than merely completing a task, for, in it, we share our ways of thinking and feeling. (2009, p. 48)

> *"Creating a systemic approach to student engagement ensures that student engagement is a priority of all adults in the school community, provides the structures to support student engagement, and ensures that all students have the opportunity to become engaged in their school community. This systemic approach addresses the multiple reasons students are disengaged, including a reassessment of curriculum and pedagogies to increase engagement with academic content; reconsidering the structure of schools to ensure each student has the opportunity to have a meaningful relationship with at least one adult in the school; and providing professional development to ensure teachers acquire the knowledge and skills to employ quality engagement strategies." (Education Commission of the States, 2007, p. 3)*

In Summary

Reasons why students are reluctant learners are often complex. Educators need to look not only at students in isolation but also at the interaction between students and the classroom/school environment. Students need both challenge and support. They need to be actively engaged, with instructional approaches designed to maximize the possibilities for engagement. They need to feel safe so that they can take risks instead of retreating from participation. By focusing efforts on both the students and the learning environment, educators are more likely to achieve their goal of motivating reluctant students. Finally, Bartholomew reminds us that encouraging student motivation should be viewed as an ongoing process:

> Fire building is an apt metaphor for what we hope to accomplish with students—not igniting a Roman candle that quickly burns out, but creating a blaze that burns steadily on its own. (2008, p. 55)

References

Bartholomew, B. (2008, March). Sustaining the fire. *Educational Leadership*, 55-60.

Boekaerts, M. (2002). *Motivation to learn.* Brussels, Belgium: International Academy of education. Retrieved from http://www.ibe.unesco.org/publications/EducationalPracticesSeriesPdf/prac10e.pdf

Brewster, C., & Fager, J. (2000). *Increasing student engagement and motivation: From time-on-task to homework.* Portland, OR: Northwest Regional Educational Laboratory. Retrieved from http://educationnorthwest.org/webfm_send/452.

Center on Innovation & Improvement. (2008). *Training for instructional leaders: Effective teaming, collegial learning, instructional planning, instructional delivery.* Lincoln, IL: Author.

DiCintio, M. J., & Gee, S. (1999, July). Control is the key: Unlocking the motivation of at-risk students. *Psychology in the Schools*, 231-237.

Dolezal, S. E., Welsh, L. M., Pressley, M., & Vincent, M. M. (2003, January). How nine third-grade teachers motivate student academic engagement. *The Elementary School Journal*, 239-267.

Education Commission of the States. (2007, September). Student engagement. *The Progress of Education Reform 2007.* Denver, CO: Education Commission of the States.

Educational Research Service. (1998). *ERS the informed educator series: Enhancing student engagement in learning.* Arlington, VA: Author.

Fulk, B. M., & Montgomery-Grymes, D. J. (1994, September). Strategies to improve student motivation. *Intervention in School and Clinic*, 28-33.

Gehlbach, H., & Roeser, R. W. (2002, January). The middle way to motivating middle school students: Avoiding false dichotomies. *Middle School Journal*, 39-46.

Good, T. L. & Brophy, J. E. (2008). *Looking in classrooms.* Columbus, OH: Allyn & Bacon/Merrill Education.

Hebb, J. L. (2000, March). Reluctant readers reading. *English Journal*, 22-25.

Herzog, J. M. (2002). *Motivating reluctant learners.* Handout from AHEA Convention in Pittsburgh, PA. Retrieved from http://www.abhome-ed.org/motivating.html

Martino, L. R. (1993, May). A goal-setting model for young adolescent at-risk students. *Middle School Journal*, 19-22.

Mendler, A. N. (2002, January). Making the connection: Building trust, encouraging success, and breaking down barriers between educators and students. *Virginia Journal of Education*, 7-10.

Muir, M. (2001, November). What engages underachieving middle school students in learning? *Middle School Journal*, 37-43.

National Research Council. (2003). *Engaging schools: Fostering high school students' motivation to learn.* Washington, DC: The National Academies Press.

Ornstein, A. C. (1994, July). Yearning to learn. *The Executive Educator*, 27-30.

Rahal, M. L. (2010). *ERS focus on: Identifying and motivating underachievers.* Alexandria, VA: Educational Research Service.

Shore, K. (2001, November). Motivating unmotivated students. *Principal*, 16-20.

Sullo, B. (2007). *Activating the desire to learn.* Alexandria, VA: Association for Supervision and Curriculum Development.

Tufly, C. (2001, October). An alternative to failure. *Principal Leadership*, 39-41.

VanDeWeghe, R. (2009). *Engaged learning.* Thousand Oaks, CA: Corwin Publications.

Implications for Our School: Questions for Discussion and Reflection

- Are reluctant learners a problem in our school? Do we see them more often in specific grades or content areas—or among specific groups of students?

- If we answered "yes" to any of the questions above, are there any patterns in the lack of engagement that might point the way to addressing the problem?

- Have we ever asked students questions such as those suggested by Mike Muir on p. 37? Brainstorm additional questions that could form the basis for discussions with students.

- Talk about the quote from the Education Commission of the States (in the box on page 39). What implications might this have for our school?

Follow-up and Action Items

_____

_____

_____

_____

_____

_____

_____

_____

_____

_____

_____

_____

Chapter 5

Culturally Responsive Teaching

Culturally responsive instruction can support school efforts to help an increasingly diverse student population meet rigorous standards.

Cultural diversity is the norm for many schools today and, for schools, this diversity often presents a difficult challenge that directly impacts efforts to have all students achieve at high levels. The achievement gap too often seen between students of different racial, ethnic, and cultural backgrounds in our schools makes it essential for educators to learn all they can about barriers to learning that some of their students experience. Although culture is only one of these barriers, it is one that schools can address.

Why Culture Matters

All children grow up within a cultural environment that influences how they present themselves, understand the world, and interpret experiences. A child's cultural context can affect how he or she processes and organizes information, communicates verbally and nonverbally, and perceives physical and social environments. Each of these factors in turn can shape a child's learning patterns and affect later school experiences (National Academy of Sciences, 1994).

Trumbell, Rothstein-Fisch, and Greenfield remind us of how interwoven culture is in our daily lives—and in the daily lives of schools:

> Culture is like the air we breathe, permeating all we do. And the hardest culture to examine is often our own, because it shapes our actions in ways that seem second nature.... Like individuals and groups, schools have cultures, too. These usually mirror the culture of the dominant society. We know the struggle many children and their parents face in learning English as a second language, and we understand that refugees from troubled homelands often bring emotional burdens. But we may not realize what an enormously difficult transition many must make in learning to decipher a new culture. This is often true, too, for native-born American children when the cultural values at home differ significantly from those of school. (2000, p. 2)

43

Koki explains the impact of cultural differences on education in commonsense terms:

> Perhaps one of the most important findings about learning is that comprehension is not transferred directly from a source—the teacher—to a learner. Instead, the brain "filters" information to make sense of it in light of what the learner already knows. In today's diverse classrooms, students have many experiences and knowledge bases that may not be familiar to teachers from the "mainstream" culture. Researchers suspect that many teachers—whether they are dealing with minority children who are geographically isolated or inner-city children in a highly urban setting—may inadvertently overlook what children already know, and thus fail to connect the information or skills the children need to have with the children's prior experiences. (n.d., p. 3)

Culture does *not* determine a child's ability or intelligence, but it can produce many different ways of knowing and learning. Even the youngest children bring knowledge and experience with them to school, and effective teachers design instruction so that these are "acknowledged, valued, and incorporated in the classroom" (Ladson-Billings, 1994).

> *Culture does not determine a child's ability or intelligence. But it can produce many different ways of knowing and learning.*

The Classroom as a Culture

We often think of culture as something other people have, something unfamiliar. However, each of us is a product of our own culture, one that may be almost invisible to us since we are so used to it. For teachers as well as students, it is "the lens through which we look at the world… it influences how we process learning, solve problems, and teach." Typically, it also "becomes the norm by which we measure all others' behavior" (Edwards, Ellis, Ko, Saifer, & Stuczynski, 2004, p. 6).

In addition, there is a dominant culture in our country, one reflecting predominantly European-American, middle class norms. This culture has a significant impact on "the content of school curricula, assumptions about background knowledge, teaching approaches, classroom interaction, classroom routines, and parental participation" (Quinn, 2001, p. 48).

Finally, it helps to understand that teaching is a cultural activity. Every day, every class period, every minute, teachers and students engage in a "dance" composed of a combination of expectations, communications, and behaviors. When the participants in this dance all come from similar backgrounds and experiences, even subtle, implicit messages are likely to be understood, and all members of the classroom community can focus on learning.

However, in classrooms characterized by a variety of cultures, such messages may not always be understood as they were intended. Students may not "share meaning" with the teacher (Nelson-Barber & Estrin, 1995, p. 13). Zion, Zion, and King talk about this:

> All of our learning and teaching is framed within the context of our culture. Often, students' cultural backgrounds and experiences do not match the dominant culture of schools, and they may become disengaged from learning.... It is the responsibility of the school/teacher to uncover the disconnects between school and home culture, and to adjust learning opportunities to correspond. (2008, p. 19)

"Children whose cultural orientations match the one that is rewarded in school (i.e., independence, individual identity, competition) experience more academic success than those with different cultural orientations (i.e., interdependence, group identity, group success). Lack of understanding of these differences often leads to negative consequences for students, including disproportionate representation in special education, overreferral to discipline, underrepresentation in advanced academic and gifted programs, and high retention and dropout rates." (Guerra & Nelson, 2009, p. 358)

Learning About Culture

Teachers who serve each day as cultural mediators know the challenge goes beyond language. Even as they try to help immigrant students navigate a new system of education, their own teaching methods and most routine classroom expectations can come into conflict with children's cultural ways of knowing and behaving. For example, a student may resist offering the right answer after another student has answered incorrectly to avoid potentially embarrassing that person in front of the group. A student raised to value consensus may find decisions made by majority rule inconsiderate or even unfair, instead of simply democratic (Trumbell et al., 2000, p. 2).

Making the Classroom Hospitable

One way in which cultures may vary is in their orientation toward valuing the community—the collective—over individuals. Teachers involved with the Bridging Cultures project have experimented with specific ways to make their classrooms more "culture friendly" for students with a more collectivistic orientation. Here are some simple changes that capitalize on children's values of helping and sharing:

- Select two classroom monitors rather than one, and allow them to work together.

- Allow students to help one another study vocabulary (students with greater English proficiency help those with lesser proficiency).

- Allow students to work in small groups to preview their homework assignments and discuss possible strategies for problems to ensure that all understand the assignment. (This also helps students whose parents may not be able to read the assignment in English.)

- Use choral reading, as well as individual reading.

- Have more than one "child of the week," so that the attention is shared.

- Share cleanup of the whole room at once, rather than having each group clean up one activity center before the children move to another (observed in a kindergarten classroom).

- Allow joint "ownership" of classroom crayons rather than a box per child (Trumbell et al., 2000, p. 11).

Cultural Orientations That May Affect Student Behavior	
Individualistic Perspective	**Collectivistic Perspective**
Student should "achieve his or her potential" for the sake of self-fulfillment.	Student should "achieve his or her potential" in order to contribute to the social whole.
Student should work independently and get his or her own work done. Giving help to others may be considered cheating.	Student should be helpful and cooperate with his or her peers, giving assistance when needed. Helping is not considered cheating.
Student should be praised frequently to build self-esteem. The positive should be emphasized whenever possible.	Student should be given feedback for improvement. Praise should be stated in terms of student's ability to help family or community.
Student should attain intellectual skills in school (education as schooling).	Student should learn appropriate social behaviors and skills as well as intellectual skills (education as upbringing).
Student should engage in discussion and argument to learn to think critically (constructivist model).	Student should be quiet and respectful in class because he will learn more (transmission model).
Property belongs to individuals, and others must ask to borrow or share it.	Much property is communal and not considered the domain of an individual.
Teacher manages behavior indirectly or emphasizes student self-control.	Teacher has primary authority for managing behavior but also expects peers to guide each other's behavior.
Parent is integrally involved with student's academic progress.	Parent believes that it is teacher's role to provide academic instruction to student.

Source: Trumbell & Pacheco, 2005, p. 94.

Caution: One Size Does Not Fit All

While information about cultural characteristics is critical to the process of making classrooms more culturally sensitive, caution is also in order. It is still essential to regard every student as an individual. Within any given ethnic group, individuals vary greatly in their experiences, beliefs, individual preferences, and personalities. Gutierrez and Rogoff (2003) also point out that an individual's "style" is neither a trait independent of context nor even constant over time.

We should also realize that problems of cultural conflicts are not always limited to foreign-born children or children from certain ethnic or racial groups. Addressing only the needs of these children will ignore the differences in life experiences that might exist between, for example, native middle-class and low-income children. These children can vary by more than just the academic or prereading skills they bring to school. Variations might include adult/child interaction patterns, behaviors considered appropriate for children, and family expectations with regard to home-school relationships. These are all part of the child's culture, and for some children that culture may be one that does not mesh easily with the school culture.

Standards-Based Education and Cultural Diversity

Saifer, Edwards, Ellis, Ko, and Stuczynski write about teachers using a relatively new approach—culturally responsive, standards-based (CRSB) teaching. These teachers work to consciously and explicitly integrate:

> two important aspects of education: culturally responsive teaching and standards-based teaching. Much has been written about culturally responsive and standards-based teaching separately, but it is the integration of the approaches that is critical to the goal of high achievement for all students. Culturally responsive teaching addresses the needs of students by improving motivation and engagement, and standards-based teaching provides all students with the opportunity for rigorous, high-level learning. CRSB teaching means doing both, *together*. (2005, p. 2)

Educators agree that high standards should be applied to all students, regardless of their culture. However, the current focus on standards—the *what* that students should know—should not be viewed as limiting *how* the content must be taught.

> Although the curriculum may be dictated by the school system, teachers teach it. Where the curriculum falls short in addressing the needs of all students, teachers must provide a bridge. (Richards, Brown, & Forde 2004, p. 8)

Obviously, the issue involves equity as well as standards, since "if instruction reflects the cultural and linguistic practices and values of only one group of students, then the other students are denied an equal opportunity to learn" (Richards et al., 2004, p. 8). In Gaitan's view, "The goal is to orient the learning setting to equitably serve the students from nondominant cultures" (2006, p. 154).

> *"Culturally responsive, standards-based teaching draws on the experiences, understanding, views, concepts, and ways of knowing of the students who are in a particular class or school." (Saifer & Barton, 2007, p. 25)*

The challenge for teachers, then, is developing an approach to teaching that supports all students. Terms often used to describe such teaching are culturally responsive or culturally sensitive. Johnson and Protheroe talk about this:

> Culturally sensitive instruction seeks an educationally productive balance between commonality and diversity in heterogeneous schools and classrooms. Commonality is emphasized through the universal acquisition of a common set of basic skills necessary to function in school and in mainstream society. The cultural diversity present in the classroom is also recognized, respected, and used as an instructional resource. In culturally sensitive instruction, teachers regard the academic success of all students as fundamental. They seek to incorporate appropriate instructional strategies and create learning environments that most effectively motivate and teach each student to succeed. (2003, p. 4)

Strong, Silver, and Perini agree with the need to recognize that "common curriculum does not imply a common instructional method" (2002, p. 65) and broaden the discussion past issues of culture to those of learning styles:

> Some students learn more visually; others require discussion; still others favor direct instruction or project work. Attempting to elevate any one instructional strategy above the others guarantees that students whose learning styles differ from the common delivery system will suffer. A child who needs an imaginative approach to learning, or one who learns through conversation and dialogue, will not acquire the learning he needs and will therefore appear more and more disabled because of the school's refusal to address that learning style. (2002, p. 65)

> *"The way we teach profoundly affects the way students learn." (Protheroe & Turner, 2003, p. 4)*

Using Knowledge About Culture to Strengthen the Teaching-Learning Connection

Simply learning about cultures represented in your classroom is not enough, since "the way we teach profoundly affects the way students learn" (Protheroe & Turner, 2003, p. 4). The next step is finding ways to incorporate this knowledge into your teaching practices. Williams (2006) asks, "Is culturally relevant teaching different from good teaching in general?" and then responds:

Good teaching includes such factors as providing a caring environment, having content knowledge and pedagogical knowledge, and practicing skillful classroom management. However, all of these factors may coexist with the implicit goal of promoting the majority culture. For many children who are not part of the majority culture, this approach can create dissonance, which may inhibit their ability to benefit fully from otherwise good teaching and further exacerbate existing gaps in learning curriculum content. Culturally relevant teaching, on the other hand, includes all that is considered good teaching but also takes the learner's cultural background into consideration, building on the student's experiences and affirming his or her cultural identity. (p. 12)

Thus, culturally sensitive teaching does incorporate many elements commonly recognized as "good teaching." For example, Moir suggests that "teachers who consistently get results with all groups of students have strong content knowledge, an array of effective strategies, draw on prior knowledge of their students, see the range of student abilities and differentiate instruction, and constantly examine their own attitudes about race, class, and culture" (2002, p. 1). Use of a variety of teaching strategies is key to culturally sensitive instruction, an approach that also helps to meet the needs of a wider range of students regardless of their cultural backgrounds.

Finally, another challenge for teachers "involves striking a balance between demonstrating respect and understanding for culturally divergent students and preparing these students to participate successfully in formal school settings" (Ellison, Boykin, Towns, & Stokes 2000, p. 3).

Four Keys to Culturally Sensitive Instruction

Teachers who have worked to make their classrooms more culturally sensitive would agree that the process is not always easy. It takes standing back and consciously reflecting on the way you teach—then asking whether your approach is successful with all your students. From that perspective, the features of culturally sensitive instruction are closely aligned with what we recognize as good teaching. For example, the first significant feature of culturally sensitive instruction is its pro-student philosophy. All students are seen as having the inherent resources and ability to experience academic success. The idea is to capitalize on each child's strengths, viewing cultural ways of learning as resources to be used rather than deficits to be remedied.

The second feature of culturally sensitive teaching is its development from a basic premise: There is no single best teaching method that will effectively reach all students at all times. Effective teachers diversify their instruction in response to individual students' interests, personalities, and abilities—taking into account their differences in culture while not ignoring their need to learn skills necessary for success in the larger community.

For example, to assist students who do not initially respond well to mainstream techniques, instructional methods that are more "culturally compatible" can be used initially to present new or difficult material—a form of scaffolding. Mainstream methods can then be employed to further develop concepts, reinforce learning, and assist with skill mastery.

A third key feature of culturally sensitive instruction is its adherence to the "principle of least change" (Jordan, 1985). This framework suggests that only the minimum number of changes necessary to produce desirable learning should be undertaken at any given time. Such a framework helps to make change a clearly defined, focused, and manageable process. In other words, teachers should not attempt to duplicate the cultural environment of their students' homes.

Finally, the fourth characteristic of culturally sensitive instruction is its emphasis on high expectations and high academic standards for all children. Strong et al. (2002) make clear that the current focus on standards—the *what* that students should know—should not be viewed as limiting *how* the content should be taught. The key to success in diverse classrooms becomes "modifying the *means* used to achieve learning outcomes, not changing the intended outcomes themselves" (Gilbert & Gay, 1985).

Although these four characteristics highlight the need to mesh culture and instruction, the appropriate place to begin is to focus on what we know about both learning and good teaching and then use that knowledge as the bedrock for designing effective student-teacher interaction. It can serve as a reminder of how important it is for teachers to understand—and design their instruction around—the strengths, weaknesses, and needs of all of their students. It also suggests that teachers using a variety of teaching approaches in their classrooms may already be incorporating many culturally compatible elements into their instruction.

For example, researchers at the Center for Research on Education, Diversity, and Excellence (CREDE) propose the following five standards for effective pedagogy as "critical for improving learning outcomes for all students, and especially those of diverse ethnic, cultural, linguistic, or economic backgrounds":

- *Joint productive activity* that also might include instruction on how students should work in groups;

- *Language development*, with efforts made to link students' natural language with the language of the classroom;

- *Contextualization*—making meaning by connecting school instruction to children's lives—not only provides students with concrete examples of the concepts being learned but also assumes that teachers will learn more about their students;

- *Challenging activities* that teach complex thinking and motivate even students typically considered at risk; and,

- *Instructional conversation*, in which teachers encourage students to engage in purposeful dialogue (Doherty et al., 2004).

Although most educators will recognize the instructional strategies described above as simply indicators of good teaching, the CREDE researchers emphasize they may be especially helpful to students from nonmainstream cultures.

Finally, one aspect of culturally responsive teaching is simply being more self-aware and in touch with the "feel" of the classroom from the perspective of culture. Saifer et al. describe this as "being conscious of the dynamics inherent when cultures interact—paying attention to the feelings in the pit of our stomach, confronting our prejudices, and refining our perceptions" (2005, p. 35).

Integrating Culture Into Classroom Practices

Pewewardy (1999) offers the following suggestions to guide teachers' efforts toward more culturally sensitive teaching:

- Understand and use students' prior cultural knowledge as a foundation in the teaching and learning process.

- Ask whether classroom practices are compatible with students' language patterns, cognitive functioning, motivation, and the social norms and structures to which they are accustomed.

- Make an effort to integrate the strengths that students bring with them—for example, experiences with storytelling—into instruction.

- Realize that teachers might sometimes need to be "cultural mediators" and provide assistance through the use of questions, feedback, and scaffolding.

- Ask if the approaches used to assess students reflect the diversity of student strengths and styles.

Embedded in these suggestions is the need for teachers to carefully study their own practices—even though these practices might have been successful with most of the students they taught in the past—and to think about them in terms of a more diverse classroom.

Some Inaccurate Beliefs About Culturally Relevant Pedagogy

- Only teachers of color can be culturally relevant.

- Culturally relevant teachers are more concerned about personal relationships with their diverse students than effective classroom management.

- The purpose of culturally relevant pedagogy is to help diverse students "feel good" about themselves.

- Culturally relevant teachers attend primarily to learning styles (e.g., by addressing African American male students' need for kinesthetic activities or allowing Asian students to work alone).

- Culturally relevant pedagogy is not helpful for teaching White students (Irvine, n.d., p. 1).

In Summary

Delpit (1995) reminds us that the goal is not how teachers can create the perfect "culturally matched" learning situation for each ethnic group, but rather how to recognize when there is a learning problem for a particular child and then to devise an approach that eliminates the barrier. And Au (1980) has a commonsense message for teachers who are trying to expand their repertoire of teaching strategies to connect with a broader spectrum of students. In her view, "[t]he specific strategies teachers use are not so important as *whether or not the strategies make good sense to the children*" [emphasis added].

While advocates of culturally sensitive instruction accept that culture conflicts cannot be held wholly responsible for low achievement among some cultural and racial groups, they are also firm in their belief that addressing them can make a positive difference. Combined with high expectations for students, an awareness of cultural differences and the implementation of even small-scale changes in instructional practices can improve teacher-student communication and help to create supportive environments that maximize student achievement.

Diversity in our schools is both an opportunity and a challenge. The more we know about the implications of culture and learning, the more we can effect productive solutions to maximize academic achievement for diverse learners and prepare all students for a future in a global society. Teachers can help to minimize culture conflict and maximize the potential for effective teaching and learning by consciously examining their own behaviors and those of their students.

References

Au, K. H. (1980). Participation structures in a reading lesson with Hawaiian children: Analysis of a culturally appropriate instructional event. *Anthropology & Education Quarterly, 11*(2), 91-115.

Delpit, L. (1995). *Other people's children: Cultural conflict in the classroom.* New York: The New Press.

Doherty, R., Echevarria, J., Estrada, P., Goldenberg, C., Hilberg, R. S., Saunders, W. M., et al. (2004). *Research evidence: Five standards for effective pedagogy and student outcomes* (Technical Report No. G1). Santa Cruz, CA: Center for Research on Education, Diversity, and Excellence. Retrieved from http://gse.berkeley.edu/research/crede/pdf/g1_2004.pdf

Edwards, K., Ellis, D., Ko, L., Saifer, S., & Stuczynski, A. (2004). *Classroom to community and back: Using culturally responsive standards-based (CRSB) teaching to strengthen family and community partnerships and increase student achievement.* Retrieved from http://educationnorthwest.org/webfm_send/619

Ellison, C. M., Boykin, A. W., Towns, D. P., & Stokes, A. (2000). *Classroom cultural ecology: The dynamics of classroom life in schools serving low-income African American children.* Washington, DC: Howard University. Retrieved from http://www.csos.jhu.edu/crespar/techReports/Report44.pdf

Gaitan, C. D. (2006). *Building culturally responsive classrooms: A guide for K-6 teachers.* Thousand Oaks, CA: Corwin Press.

Gilbert, S. E., & Gay, G. (1985). Improving the success in school of poor black children. *Phi Delta Kappan, 67*(2), 133–37.

Guerra, P. L., & Nelson, S. W. (2009, January). Changing professional practice requires changing beliefs. *Phi Delta Kappan, 90*(5), 354-359.

Gutierrez, K. D., & Rogoff, B. (2003, June/July). Cultural ways of learning: Individual traits or repertoires of practice. *Educational Researcher, 32*(5), 19-25.

Irvine, J. J. (n.d.) *Culturally relevant pedagogy: A primer* [Facilitator's Guide]. Montgomery, AL: Teaching Diverse Students Initiative, Southern Poverty Law Center.

Johnson, L., & Protheroe, N. (2003). *What we know about: Culture and learning.* Arlington, VA: Educational Research Service.

Jordan, C. (1985). Translating culture: From ethnographic information to educational program. *Anthropology and Education Quarterly, 16*(2), 105-123.

Koki, S. (n.d.). *New research on learning indicates need for cultural awareness among educators* (PREL Briefing Paper). Honolulu: Pacific Region Educational Laboratory. Retrieved from http://www.prel.org/products/Products/New-research.pdf

Ladson-Billings, G. (1994). *The dreamkeepers: Successful teachers of African-American children.* San Francisco: Jossey-Bass Inc.

Moir, E. (2002, Spring). Preparing new teachers to meet the challenge. New Teacher Center Reflections, *5*(1).

National Academy of Sciences. (1994). *Cultural diversity and early education: Report of a workshop.* Washington: Author.

Nelson-Barber, S., & Estrin, E. T. (1995). *Culturally responsive mathematics and science education for native students.* San Francisco, CA: Far West Laboratory for Educational Research and Development.

Pewewardy, C. (1999). Culturally responsive teaching for American Indian students. In E. R. Hollins & E. I. Oliver (Eds.), *Pathways to success in school.* Rahway, N.J.: Lawrence Erlbaum Associates.

Protheroe, N., & Turner, J. (2003). *ERS informed educator: Culturally sensitive instruction.* Arlington, VA: Educational Research Service.

Quinn, A. E. (2001, March). Moving marginalized students inside the line: Cultural differences in the classroom. *English Journal, 90*(4), 44-50.

Richards, H. V., Brown, A. F., & Forde, T. B. (2004). *Addressing diversity in schools: Culturally responsive pedagogy.* Denver, CO: National Center for Culturally Responsive Educational Systems.

Saifer, S., & Barton, R. (2007, September). Promoting culturally responsive standards-based teaching. *Principal Leadership, 8*(1), 24-28.

Saifer, S., Edwards, K., Ellis, D., Ko, L., & Stuczynski, A. (2005). *Classroom to community and back: Using culturally responsive, standards-based teaching to strengthen family and community partnerships and increase student achievement.* Portland, OR: Northwest Regional Educational Laboratory.

Strong, R. W., Silver, H. F., & Perini, M. J. (2002). *Teaching what matters most: Standards and strategies for raising student achievement.* Alexandria, VA: Association for Supervision and Curriculum Development.

Trumbell, E., Rothstein-Fisch, C., & Greenfield, P. M. (2000). *Bridging cultures in our schools: New approaches that work* (WestEd Knowledge Brief). San Francisco: WestEd.

Trumbell, E., & Pacheco, M. (2005). *The teacher's guide to diversity: Building a knowledge base. Volume I: Human development, culture, and cognition.* Providence, RI: The Education Alliance at Brown University. Retrieved from http://www.alliance.brown.edu/pubs/teach_guide_diversity/tgd_humdevcult.pdf

Williams, B. (2006, Fall). Lessons along the cultural spectrum. *Journal of Staff Development, 27*(4), 10-14.

Zion, S., Zion, T., & King, K. (2008). *Academy 2: Culturally responsive classrooms, Module 2: Culturally responsive pedagogy and practice* [Facilitator's Manual]. Tempe AZ: National Center for Culturally Responsive Educational Systems, Arizona State University.

Implications for Our School: Questions for Discussion and Reflection

- How can we learn more about how specific cultural mismatches between school and our students' life experiences might be impacting their ability to learn?

- Talk about the possible balancing act between adapting classroom practices to better match students' cultural framework and the need to prepare the student to operate effectively in the mainstream culture.

- Au talks about the need for instructional strategies to "make good sense to children." As a student, did you ever experience instruction that didn't make good sense to you? Describe it briefly.

- Have you observed any student behavior in your classroom that varies from the norm and that might have its roots in the student's cultural experiences? Is this a behavior you can build on to help support the student's learning?

- Visit the page on the Teaching Tolerance Web site that discusses "Commonly Held Beliefs that Influence Teachers' Work with Diverse Students" (http://www.tolerance.org/tdsi/cb_intro) and discuss your experiences or thoughts about these beliefs.

Follow-up and Action Items

_____

_____

_____

_____

_____

_____

_____

_____

_____

_____

_____

Chapter 6

Response to Intervention in Middle and High Schools

Although implementing a Response to Intervention framework may be challenging in middle and high schools, its core elements can help schools more effectively address the needs of struggling students.

Until recently, Response to Intervention (RTI) has been seen as primarily an elementary school initiative, but now middle and high schools are looking at the approach—some voluntarily as a support for struggling students and some in response to state or district requirements. Regardless of the reason, RTI is a topic of interest for many secondary schools.

In essence, RTI is a shift away from a discrepancy approach that focuses primarily on identifying students who are already exhibiting learning problems to one that includes "comprehensive, data-based prevention" as a core element (Center for Comprehensive School Reform and Improvement, 2008). It is "not a program or a specific strategy, but a prevention framework" (Crockett & Gillespie, 2007, p. 6). It is also intended to be "a schoolwide effort to refocus attention from identifying deficiencies in students to identifying scientifically-based instructional practices that support the learning of all students" (Duffy, 2007, p. 7). At its most basic,

> The goal of the entire process is *accelerating learning for all*. An essential assumption of RTI is that all students can learn, and will, given the right opportunities. It cannot be stressed too much, at the outset and throughout, that *RTI is about general education*. Some of its origins are in special education research and practice, and its federal funding began there, but it is intended to apply to every child. (Renaissance Learning, 2009, p. 1)

Ehren, Ehren, and Proly stress that "RTI is not a one-size-fits-all model for educational reform" (2009, p. 3). Instead, they see it as a framework. In their view, a critical strength of this framework is that it:

> provides a structure within which to establish a well-integrated system across general, compensatory, and special education. It is a golden opportunity to deconstruct the silos that often exist in schools with programs and processes and to create a unitary system for addressing student needs. The objective is that students receive what they need, when they need it. (Ehren et al., 2009, p. 56)

Because of its broad-based potential as a lever for improvement, Crockett and Gillespie view RTI as "a hot topic for school leaders, and for good reason. Momentum is building behind the use of RTI as a promising approach to strengthening instruction" (2007, p. 1).

> *"RTI is about general education." (Renaissance Learning, 2009, p. 1)*

Ehren et al. (2009) describe RTI as having three broad purposes—prevention of learning failure, intervention to assist struggling students, and, in many schools, determination of a student's eligibility for special education services:

- *"Prevention*—The prevention aspect of the RTI framework begins with high-quality core instruction to ensure that any problems students may be experiencing are not related to ineffective teaching practices. For students having academic or behavioral problems, the idea is to promote success before a cycle of failure begins.… Prevention is addressed within an RTI framework by employing screening of all students. Student progress is then continuously monitored throughout a school year.

- *Intervention*—Once a student is identified as not meeting predetermined benchmarks after receiving high-quality core instruction, additional supports are provided to the student.… Initial intervention often occurs in small groups and may take place in the regular education classroom or elsewhere.… The student's responsiveness to this intervention is closely monitored through data collection and analysis. The frequency and duration of interventions can be altered depending on student progress. Then, if the student is showing little progress, the intervention program may increase in intensity to focus on individual needs. If insufficient progress is seen after a predetermined period of time, the student may be referred for further evaluation and possible special education placement.

- *Determination of Learning Disabilities*—Within an RTI framework, when a student is not sufficiently responsive to high-quality core instruction and interventions in subsequent tiers within general or compensatory education, it may indicate the need for special education services. In such a case, the data gathered during progress monitoring throughout preliminary tiers may be used as part of the process for determination of learning disability. Hence, lack of responsiveness to intervention can be used as part of a comprehensive evaluation process." (Ehren et al., 2009, pp. 8-9)

What Does RTI Look Like?

Discussions about RTI often begin with a description of structural elements typically called tiers. Starting here makes sense if the discussion also addresses some of the theoretical underpinnings. Specifically, what are the tiers meant to do and how do they fit with one another? Ehren et al. describe them as "levels along a continuum of intensity for instruction and intervention" (2009, p. 25).

The tiers are usually depicted as fitting within a triangle, with Tier 1 fitting at the broad end and including most of the students in the school. While different implementations of RTI may include three to five tiers, three is most typical. A three-tiered RTI "triangle" (see Figure 6.1 below) assumes that:

> 80% of students will reach performance benchmarks within the core instructional program—
> "Tier 1." If Tier 1 instruction is not working for roughly that percentage of students, there
> will never be enough resources in Tier 2 and Tier 3 to make up for it. Therefore, evaluation
> of the core instructional program is the "fork in the road." If core programs are working for
> 80%, then Tiers 2 and 3 can help the rest of the kids catch up. If they are not working, then
> the first job is "Fix Tier 1" (while, at the same time, delivering as much intensive intervention
> as resources will allow to the students in critical need of more intervention). (Renaissance
> Learning, 2009, p. 11)

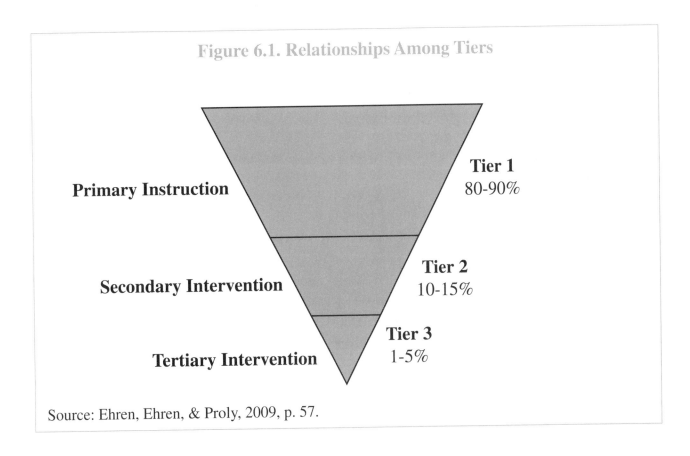

Figure 6.1. Relationships Among Tiers

Primary Instruction

Tier 1
80-90%

Secondary Intervention

Tier 2
10-15%

Tertiary Intervention

Tier 3
1-5%

Source: Ehren, Ehren, & Proly, 2009, p. 57.

Ehren et al. see a problem with using a triangle to describe the "placement" of students within an RTI-driven system since:

> it may be interpreted as a linear process, and it really is not. Students do not drop out of Tier 1 when they move to Tier 2. However, students may not be participating in Tier 2 if they are in Tier 3. (2009, p. 57)

They present a different graphic to describe the interaction among tiers and talk about this interaction in practice (see Figure 6.2):

> This circular depiction shows that Tier 2 and 3 take place within the context of Tier 1. This is meant to show that Tier 1 doesn't end when Tiers 2 or 3 are initiated. You will notice that a small part of Tier 3 falls outside of Tier 1, which is meant to signify the very small percentage of students in special education who are not in general education. This would only apply in approaches where special education is considered as part of Tier 3. (Ehren et al., 2009, p. 57)

Figure 6.2. Relationships Among Tiers

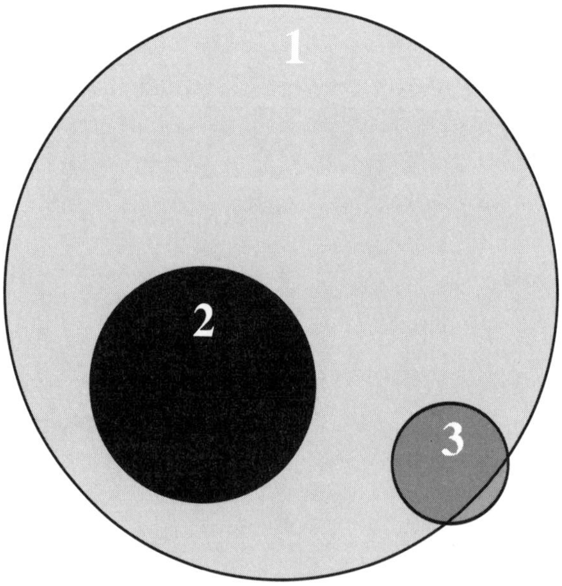

Source: Ehren, Ehren, & Proly, 2009, p. 57.

Tier 2 Interventions—Some Possibilities

Although many people think of individualized interventions as the crux of RTI, it is the more standardized interventions used in tier II that directly determine the success of the model. The hallmark of tier II is small-group interventions. Students receive interventions on the basis of their needs with a standardized approach to interventions....

Tier II interventions at the secondary level are often implemented in specially designed courses, but how those courses function depends on the characteristics of the individual school. Schools that use a 50-minute (or one-hour) course block could provide a course in remedial reading instruction for students who are struggling readers in addition to regular literacy instruction. A common model used in high schools is to schedule the remedial course simultaneously with a content area, such as social studies, and use the social studies curriculum as the instructional material. For example, 25 minutes might be dedicated to content-area instruction and 25 minutes to comprehension or decoding strategies applied to the content-area text. This would allow students to transfer back and forth between the courses (flexible grouping) with relatively little disruption.

A block schedule of 90 minutes could incorporate 30 minutes of reading enrichment in which students with strong or average reading skills would read independently and the teacher could run a small flexibly grouped remedial intervention in the same room. Alternatively, a reading specialist could co-teach a course and provide remediation or could run a small group in a different setting. The latter would allow the reading specialist to conduct three groups, lasting 30 minutes each, within the same 90-minute block.

Because these are small groups, the tutor-to-student ratio should be between 6 and 10 students for each instructor. Thus, one teacher and one paraprofessional (or two teachers) could teach up to 20 students, or one reading specialist could pull out up to 10 students at any one time.

Excerpted from Burns, 2008, pp. 13-14.

Shinn, Phillips, and March (2008) talk about the "high school problem" in regard to the need for use of an RTI approach, using the tiers to make their point. In their view, too little attention is paid to instruction that would "fit" in Tier 1, with a critical need to improve teacher effectiveness with diverse student needs. Often, few to no Tier 2-like options exist, and the Tier 3-type interventions include options (such as content area tutoring or help with homework) typically identified by research as having weak effects on remediation of student problems. They suggest that improvement of the skills of general education teachers to deal with a wide range of student abilities through strong and ongoing staff development should be a primary focus for high schools.

Core Elements

In addition to the tier structure, an implementation of RTI has some common elements, "although RTI can be shaped to fit the philosophy, personnel, experience, and needs of a given school" (Canter, Klotz, & Cowan, 2008, p. 14). Understanding these core elements can help a school plan its own implementation of the process. Mellard (2004) provides a brief description of these:

1. *"High quality classroom instruction.* Students receive high quality instruction in their general education setting. Before students are singled out for specific assistance, one has to have an assurance that the typical classroom instruction is of high quality. This quality can be assessed by comparing students' learning rates and achievement in different classrooms at the same grade level.

2. *Research-based instruction.* General education's classroom practices and the curriculum vary in their efficacy. Thus, ensuring that the practices and curriculum have demonstrated their validity is important. If not, one cannot be confident that students' limited gains are independent of the classroom experiences.

3. *Teacher assessment of classroom performance.* General education instructors and staff assume an active role in students' assessment in the general education curriculum. This feature emphasizes the important role of the classroom staff in designing and completing student assessments rather than relying on externally developed tests (e.g., state or nationally developed tests).

4. *Universal screening.* School staff conducts universal screening of academics and behavior. This feature focuses on specific criteria for judging the learning and achievement of all students, not only in academics but also in related behaviors (e.g., class attendance, tardiness, truancy, suspensions, and disciplinary actions). Those criteria are applied in determining which students need closer monitoring or an intervention.

5. *Continuous progress monitoring.* In RTI models, one expects students' classroom progress to be monitored continuously. In this way, staff can readily identify those learners who are not meeting the benchmarks or other expected standards. Various curriculum-based assessment models are useful in this role.

6. *Research-based interventions.* When students' screening results or progress monitoring results indicate a deficit, an appropriate instructional intervention is implemented, perhaps an individually designed instructional package or a standardized treatment.... These interventions might include a "double-dose" of the classroom instruction or a different instructional method. These interventions are not adaptations of the current curriculum or accommodations, because one would expect those procedures to be implemented already. These research-based interventions are 8 to 12 weeks in length and are designed to increase the intensity of the learner's instructional experience.

7. *Progress monitoring during interventions.* School staff use progress-monitoring data to determine interventions' effectiveness and to make any modifications as needed. Carefully defined data are collected, perhaps daily, to provide a cumulative record of the learner's response to the intervention.

8. *Fidelity measures.* While the interventions are designed, implemented, and assessed for their learner effectiveness, fidelity measures are completed that focus on [teachers] . . . The fidelity measure provides the information that the intervention was implemented as intended and with consistency."

Effective Use of Data

Effective data use is central to implementation of RTI since "progress monitoring data inform decisions about when to adjust instruction, when to stay the course, and when to exit a student from intervention" (Hall, 2008, p. 29). Ehren et al. describe the two major types of assessments that need to be incorporated in an RTI process:

Universal Screening—The way schools identify students in need of Tier 2 intervention is to conduct screenings. Students who score below a certain prescribed point on the screening either receive intervention immediately or their progress is monitored for several weeks. In the latter case, students' growth rates are tracked to see if they are making sufficient progress in their classrooms. If they are not, they move to Tier 2.

Progress Monitoring—Progress monitoring is the process of assessing students' academic performance or behavior on a regular basis to evaluate the effectiveness of instruction and intervention…. It can be implemented with individual students or an entire class. Students' current levels of performance are determined and goals are identified for learning that will take place over time. The student's academic performance is measured on a weekly or monthly basis. Progress toward meeting the student's goals is measured by comparing expected and actual rates of learning. Based on these measurements, teaching is adjusted as needed. Typically the more intense the intervention, the more frequent the measures are taken. (2009, p. 58)

> *"Is RTI possible in secondary schools? According to secondary educators who are implementing RTI models, the answer is 'Yes.'" (Center for Comprehensive School Reform and Improvement, 2008)*

RTI in Secondary Schools

While a brief review of core elements of RTI makes it clear that most of these elements, such as data use to diagnose student problems, provision of instructional interventions, and so on, are familiar to secondary school educators, there are differences between elementary schools in which most of the RTI work to date has been done and secondary schools. For example, in elementary schools, instruction focuses on helping students learn to read and most skills-based instruction is provided by only one to two teachers for each student. In secondary schools, instruction shifts to helping students read to learn, with reading a critically needed skill in content-area classes, and students may interact with five or more content-area teachers a day (Hughes & Deshler, 2007).

Ehren (n.d.) talks about some of the special challenges faced by high schools as they work to develop an effective implementation of RTI:

> What increases the challenge at the secondary level is the complexity of the organization and the nightmare of scheduling, especially in high schools. The definition of tiers is an issue—who, what, how, and for how long? How intensive should the third tier be before it can be considered "specialized" and, therefore, more appropriately a special education service?
>
> Developing structures to deliver intervention within the framework of middle, junior, and high school in ways that are palatable to adolescents can be difficult. For example, the one-on-one tutorial approach used in elementary schools during the school day may be disruptive to the operation of a typical middle or high school and may also be met with resistance from adolescents who would prefer not to be singled out....
>
> Also, it is difficult (although not impossible) for secondary schools to promote flexible movement across tiers within a semester course schedule. Then, too, in high school there is the issue of credits; students must be sure to take the courses they need to earn a diploma. If a student needs substantial intervention, he or she may not be able to meet graduation requirements in the 4 years typically allotted for high school.

Khan and Mellard add some additional practical challenges that secondary school leaders will need to address as their schools implement RTI:

> *Collaboration*—One of the practical obstacles to implementing RTI in middle and high schools is the development and sustainability of collaboration among grade levels, content areas, support staff, Title I administrators, reading specialists, general education teachers, special education staff, and administrators. If educators are unwilling to share data and ways to help children learn better, interventions in the RTI process are stymied.
>
> *Time*—Another key factor that presents a challenge is the issue of time; teachers need to have enough time to work collaboratively, as well as to prepare formative assessments, review data, and implement interventions. Teachers need to have administrative support in developing workable solutions to this problem. Flexible and/or creative scheduling, a challenge particularly at the high school level, is a necessary component to implementing RTI. (2008, p. 4)

However, even taking into account differences between elementary and secondary schools, educators at the secondary level should ensure that the RTI process "utilizes the same principles of universal screening, prompt tiered intervention, and progress monitoring" (Renaissance Learning, 2009, p. 16).

Support for Literacy

Since effective reading skills are critical to student success in content-area instruction, a primary focus for RTI work in most secondary schools will be literacy. Hughes and Deshler (2007) suggest that schools routinely assess—using a universal approach to screening—to develop a literacy profile of all students in the school. Elements of the assessment should generate data about word analysis skills, reading fluency, and comprehension. In addition, all teachers should be provided with professional development on instruction to help students develop the skills needed for reading and comprehension of academic texts as well as vocabulary and concept development. This support for students becomes part of and is embedded in Tier 1 instruction provided to all students.

McInerney and Mellard provide some questions schools can use to help them develop an RTI-ready framework for literacy instruction and supports:

- What happens for those students who are reading below the 4th-grade level?

- What is in place across a school staff to ensure that students will get the "critical" content in spite of their literacy skills?

- What happens for students who know how to decode but can't comprehend well?

- What steps have been taken to ensure that powerful learning strategies are embedded across the curriculum?

- What happens for students who have language problems? (2008).

Scheduling

Renaissance Learning characterizes scheduling issues as "trickier" at the secondary than the elementary level. In general, the type of schedule used for interventions depends on the general schedule a school uses:

- "Traditional day schedule (40-50 minute periods for individual subjects): The school selects a period during the day—sometimes homeroom period, if it is long enough—during which students can receive additional instruction and/or practice. Usually the subject addressed is reading, but the same approach can work with math. The challenge in this 'homeroom' approach is that usually there are insufficient instructional resources available to provide flexible grouping during the period, so the standard protocol intervention must be selected with special care" (2009, p. 16).

- "Block schedule (90-minute periods with multiple teachers): Reading interventions can be scheduled into block classes with one of the teachers managing the Tier 2 activity while the other teachers work with the Tier 1 program or enrichment activities. Most subject areas incorporated into block scheduling approaches lend themselves to reading assignments geared to the content area" (2009, p. 16).

Implementation Issues

Efforts at implementation at the high school level will need to take both the special environment of high schools and the significant impact that RTI will have on school processes and staff roles into account. Hall also cautions that "implementing RTI is a 3- to 5-year effort. Your staff needs to believe that RTI is here to stay and is not the 'idea du jour'" (2008, p. 42). Finally, school leaders should build in mechanisms to ensure that both the process of RTI and its various elements are working as intended:

> The concept of fidelity of implementation is routinely mentioned in much of the literature on RTI. Unless a school implements the components of the RTI framework with fidelity, the process will not be helpful in preventing school failure, engaging in data-based decision making, or informing instructional practice. (Mellard & Johnson, 2008, p. 142)

Where Should Our School Start?

Schools beginning the process of implementing RTI may rightfully see it as a daunting process. Crockett and Gillespie suggest that schools begin by "building a leadership team of key personnel, including general and special education teachers, psychologists, and other support staff, to evaluate school readiness for adopting RTI and to maximize the chances of using the approach effectively" (2007, p. 4).

Ehren et al. feel that a key component in this evaluation of readiness should be assessing school assets that can help support the RTI framework:

> It is very likely that beginning an RTI initiative will not mean that you are starting from scratch. You may have several building blocks already in place that will serve as a foundation. Think of RTI as a framework for integrating the good things you are doing to meet students' needs and for guiding improvement efforts. Taking stock in your current status provides cues for start up and helps you to feel that RTI is doable. Looking at the practices you currently employ and the beliefs upon which your educational approach is based helps set the stage for an RTI approach. (2009, p. 39)

Crockett and Gillespie agree that, "realizing the benefits of a schoolwide RTI model starts with using practices that are already in place" (2007, p. 6). Research done at RTI implementation model sites provides support that this commonsense approach can work. If existing school resources are used, implementation of RTI "does not require a wrenching overhaul but can build on existing frameworks within a school and can be implemented in stages that meet students' needs and staff members' capacities" (Canter, Klotz, & Cowan, 2008, p. 15).

In Summary

Issues related to implementation of RTI—of embedding its approaches into the everyday work of schools—are undeniably complex. However, the bottom line is whether the approach will strengthen instruction and make it more likely that all students will succeed. Alonzo, Tindal, and Robinson feel that, properly implemented, RTI *can* have a positive impact:

> Although it was not originally billed as such, a positive unintended consequence of using an RTI approach schoolwide is that it may result in better targeted, more appropriate instruction for all students, thereby reducing the achievement gap. (2008, p. 2)

Ehren et al. recognize that the shift to an RTI-driven approach will require patience, perserverance, and leadership, especially since "teachers and support personnel will have to adapt to new roles and processes and this will take time" (2009, p. 63). However, on a positive note:

> RTI *can* succeed because, properly understood, it is fundamentally practical. . . . It is not based on new theories or experimental ideas. Rather, it is a way of putting into practice the things that research has always taught us we should be doing—a way of *taking what works and making it workable.* (Renaissance Learning, 2009, p. iii)

References

Alonzo, J., Tindal, G., & Robinson, Q. (2008, Winter). Using schoolwide Response to Intervention to close the achievement gap in reading. *ERS Spectrum, 26*(1), 1-9.

Burns, M. K. (2008, March). Response to Intervention at the secondary level. *Principal Leadership*, *8*(7), 12-15.

Canter, A., Klotz, M. B., & Cowan, K. (2008, February). Response to Intervention: The future for secondary schools. *Principal Leadership*, *9*(2), 12-15.

Center for Comprehensive School Reform and Improvement. (2008). *Response to Intervention: Possibilities for service delivery at the secondary school level.* Retrieved from http://www.centerforcsri.org/index.php?Itemid=5&id=559&option=com_content&task=view

Crockett, J. B., & Gillespie, D. N. (2007, Fall). Getting ready for RTI: A principal's guide to Response to Intervention. *ERS Spectrum, 25*(4), 1-9.

Duffy, H. (2007). *Meeting the needs of significantly struggling learners in high school: A look at approaches to tiered intervention.* Washington, DC: National High School Center. Retrieved from http://www.betterhighschools.org/docs/NHSC_RTIBrief_08-02-07.pdf

Ehren, B. J. (n.d.). *Response to Intervention in secondary schools: Is it on your radar screen?* Retrieved from http://www.rtinetwork.org/Learn/Why/ar/RadarScreen

Ehren, B. J., Ehren, T. C., & Proly, J. L. (2009). *Response to Intervention: An action guide for school leaders*. Alexandria, VA: Educational Research Service.

Hall, S. (2008). *Implementing Response to Intervention*. Thousand Oaks, CA: Corwin Press.

Hughes, C., & Deshler, D. (2007). *RTI in middle and high school: How will the game play out?* Presentation at the annual meeting of the Council for Exceptional Children in Louisville, KY. Retrieved from http://www.nrcld.org/about/presentations/2007/RTI_Secondary.pdf

Khan, C., & Mellard, D. (2008). *RTI in the language of a classroom teacher: Improving student success through collaboration*. Lawrence, KS: National Center on Response to Intervention. Retrieved from http://www.betterhighschools.org/docs/TeacherLanguage1-%20RTI-2.pdf

Mellard, D. (2004). *Understanding Responsiveness to Intervention in learning disabilities determination*. Retrieved from http://www.nrcld.org/about/publications/papers/mellard.html

Mellard, D. F., & Johnson, E. (2008). *RTI: A practitioner's guide to implementing Response to Intervention*. Thousand Oaks, CA: Corwin Press and National Association of Elementary School Principals.

McInerney, M., & Mellard, D. (2008). *Tiered intervention at the high school level*. Presentation at the National High School Center's Summer Institute in Washington, DC. Retrieved from http://www.betterhighschools.org/SI08/TieredIntervention.asp

National Association of State Directors of Special Education. (2006). *Myths about Response to Intervention (RTI) implementation*. Retrieved from http://www.nasdse.org/Portals/0/Documents/Download%20Publications/Myths%20about%20RtI.pdf

National High School Center. (n.d.). *Tiered intervention on the high school level* (Ask the Expert). Retrieved from http://www.betterhighschools.org/expert/ask_tiered.asp

Renaissance Learning. (2009). *Making RTI work: A practical guide for using data for a successful "Response to Intervention" program*. Wisconsin Rapids, WI: Renaissance Learning.

Shinn, M. R., Phillips, M., & March, R. (2008). *Implementing Response to Intervention (RTI) in a problem-solving model at the secondary level*. Presentation at the annual meeting of the National Association of School Psychologists in New Orleans, LA. Retrieved from http://successfulschools.org/wp-content/uploads/marknasphandouts.pdf?phpMyAdmin=168c4a6ce7f3t76b9b6da

Implications for Our School: Questions for Discussion and Reflection

- Do the approaches we currently have in place identify struggling students soon enough to provide them with the supports they need in a timely fashion? If not, what are some of the problems we're seeing?

- Have we built in systems to evaluate whether a student is making acceptable progress when he or she is provided with an intervention?

- Is there a system that encourages routine sharing of information and expertise among teachers and other staff members regarding the progress—or lack of it—of individual students?

- Are we satisfied that our Tier 1 approaches—regular classroom instruction—are providing a solid base for all students? Do content-area teachers receive the training and support they need to address difficulties faced by students struggling with literacy issues?

Follow-up and Action Items

_____

_____

_____

_____

_____

_____

_____

_____

_____

_____

_____

_____

Chapter 7

Supporting English Language Learners

English Language Learners need the support of both English as a Second Language and regular classroom teachers to succeed.

Over the past few decades, schools across the country have experienced an upsurge in the numbers of students who come to them speaking little to no English. In addition, some of these students have had little formal experience with schooling. Making this trend even more challenging is the requirement that many of these students are required to participate in standardized testing before they are proficient in English.

There has also been a shift in expectations in many schools and districts away from viewing English Language Learners (ELLs) as the sole responsibility of English as a Second Language (ESL) teachers toward shared responsibility with classroom teachers, even for students still struggling with English. Thus, regular education teachers find themselves needing to provide support for ELLs, even though "for the most part, teachers' training, skills, and experiences have not prepared them for working with students for whom English is not their primary language" (Elfers et al., 2009, p. 29). To provide effective instruction, teachers need to learn about second language acquisition and how it might affect students' learning, how to support ELL students' acquisition of English, and also how to implement instructional strategies that can help these students learn required content.

Second Language Acquisition

Teachers today need some familiarity with the basic concepts of second language acquisition in order to provide ELLs with appropriate instruction. Not surprisingly, one of the most discussed topics is how long it takes for ELLs to become proficient in English. According to a leading authority in the field, Jim Cummins, it takes ELLs 1 or 2 years to become proficient in basic interpersonal communicative skills (BICS) and 5 to 7 years to develop cognitive academic language proficiency (CALP; Cruz, Nutta, O'Brien, Feyten, & Govoni, 2003; Kottler & Kottler, 2002). BICS and CALP are better known as social English and academic English. Social English refers to the more casual English typically spoken with friends. Academic English is more formal and includes the words that students learn in content-area classes, such as math, science, and social studies. Cummins suggests that academic English is more complex because it includes more difficult concepts, "low-frequency and technical words," and "increasingly sophisticated grammatical constructions" (2006, p. 60).

A frequent misconception about ELLs is that they should be able to read or write English as well as they can speak it. Often a teacher who hears a student speaking fairly fluently will assume that he or she is completely proficient. In reality, students who are able to converse fluently will still have trouble reading and writing in English for some time. It is also much more difficult for ELLs to become fluent in academic English, in part because these words tend to have little context, whereas casual conversation typically has a great deal of context, such as "gestures, facial expressions, and intonation" (Rea & Mercuri, 2006, p. 11). Without understanding this, teachers (or parents) may wrongly assume that an ELL student who is not doing well in school has a learning disability, is not motivated, or is lazy (Hill & Flynn, 2006).

The amount of time needed to learn English can vary greatly depending on each student's particular circumstances and background. Harper and de Jong (2004) caution teachers to be aware of personal, affective, and sociocultural factors that may affect students' progress. Some factors that may affect students' language acquisition include their prior schooling experiences and academic achievement, their family's expectations and support, the language(s) spoken at home, their level of anxiety, and whether they are literate in their native language. For instance, ELLs who did not attend school regularly before coming to the United States and are not literate in their native language will likely have a more difficult time becoming fluent in English than ELLs who have had several years of formal schooling.

Language Acquisition Versus Learning Disabilities

It is also important to note that indicators of learning disabilities can be misinterpreted as difficulties with second language acquisition. Differentiating between the two can be difficult because "students learning a second language and students with learning disabilities often exhibit similar difficulties with learning, attention, social skills, and behavioral and emotional balance" (Salend & Salinas, 2003, p. 36). When trying to determine whether an ELL has a learning disability or a problem with second language acquisition, it can sometimes help to have an understanding of the student's culture, since "some behaviors that appear to indicate LD [learning disabilities] might be typical for the child's cultural background" (Collier & Hoover, in Klingner, Artiles, & Barletta, 2006, p. 114). The student's ESL teacher will be able to tell content-area teachers whether the same problems are surfacing when the student uses his or her native language. If a student who is falling behind in the mainstream classroom is doing well in the ESL class, it is an indication that the child may be having trouble with second language acquisition as opposed to a learning disability.

Is There a "Critical Period" for Learning Languages?

Another widely discussed topic is whether there is an age range, or critical period, during which people can learn languages more easily. Although researchers have not been able to come to a consensus, it appears that there are benefits and disadvantages for both younger and older students. Some research has shown that younger students "are more likely to attain native-like proficiency"; however, "they are also more likely to lose proficiency in their first language" (Mikow-Porto et al., 2004, p. 39). While older students may be at a disadvantage because they have less time to catch up to their peers, they also have the advantage of "a well-developed cognitive and conceptual system" and may have already developed literacy and numeracy skills through prior schooling (Peregoy & Boyle, 2005, p. 63).

Supporting Students' Second Language Acquisition

ELLs in mainstream classrooms need to catch up to their peers as quickly as possible. These students do not have time to learn English before beginning to learn subject content. Much of the professional literature suggests that learning English through content-area teaching is actually beneficial for ELLs. According to Rea and Mercuri, researchers "have discovered that most language is acquired, not learned," and, therefore, teachers should "focus on strategies that foster acquisition" not grammar drills (2006, p. 9).

Teaching ELLs English through content rather than grammar lessons has several benefits. The largest is obvious—they are learning English and content at the same time. In addition:

- "Students learn the academic vocabulary of each content area.

- Language is kept in its natural context.

- Students have reasons to use language for real purposes" (Freeman, Freeman, & Mercuri, in Rea & Mercuri, 2006, p. 75).

Throughout the professional literature, researchers and educators stress the need to provide ELLs with "comprehensible input"—a concept developed by Krashen and Terrell (in Mora, 2006). Put simply, the language used during classroom instruction needs to be modified to make it understandable for ELLs. According to Mora, teachers should use language with "grammatical structures and vocabulary [that are] one 'stage' or level above the student's current level of productive language ability" (2006, p. 31). If teachers use language that is too complex for students, it will diminish their ability to learn vocabulary and language structures. However, Krashen and Terrell (in Hill & Flynn, 2006) suggest that, in order to progress, an ELL needs to be exposed to language that "includes some of the structures that are part of the next stage of acquisition" and should be "encouraged to use language that reflects that more advanced stage" (p. 16). Therefore, it is important for teachers to understand their students' varying levels of proficiency not only to provide comprehensible input, but also to determine how to help students progress.

A key aspect of supporting ELLs' oral language development is simply exposing them to English and providing them with ample opportunities to use English through assignments and interactions. Swain (in Hill & Flynn, 2006) refers to speaking as output and notes that students who are not given ample chance to speak in class are less likely to achieve a high level of proficiency. Bear in mind that exposure alone will not make students proficient in English. Harper and de Jong remind us that, "Teachers need to draw students' attention to the structure of the English language used in specific academic contexts and provide appropriate feedback that ELLs can use to further their oral and written academic language development" (2004, p. 154). Finally, it is especially important that teachers with ELL students in their classrooms explicitly teach content-area vocabulary and provide all students with opportunities to practice using the new words (Haynes & Zacarian, 2010).

Using Instructional Strategies That Provide Special Support for ELLs

Typically, effectively communicating with ELLs will be the biggest hurdle for teachers. Fortunately, there are many simple techniques that can be used to enhance comprehension for ELLs. The first step is to think about how you speak to students. Speaking loudly will not help ELLs understand you, but speaking slowly and repeating what you say can (Cruz et al., 2003; Lessow-Hurley, 2003). Instead of just simplifying concepts, teachers can help ELLs comprehend what they mean by describing it in several different ways or by providing multiple examples to illustrate the concept.

How teachers ask questions is another important element of teaching style. It is crucial that teachers ask questions often to check ELLs' comprehension (Cruz et al., 2003). In addition, to encourage ELL participation, teachers should make sure that they have enough time to answer questions. They must first translate what has been said before they are able to generate an answer to the question posed. Finally, teachers should not assume that a lack of questions from students means that they have fully grasped the lesson.

While it is important to try to boost ELLs' comprehension by simplifying, teachers should not do so to the detriment of their learning. In some cases, lessons are so oversimplified that ELLs are presented with little or no information that is relevant to what their classmates are studying. During a class observation, Iddings found evidence of this:

> … while some students in the class were researching the solar system and discussing the moons of Jupiter, Venus's veil, and the canals of Mars, the ELLs' lesson had been reduced to the recitation of the words *closest, bigger, far, farther,* and *near*: words that do not necessarily bear much relationship to the solar system per se. (2005, p. 175)

Teachers should challenge ELL students, but at the same time, ensure that they are capable of handling the assignment.

Instructional Materials

Teachers should also consider the instructional materials used with ELLs. Teachers will almost certainly have to modify the instructional materials used with some of these students. This is especially true for secondary teachers whose subjects generally require textbooks or other materials with numerous specialized words and new concepts.

One way to think about altering materials and assignments is by considering the four "loads" described by Meyer (2000): the cognitive load, cultural load, language load, and learning load. The *cognitive load* is the number of concepts in a text or other instructional material that are new to a student. The *culture load* refers to the amount of (American) cultural knowledge that the student will need to understand the text. The *language load* is the number of complicated words or sentence structures used in the text. Finally, the *learning load* refers to the level of English proficiency a student needs to complete classroom activities. A learning load would be too high if it requires language skills that ELLs do not have to complete the task.

74

Any of these loads can act as barriers to comprehension if they are too heavy. When ELLs are overwhelmed by too much new or difficult information, they will be unable to comprehend lessons and, therefore, unable to keep up with their peers. One way teachers can combat this problem is by reviewing the text to identify concepts or vocabulary that may be difficult for ELLs. Then this information should be previewed with students to provide them with some background knowledge of the subject. Another option is to use visual aids or graphic organizers to help students better understand challenging concepts. In addition, Echevarria and Graves (2005) suggest outlining or rewriting the text, using audiotapes, and/or finding alternative materials if necessary.

Effective Teaching Strategies

Although the strategies highlighted below are all good instructional practices for students in general, they can provide much needed special support for ELLs. Since each of these strategies can be modified for a range of ability levels, they are especially useful for mainstream teachers with linguistically and culturally diverse classrooms.

Scaffolding: Begin by assessing just how much support ELL students need, and then provide it through scaffolding. Supports should be removed as students no longer need them, an approach that gradually increases their ability to operate successfully in situations where no special supports are available. Instructional strategies could include, for example, using visual aids and previewing vocabulary.

Contextualizing: When teachers contextualize lessons, they provide students with a framework—with clues—they can use to help them understand new words and concepts. This is especially important when working with ELLs who have a low level of English proficiency. For example, teachers might use visual aids such as pictures, maps, or graphs to provide a structure for the concepts being discussed. Another way to add context is to use gestures, facial expressions, and body language to convey meaning when speaking to students. Finally, manipulatives—both real and virtual ones provided through computer programs—can help to make concepts more concrete.

Modeling: When teachers model assignments or activities for students, it can help increase student understanding of expectations, clarify directions, and demonstrate a finished product (Walter, 2004). Techers can use modeling in a number of different ways to support ELLs. It can be as simple as demonstrating how to perform a task or talking to provide a model of correct grammar and pronunciation for students. In addition, teachers can model thinking processes or problem solving, which is particularly helpful for ELLs. Even students can help. During class discussions, native-speaking students can model skills such as discussing literature. In this way, ELLs gain access to the ways that their peers express their feelings and reactions—which may be very different from their teacher.

Using Prior Knowledge and Providing Background Information: Even if students do not have prior knowledge of a specific concept, they may still have useful knowledge that teachers can tap into to help them understand new information. For example, ELLs may be unfamiliar with the (American) Civil War, but if they have studied, or experienced, a different war, that prior knowledge will help inform their understanding of the Civil War (Short & Echevarria, 2004/2005). Teachers can also activate prior knowledge through questioning, visual aids, or prereading guides. Echevarria and Graves suggest a simple three-phase strategy for building and using prior knowledge: (1) leading a whole group brainstorming session, (2) "providing direct experiences" (such as videos) and "information-gathering opportunities," and (3) providing an opportunity (such as a research paper) for students to connect the background knowledge with new information (2005, p. 227).

Cooperative Learning: One of the best reasons to use collaborative or cooperative work with ELLs is that it will expose them to both social and academic English. During the peer interactions, students will have many opportunities to listen to other points of view and practice speaking in context-rich, and therefore more comprehensible, situations. In addition, group discussions will facilitate the repetition of vocabulary words. And students who may not understand a word or concept are able to get clarification from their peers (Peregoy & Boyle, 2006).

Themed Units: Although they have typically been used in elementary classrooms, themed units can provide benefits for students at all ability and grade levels. This is especially true for ELLs, who may be overwhelmed in classrooms where the content areas are not connected. Since they often only understand a small portion of what is being said, ELLs may struggle to decipher what they should be doing when the class has moved to a new topic (D. E. Freeman & Y. S. Freeman, 2006). Themed units allow ELLs to follow along more easily.

Fostering Development of Reading and Writing Skills: Obviously, in order to become proficient in all aspects of English, ELLs will need plenty of opportunities to practice. A simple way of developing students' literacy skills is by reading aloud to them regularly. Through read alouds, teachers can boost ELLs' interest in a variety of genres, introduce them to the rhythm of English, and provide examples of the "conventions of written English" (Peregoy & Boyle, 2005, p. 408). Modeling can also be used to help ELLs develop their writing skills. For instance, Richard-Amato and Snow (2005) suggest that providing ELLs with examples of former students' writing may help them understand both different forms of writing and teachers' expectations.

In Summary

As the number of ELLs in mainstream classrooms increases, teachers will require a basic understanding of second language acquisition as well as a working knowledge of instructional strategies that are particularly effective for these students. These teachers will need to carefully assess an individual ELL and respond to them with appropriate teaching strategies and language supports. Although it undoubtedly will be a challenge to implement the multiple changes needed, it is also clear that, without them, many ELLs are unlikely to overcome the language barrier and succeed academically.

References

Cruz, B. C., Nutta, J. W., O'Brien, J., Feyten, C. M., & Govoni, J. M. (2003). *Passport to learning: Teaching social studies to ESL students.* Silver Spring, MD: National Council for the Social Studies.

Cummins, J. (2006). How long does it take for an English Language Learner to become proficient in a second language? In E. Hamayan & R. Freeman (Eds.), *English language learners at school* (pp. 59-61). Philadelphia: Caslon Publishing.

Echevarria, J., & Graves, A. (2005). Curriculum adaptations. In P. A. Richard-Amato & M. A. Snow (Eds.), *Academic success for English Language Learners: Strategies for K-12 mainstream teachers* (pp. 224-247). White Plains, NY: Longman.

Elfers, A. M., Stritikus, T., Calaff, K. P., Von Esch, K. S., Lucero, A., Knapp, M. S., et al. (2009). *Building systems of support for classroom teachers working with second language learners.* Seattle, WA: University of Washington College of Education. Retrieved from http://depts.washington.edu/ctpmail/PDFs/ELLStudy-July2009.pdf

Freeman, D. E., & Freeman, Y. S. (2006). Teaching language through content themes: Viewing our world as a global village. In T. A. Young & N. L. Hadaway (Eds.), *Supporting the development of English learners* (pp. 61-78). Newark, DE: International Reading Association.

Fu, D. (2004). Teaching ELL students in regular classrooms at the secondary level. *Voices from the Middle, 11*(4), 8-15.

Garcia, E. (2006). When should an English Language Learner begin to read and write in English? In E. Hamayan & R. Freeman (Eds.), *English Language Learners at school* (pp. 144-146). Philadelphia: Caslon Publishing.

Genesee, F. (2006). How do English Language Learners acquire a second language at school? In E. Hamayan & R. Freeman (Eds.), *English Language Learners at school* (pp. 65-66). Philadelphia: Caslon Publishing.

Gibbons, P. (2005). Writing in a second language across the curriculum. In P. A. Richard-Amato & M. A. Snow (Eds.), *Academic success for English Language Learners: Strategies for K-12 mainstream teachers* (pp. 275-310). White Plains, NY: Longman.

Harper, C., & de Jong, E. (2004). Misconceptions about teaching English-Language Learners. *Journal of Adolescent & Adult Literacy, 48*(2), 152-162.

Haynes, J., & Zacarian, D. (2010). *Teaching English Language Learners across the content areas.* Alexandria, VA: ASCD.

Hill, J. D. & Flynn, K. M. (2006). *Classroom instruction that works with English Language Learners.* Alexandria, VA: Association for Supervision and Curriculum Development.

Iddings, A. C. D. (2005). Linguistic access and participation: English Language Learners in an English-dominant community of practice. *Bilingual Research Journal, 29*(1), 165-183.

Klingner, J. K., Artiles, A. J., & Barletta, L. M. (2006). English Language Learners who struggle with reading: Language acquisition or LD? *Journal of Learning Disabilities, 39*(2), 108-128.

Kottler, E., & Kottler, J. A. (2002). *Children with limited English: Teaching strategies for the regular classroom.* Thousand Oaks, CA: Corwin Press.

Lessow-Hurley, J. (2003). *Meeting the needs of second language learners: An educator's guide.* Alexandria, VA: Association for Supervision and Curriculum Development.

Meyer, L. (2000). Barriers to meaningful instruction for English learners. *Theory Into Practice, 39*(4), 228-236.

Mikow-Porto, V., Humphries, S., Egelson, P., O'Connell, D., Teague, J., & Rhim, L. (2004). *English Language Learners in the Southeast: Research, policy & practice.* Retrieved from http://www.serve.org/_downloads/publications/ell.pdf

Mora, J. K. (2006). Differentiating instruction for English learners: The four-by-four model. In T. A. Young & N. L. Hadaway (Eds.), *Supporting the development of English learners* (pp. 24-40). Newark, DE: International Reading Association.

Peregoy, S. F. & Boyle, O. (2005). *Reading, writing, and learning in ESL: A resource book for K-12 teachers.* Boston: Pearson/Allyn & Bacon.

Rea, D. M., & Mercuri, S. (2006). *Research-based strategies for English Language Learners: How to reach goals and meet standards, K-8.* Portsmouth, NH: Heinemann.

Richard-Amato, P. A., & Snow, M. A. (2005). Instructional strategies for K-12 mainstream teachers. In P. A. Richard-Amato & M. A. Snow (Eds.), *Academic success for English Language Learners: Strategies for K-12 mainstream teachers* (pp. 197-223). White Plains, NY: Longman.

Salend, S. J., & Salinas, A. (2003). Language differences or learning difficulties: The work of the multidisciplinary team. *Teaching Exceptional Children, 35*(4), 36-43.

Short, D., & Echevarria, J. (2004/2005). Teacher skills to support English Language Learners. *Educational Leadership, 62*(4), 8-13.

Vialpando, J., Linse, C., and Yedlin, J. (2005). *Educating English Language Learners: Understanding and using assessment.* Retrieved from http://www.nclr.org/content/publications/download/32971

Walter, T. (2004). *Teaching English Language Learners: The how-to handbook.* White Plains, NY: Longman.

Implications for Our School: Questions for Discussion and Reflection

- How do we provide support for ELL students? Is the system we use for classroom teacher/ESL teacher collaboration working?

- Are there topics related to ELL students and their education that we, as a faculty, feel we need more information on? How might we get that?

- Are there ways that some parts of the school day could be restructured to provide stronger support for ELL students, perhaps through grouping by skill level for part of the day while still including ELL students in regular classrooms for other periods?

- What's not working for our ELL students? How can we address these problems?

Follow-up and Action Items

_____

_____

_____

_____

_____

_____

_____

_____

_____

_____

_____

_____

_____

Section II

Improving Teacher Effectiveness

Chapter 8
Using the Research Base About Good Teaching

The strong research base about good teaching practices provides a valuable resource for staff conversation and teacher development.

In the past decade, there has been ever-increasing interest in efforts to identify why students in certain classrooms learn at faster rates than those in others. Student characteristics obviously are part of the equation. Recently, however, researchers, along with school districts and other organizations, have used relatively new statistical approaches to focus on teacher impact on student learning. A clear lesson from these projects is that some teachers are especially effective.

Educational research is complex—perhaps none more so than efforts to link instructional approaches with student learning. Teachers are working in classrooms that vary by the ages and backgrounds of students taught, the subjects presented, and the resources available. Thus, although there may have been thousands of studies conducted over the past few decades, a challenge for researchers has been analyzing massive amounts of data in ways that could help to identify significant findings.

Several research efforts have done this type of analysis and identified critical "lessons learned" about teaching behaviors with particularly strong effects on student learning. We'll take a look here at findings from some of the most significant projects.

> *"Efforts to improve instruction must focus on the existing knowledge base about effective teaching and learning in order to succeed." (Cawelti, 2004, p. 1)*

What Helps Children Learn? The Wang, Haertel, and Walberg Analysis

Almost 20 years ago, Wang, Haertel, and Walberg (1993/94) asked the question "What helps children learn?" To address this question, they analyzed the content of materials such as books on educational inputs and outputs, compiled 91 research syntheses, and surveyed 61 educational researchers. To help provide a teacher-friendly way to summarize the data, they developed a 28-category framework of variables that might have an influence on learning and then grouped these into six general "types of influence," one of which was "student aptitude" and another "classroom instruction and climate."

What the three researchers found highlights the importance of good teaching. Averaged together, the variables making up classroom instruction and climate had almost as much impact on student learning as student aptitude. In fact, one of the teacher-related factors—classroom management—had the most impact of all 28 factors. The researchers defined classroom management as including "group alerting, learner accountability, smooth transitions, and teacher 'with-it-ness'" (1993/94, p. 76).

They went on to say "effective classroom management increases student engagement, decreases disruptive behaviors, and makes good use of instructional time" (p. 76). Other teacher-related factors with high rankings included constructive student and teacher interactions—which boost students' self-esteem and provide them with a sense of belonging in the class and school—and proportion of time spent on instruction. The researchers explain students should be "fully engaged in their academic pursuits and teachers need to make wise use of instructional time … other things being equal, the more time spent on instruction, the better" (p. 76).

Effective General Practices: The Walberg and Paik Analysis

Walberg was also involved in another analysis of research studies. This time he worked with co-researcher Paik to identify instructionally related practices identified by research that "can be applied widely to the academic subject matter of kindergarten through 12th grade … [and that] show powerful and consistent effects for students in widely varying circumstances" (2004, p. 25). The researchers emphasize the importance of the teacher in implementing these practices, because "as with all educational practices … they can be effectively or ineffectively planned and conducted, and the results will vary accordingly" (2004, p. 25). Included among the teaching strategies identified by Walberg and Paik are:

- *Aligned time on task.* Students who are actively focused on educational goals do best in mastering the subject matter. The teacher's skillful classroom management, by taking into account what is to be learned and identifying the most efficient ways to present it, increases effective study time.

- *Direct teaching.* This process emphasizes systematic sequencing of lessons, presentation of new content and skills, guided student practice, the use of feedback, and independent practice by students. The traits of teachers employing effective direct instruction include clarity, task orientation, enthusiasm, and flexibility. These teachers also clearly organize their presentations.

- *Advance organizers.* Showing students the relationships between past and present learning increases the depth and breadth of student learning. When teachers explain how new ideas in the current lesson relate to ideas in previous lessons and other prior learning, students can connect the old with the new, which helps them to better remember and understand. Similarly, alerting them to key points to be learned allows them to concentrate their attention on the most crucial parts of the lesson.

- *Teaching of learning strategies.* Delegating some control to students for learning goals and the monitoring of personal progress in achieving them yields learning gains. Some students have been found to lack this self-awareness and must be taught the skills necessary to monitor and regulate their own learning.

- *Graded homework.* Students learn more when they complete homework that is graded, commented upon, and discussed by their teachers. The role of the teacher in providing feedback—in reinforcing what has been done correctly and in reteaching what has not—is key to maximizing the positive impact of homework.

- *Mastery learning.* When there is subject matter to be learned in a sequence, thorough mastery of each step is optimal. Because of its emphasis on outcomes and careful monitoring of progress, mastery learning can save learners' time. It allows more time and remediation for students who need it. It also enables faster learners to skip material they already know (excerpted from 2004, pp. 25-36).

> *"It is what teachers know, do, and care about which is very powerful in the learning equation.... [The answer] lies in the person who gently closes the classroom door and performs the teaching act—the person who puts into place the end effects of so many policies, who interprets these policies, and who is alone with students during their 15,000 hours of schooling." (Hattie, 2003, pp. 2-3)*

Identification of "Principles of Effective Teaching": The Brophy Analysis

Although Brophy's findings identify several "principles of effective teaching," he also stresses that "no single teaching method (e.g., direct instruction, social construction of meaning) can be the method of choice for all occasions. An optimal program will feature a mixture of instructional methods and learning activities… [as well as] a supportive classroom climate and positive student attitudes towards schooling, teachers, and classmates" (2000, p. 6). Principles he describes include:

- *A supportive classroom climate.* Students learn best within cohesive and caring learning communities.

- *Opportunity to learn.* Students learn more when most of the available time is allocated to curriculum-related activities and the classroom management system emphasizes maintaining student engagement in those activities.

- *Curricular alignment.* All components of the curriculum are aligned to create a cohesive program for accomplishing instructional purposes and goals.

- *Establishing learning orientations.* Teachers prepare students for learning by providing an initial structure to clarify intended outcomes and cue desired learning strategies.

- *Coherent content.* To facilitate meaningful learning and retention, content is explained clearly and developed with emphasis on its structure and connections.

- *Thoughtful discourse.* Questions are planned to engage students in sustained discussion structured around powerful ideas.

- *Practice and application activities.* Students are provided with sufficient opportunities to practice and apply what they are learning, and to receive improvement-oriented feedback.

- *Scaffolding students' task engagement.* The teacher provides whatever assistance students need to enable them to engage in learning activities productively.

- *Strategy instruction.* The teacher models and instructs students in learning and self-regulation strategies.

- *Cooperative learning.* Students often benefit from working in pairs or small groups to construct understandings or help one another master skills.

- *Goal-oriented assessment.* The teacher uses a variety of formal and informal assessment methods to monitor progress toward learning goals.

- *Achievement expectations.* The teacher establishes and follows through on appropriate expectations for learning outcomes.

What Works in Classroom Instruction?: The Marzano, Gaddy, and Dean Analysis

As did other researchers profiled in this chapter, Marzano, Gaddy, and Dean used a research technique referred to as "meta-analysis, a strategy that combines results from a number of studies to determine the net effect of an intervention" (2000, p. 2). Their analysis identified several instructional approaches as ones that "work well with all types of subject matter knowledge" and that demonstrate a positive impact on student learning:

- *Identifying similarities and differences.* This category of instructional strategies requires "students to analyze two or more elements in terms of their similarities and differences on one or more characteristics" (p. 9) and includes approaches such as comparing, classifying, creating metaphors, and creating analogies.

- *Summarizing and note taking.* Both require students to "mentally sift through and synthesize information" (p. 27).

- *Reinforcing effort and providing recognition.* These strategies "deal with students' attitudes and beliefs and, thus, are likely to affect students' level of engagement in cognitive processes" (p. 49).

- *Homework and practice.* These strategies provide students with opportunities to deepen their proficiency and understanding.

- *Nonlinguistic representations.* "Generating mental pictures of information enhances recall and understanding" (p. 69). Examples include graphic organizers, pictures and pictographs, mental pictures, concrete representations, and kinesthetic activity.

- *Cooperative learning.* While identified as an effective instructional practice, the researchers also stress that cooperative activities should be carefully structured (for example, including the element of positive interdependence) and not overused.

- *Setting objectives and providing feedback.* "Goal setting is defined as the process of established direction and purpose" (p. 98)—a metacognitive strategy. Feedback about students' progress is "one of the most generalizable strategies a teacher can use" (p. 98) and a tool to enhance learning.

- *Activating prior knowledge.* These strategies help students retrieve what they already know and include approaches such as "cues and questions, as well as advance organizers" (p. 123).

Marzano went on to work with researchers Pickering and Pollock and identified an additional category:

- *Generating and testing hypotheses.* This category includes engaging students in projects that involve generating and testing hypotheses through, for example, problem solving or invention tasks (Marzano, Pickering, & Pollock, 2001).

Visible Learning: The Hattie Analysis

John Hattie and fellow researchers from Auckland in New Zealand conducted an analysis of over 800 meta-analyses related to achievement, a data base that reflected over 50,000 studies representing over 200 million students. Variables related to "achievement variance" were divided into six categories—student, home, schools, curriculum, teachers, and approaches to teaching (Hattie, 2008).

The researchers estimated that about 30% of the variance in student learning could be attributed to teachers. Several teacher behaviors were identified within the teacher category, with effect sizes calculated for each of these. Ranked high were the teaching approaches of:

- Providing formative evaluation—Effect size of .9, which Hattie estimates could translate into increasing the rate of student learning by almost 50%.

- Reciprocal teaching—Uses a structured dialogue between teacher and students that includes the use of summarizing, question generating, clarifying, and predicting.

- Feedback—Providing information about what (and why) the student understands and misunderstands as well as direction about how to improve (Hattie, 2008).

Hattie also talks about the importance of being a strategic teacher:

> The key ingredients of what it means to be strategic in teaching and learning relates to teachers finding ways to engage and motivate students, teach appropriate strategies in the context of various curricula domains, and constantly seeking feedback about how effective their teaching is with all students. (2008, p. 161)

> *"Effective teaching practice begins with the thoughtful and intentional design of learning that engages students intellectually and academically." (Friesen, 2009, p. 4)*

Pulling It All Together

Although the five efforts to synthesize the aforementioned research used different analytic techniques and looked at different bodies of literature, there were some common themes identified by these as well as other researchers.

For example, there were several indicators of the importance of teachers' efforts to 1) maximize the time available for instruction, 2) actively engage students, 3) demonstrate links between what students already know and what they are studying, 4) help students develop metacognitive skills, and, finally, 5) use assessment and feedback in ways that both diagnose student needs and help students focus on learning.

Efficient Use of Time

One important teacher skill that research has linked to high levels of student learning is the effective and efficient use of instructional time. One aspect of this involves effective classroom management. Classroom management is more than dealing with disruption. It is effectively organizing all elements of the classroom so that students are less likely to misbehave. Most important, it is recognizing that instruction and management must be woven together. Tanner, Bottoms, Feagin, and Bearman expand on this:

> Well-managed classrooms are organized to support the learning environment. Managing a classroom is much more than maintaining discipline; it is a complex task that involves the interaction of teachers and students and the organization of materials and space. (n.d., p. 35)

Lindberg and Swick (2002) emphasize some specific ways effective teachers successfully organize time. These teachers understand the importance of consistency for smooth transitions between subjects, classrooms, and learning activities. They explain their rules and procedures on the first day and then adhere to these throughout the school year.

In addition to such important strategies, there are even more basic efforts that help to make good use of time. For example, teachers can make efficient use of time through the following approaches:

- *Quality and Pacing of Instruction.* In their review of research focusing on teacher behavior and student achievement, Brophy and Good state that "the most consistently replicated findings link achievement to the quality and pacing of instruction" (1986, p. 360). Effective teachers structure instruction so that "students are engaged in activities that are appropriate in difficulty level and otherwise suited to their current achievement levels and needs.… [They are] effective in diagnosing and prescribing appropriate activities" (Brophy & Good, 1986, p. 360). Smith, Lee, and Newmann (2001) found that too much review—in essence, slower pacing—resulted in lower levels of student learning, apparently because it limits the time available for the presentation of new material.

- *Curriculum Alignment.* In classrooms that produce high levels of learning, "All components of the curriculum are aligned to create a cohesive program for accomplishing instructional purposes and goals" (Brophy, 2000, p. 13). The intended curriculum is taught, and materials, activities, and assessments all support this.

Actively Engage Students

Students who are active—not passive—participants in the classroom learn more. Research repeatedly demonstrates that the ways in which teachers organize instruction make a difference. Some practices that contribute to student engagement include:

- *A positive and caring learning climate, in which constructive student and teacher social interactions take place.* In these classrooms, students and teachers share common interests and values and cooperative goals are emphasized (Brophy, 2000; Wang, Haertel, & Walberg, 1993/94).

- *Attention to individual students' learning needs.* The teacher provides whatever assistance students need to enable them to engage in learning activities productively (Brophy, 2000). One way in which effective teachers accomplish this is through "coaching/scaffolding," in which the teacher supports/prompts/coaches the child, providing just as much assistance as the child needs to perform a task (Taylor, Pearson, Clark, & Walpole, 1999).

- *Use of a variety of groupings for instruction.* Students often benefit from working in pairs or small groups to construct understanding or help one another master skills (Brophy, 2000). The small groups, if ability-based, should be flexible, with periodic assessments used to review the placement of individual children.

Tanner et al. suggest that another important aspect of ensuring students are actively engaged in learning is a balance between teacher-directed instruction and student-centered learning. They provide an example:

A teacher may work with students to design a community project that requires them to collect, plot, and analyze data. Before the project begins, the teacher decides whether the students have all the skills needed to perform the task. He or she determines whether [they] need direct instruction in survey techniques and particular mathematical skills and monitors students' progress throughout the activity, providing support and additional instruction as needed. (n.d., p. 5)

Create Linkages Between Past Learning and New Content

Studies have found that the degree to which instruction builds linkages for learning strongly affects student achievement (see, for example, Center on English Learning and Achievement, 2000; Haberman, 1995).

Characteristics of such classrooms include, for instance, effective presentation of material and questioning. Effective teachers prepare students for learning by providing an initial structure to clarify intended outcomes and cue desired learning strategies. They provide students with a broad outline of the lesson before formal instruction begins, explain content clearly, and develop information with emphasis on its structure and connections. They plan questions to engage students in conversation structured around powerful ideas (Brophy, 2000).

Effective teachers also explicitly provide opportunities and encouragement for students to "apply, interpret, and integrate knowledge into prior understanding" (Smith, Lee, & Newmann, 2001, p. 11).

Development of Students' Metacognitive Skills

Protheroe and Clarke talk about *why* instruction that encourages use of metacognitive strategies is an important topic:

> Think of a student you have known who approached new types of tasks with enthusiasm and who was typically able to "figure out" how to apply what he or she already knew to tackling a new problem. Now think about another child who reads a textbook but, when asked to summarize the main points in the chapter, can present only a disjointed list of thoughts with little sense of how they fit together. In math, this child might use only one strategy when approaching a problem—even when that method repeatedly fails.
>
> Oftentimes, the difference between these two children is neither cognitive ability nor content knowledge. Instead, the second child lacks metacognitive skills. Activities such as planning, monitoring comprehension, and evaluating progress toward completion of a learning task are metacognitive in nature. Students with better-developed metacognitive skills typically have a better sense of their own strengths and needs related to the learning process. They have a larger repertoire of learning strategies—again, many of them used almost unconsciously. And perhaps most importantly, they are likely to select and use the learning strategy that is most effective in helping them address a particular learning task. (2008, p. 34)

Researchers have offered the following general conclusions about the most important elements of effective strategy instruction. First, learning skills should be taught in the context of content-area instruction, and students should be provided with meaningful opportunities to practice them. Second, the instruction about strategies should be explicitly provided. The instruction should also include elements that help students learn how to appropriately generalize use of one strategy to other tasks and classes (Hattie, Biggs, & Purdie, 1996; Kiewra, 2002). Finally, teachers should model use of learning strategies—using a "thinking aloud" approach when possible. Students should also be encouraged to ask and answer why they used particular strategies.

Effective Use of Assessment and Feedback

Effective teachers are more likely to use a variety of formal and informal assessment methods to monitor progress toward learning goals (Brophy, 2000). They use the results of these assessments to adjust instruction for both the class as a whole and for individual students.

They also provide sufficient opportunities for students to practice and apply what they are learning and—critically important—to receive improvement-oriented feedback (Brophy, 2000). They are more likely to ask open-ended questions and probe for the thinking of students to determine how they arrive at answers, thus providing many opportunities to assess for understanding or, alternately, for misunderstandings.

Such teachers understand that feedback to students helps them learn. For example, some of the research summaries briefly described here specifically mention homework not only as a way to provide students with the opportunity for practice but also as a mechanism through which teachers can identify areas a student has mastered or in which more work is needed.

Some "Red Flag" Approaches

Research can also help identify what Stronge (2002) describes as "red flag" approaches—in other words, teaching likely to be ineffective in supporting high levels of student learning. His review of the research highlights some of these; they include:

- vague instructions for seatwork, projects, and activities;

- unresponsive to student cues so that the delivery of instruction is ineffective;

- lack of variety in instructional methods used;

- seldom individualizes instruction or does so ineffectively;

- use of outdated material or terminology;

- failure to implement needed changes highlighted by peers or supervisors; and,

- slow or labored transitions between activities or lessons.

Another study, this one conducted by Dolezal, Welsh, Pressley, and Vincent (2003), identified classroom practices that undermine student motivation and have the potential for a negative impact on student learning. These include, for example:

- a competitive environment in which "winning" is stressed over working together and improving;

- few displays of student work and accomplishments;

- lack of scaffolding for students who are struggling;

- ineffective and/or negative feedback;

- lack of connection of new material to students' prior knowledge;

- lack of established routines and procedures;

- inappropriately low task difficulty or overly difficult tasks;

- poor/incomplete planning;

- slow pacing; and,

- emphasis of task completion over learning.

> *"If we improve the quality of instruction, we can improve student learning."*
> *(Lemons & Helsing, 2008, p. 15)*

In Summary

The knowledge base about the components of effective teaching provides a powerful tool for teachers. By discussing the research base, teachers can move toward expanding their repertoire of teaching strategies.

However, it's important that we wrap up with the recognition that effective teaching is more than the use of isolated strategies throughout the day. Teachers must continually make decisions about what practice to use and when. Thus, another characteristic of effective teachers is their ability to apply lessons learned from research at appropriate times.

References

Brophy, J. (2000). *Teaching*. Geneva, Switzerland: International Academy of Education. Retrieved from http://unesdoc.unesco.org/images/0012/001254/125450e.pdf

Brophy, J., & Good, T. L. (1986). Teacher behavior and student achievement. In M. C. Wittrock (Ed.), *Handbook of research on teaching* (3rd ed.) (pp. 328-378). New York: Macmillan.

Cawelti, G. (2004). Introduction. In G. Cawelti (Ed.), *Handbook of research for improving student achievement* (3rd ed.) (pp. 1-9). Arlington, VA: Educational Research Service.

Center on English Learning and Achievement. (2000, Winter). Engaging students in meaningful conversations leads to higher achievement. *Newsletter.* Retrieved from http://cela.albany.edu/newsletter.htm

Dolezal, S. E., Welsh, L. M., Pressley, M., & Vincent, M. M. (2003). How nine third-grade teachers motivate student academic engagement. *The Elementary School Journal, 103*(3), 239-267.

Friesen, S. (2009). *Teaching effectiveness: A framework and rubric*. Toronto, ON: Canadian Education Association.

Haberman, M. (1995). *Star teachers of children in poverty*. West Lafayette, IN: Kappa Delta Pi.

Hattie, J. (2003, October). *Teachers make a difference: What is the research evidence?* Presented at the University of Auckland Australian Council for Educational Research. Retrieved from http://www.acer.edu.au/workshops/documents/Teachers_Make_a_Difference_Hattie.pdf

Hattie, J. (2008). *Visible learning: A synthesis of over 800 meta-analyses relating to achievement*. New York: Routledge.

Hattie, J., Biggs, J., & Purdie, N. (1996, Summer). Effects of learning skills interventions on student learning: A meta-analysis. *Review of Educational Research*, 99-136.

Kiewra, K. A. (2002, Spring). How classroom teachers can help students learn and teach them how to learn. *Theory Into Practice*, 71-80.

Lemons, R. W., & Helsing, D. (2008, November). High quality teaching and learning: Do we know it when we see it (and when we don't)? *Education Canada*, 14-18.

Lindberg, J. A., & Swick, A. M. (2002). *Common-sense classroom management: Surviving September and beyond in the elementary classroom*. Thousand Oaks, CA: Corwin.

Marzano, R. J., Gaddy, B. B., & Dean, C. (2000). *What works in classroom instruction*. Aurora, CO: Mid-Continent Research for Education and Learning. Retrieved from http://www.mcrel.org/topics/productDetail.asp?productID=110

Marzano, R., J., Pickering, D. J., & Pollock, J. E. (2001). *Classroom instruction that works: Research-based strategies for increasing student achievement*. Alexandria, VA: Association for Supervision and Curriculum development.

Protheroe, N., & Clarke, S. (2008, November/December). Learning strategies as a key to student success. *Principal*, 33-37.

Smith, J. B., Lee, V. E., & Newmann, F. M. (2001). *Instruction and achievement in Chicago elementary schools*. Chicago: Consortium on Chicago School Research. Retrieved from http://www.consortiumchicago.org/acrobat/InstructionReport.pdf

Stronge, J. H. (2002). *Qualities of effective teachers*. Alexandria, VA: Association for Supervision and Curriculum Development.

Tanner, B. M., Bottoms, G., Feagin, C., & Bearman, A. (n.d.). *Instructional strategies: How teachers teach matters*. Atlanta, GA: Southern Regional Education Board.

Taylor, B., Pearson, D., Clark, K., & Walpole, S. (1999). *Beating the odds in teaching all children to read*. Ann Arbor, MI: Center for the Improvement of Early Reading Achievement.

Wang, M. C., Haertel, G. D., & Walberg, H. J. (1993/1994, December/January). What helps students learn? *Educational Leadership*, 74-79.

Walberg, H. J., & Paik, S. (2004). Effective practices. In G. Cawelti (Ed.), *Handbook of research for improving student achievement* (3rd ed.) (pp. 25-38). Arlington, VA: Educational Research Service.

Implications for Our School: Questions for Discussion and Reflection

- How might we incorporate use of the research base about effective teaching strategies into development opportunities for individual teachers? What about schoolwide development opportunities?

- Review the categories of strategies (such as "effective use of assessment and feedback") presented here. Is there one that should be the focus for teacher development in our school?

- Review the "red flag" approaches discussed on pp. 91-92. How might we ensure that these practices are not used in our school?

Follow-up and Action Items

_____

_____

_____

_____

_____

_____

_____

_____

_____

_____

_____

_____

_____

Chapter 9

Teacher Efficacy: What Is It and Why Does It Matter?

Teachers' confidence in their own ability to promote learning can affect their ability to successfully teach all students. Together, a school staff can help develop a sense of efficacy across the entire school.

More than 30 years ago, studies conducted by the RAND Corporation asked teachers to express their degree of agreement or disagreement with the following two statements:

- "When it comes right down to it, a teacher really can't do much because most of a student's motivation and performance depends on his or her home environment."

- "If I try really hard, I can get through to even the most difficult or unmotivated students." (Armor et al., 1976, in Henson, 2001)

The attitudes reflected in teachers' responses to these statements initiated the concept of *teacher efficacy*—"teachers' confidence in their ability to promote students' learning" (Hoy, 2000, p. 2). Some researchers suggest that the more precise term would be *teacher sense of efficacy*. After all, what is being discussed is a teacher's *sense* of competence—not some objective measure of actual competence. From a practical standpoint, there are two important questions related to this theoretical construct:

- How does a teacher's sense of efficacy affect his or her teaching?

- Can it, through its impact on teaching, affect student achievement?

Over the years since the concept was first developed, researchers have helped to provide answers to both these questions. In his review of research, Jerald (2007) highlights some teacher behaviors found to be related to a teacher's sense of efficacy. Teachers with a stronger sense of efficacy:

- Tend to exhibit greater levels of planning and organization;

- Are more open to new ideas and are more willing to experiment with new methods to better meet the needs of their students;

- Are more persistent and resilient when things do not go smoothly;

- Are less critical of students when they make errors; and,

- Are less inclined to refer a difficult student to special education.

> *"Teachers who set high goals, who persist, who try another strategy when one approach is found wanting—in other words, teachers who have a high sense of efficacy and act on it—are more likely to have students who learn." (Woolfolk, in Shaughnessy, 2004, p. 156)*

Researchers interested in the topic of efficacy have worked to develop longer and more focused instruments to get at the beliefs the first two RAND survey items were intended to measure. Their work has also increased our understanding of the concept. It is now generally thought that the construct of efficacy comprises two types of beliefs. The first, *personal* teaching efficacy, relates to a teacher's own feeling of confidence regarding his or her teaching abilities. The second, often called *general* teaching efficacy, "appears to reflect a general belief about the power of teaching to reach difficult children" (Hoy, 2000, p. 7). Researchers have also found that these two constructs are independent. Thus, a teacher may have faith in the ability of teachers to reach difficult children in general, while lacking confidence in his or her personal teaching ability.

How Do Teachers Develop a Sense of Efficacy?

An important factor determining a teacher's sense of efficacy is, not surprisingly, experience—or what Bandura (1977), a leader in the development of self-efficacy theory, calls *performance accomplishments.* Has the teacher been able to make a difference in student learning? Hoy suggests that "some of the most powerful influences on the development of teacher efficacy are mastery experiences during student teaching and the induction year." Thus, "the first years of teaching could be critical to the long-term development of teacher efficacy" (2000, p. 2).

Building on the work of Bandura, Hoy (2000) discusses other factors that can impact a teacher's sense of efficacy:

- *Vicarious experiences.* For example, a teacher might observe another teacher using a particularly effective practice and thus feel more confident that, through its use, she could be more successful in reaching her students.

- *Social persuasion.* In a school setting, this could take the form of either pep talks or feedback that highlights effective teaching behaviors while providing constructive and specific suggestions for ways to improve. However, such "persuasion" is likely to lose its positive impact if subsequent teacher experiences are not positive.

Hoy views the school setting itself—especially the ways in which new-to-the-profession teachers are socialized—as having a potentially powerful impact on a teacher's sense of efficacy. For example, is a new teacher encouraged to view asking for help as not only normal, but desirable? This can be an important way to ensure that a new teacher does not experience a series of failures that in turn affect mastery experiences, the prime determinant of a sense of efficacy.

> *"A strong sense of collective efficacy in a school creates a powerful set of norms and behavioral expectations that reinforce the self-efficacy beliefs of teachers." (Hoy, Tarter, & Hoy, 2006, p. 430)*

Collective Efficacy

Some researchers have taken the concept of teacher efficacy to another level and developed a complementary construct called collective teacher efficacy. Goddard, Hoy, and Hoy (2000) define this as "the perceptions of teachers in a school that the efforts of the faculty as a whole will have a positive effect on students" (p. 480), with the faculty in general agreeing that "teachers in this school can get through to the most difficult students" (p. 487). In the view of these researchers, "teachers' shared beliefs shape the normative environment of schools … [and] are an important aspect of the culture of the school" (p. 502).

Veteran educators have likely experienced some of the effects of a strong positive—or negative—sense of collective efficacy. Teachers in a school characterized by a can-do, "together we can make a difference" attitude are typically more likely to accept challenging goals and be less likely to easily give up. In contrast, teachers in a school characterized by a low level of collective efficacy are less likely to accept responsibility for students' low performance and more likely to point to student risk factors, such as poverty and limited knowledge of English, as causes.

> *Teachers in a school characterized by a can-do, "together we can make a difference" attitude are typically more likely to accept challenging goals and be less likely to easily give up.*

Finally, as with an individual teacher's sense of efficacy, there is a positive relationship between collective efficacy and student achievement. For example, a study conducted by Hoy, Sweetland, and Smith found that collective efficacy "was more important in explaining school achievement than SES [socioeconomic status]" and highlighted the finding's practical significance "because it is easier to change the collective efficacy of a school than it is to influence the SES of the school" (2002, p. 89).

In their summary of research on collective efficacy, Brinson and Steiner suggest that a school's strong sense of collective efficacy can also have a positive impact on parent-teacher relationships since "a staff that is confident in their own abilities and in their effectiveness … is more likely to welcome parental participation." Finally, it can help to build teacher commitment to the school with individual teachers more likely to "share what they know with others" (2007, p. 3).

> *"It seems likely that personal teaching efficacy promotes collective efficacy, which reinforces personal teaching efficacy." (Hoy, Sweetland, & Smith, 2002, p. 91)*

School Leaders' Role in Building a Sense of Efficacy

Although much of teachers' sense of individual and collective efficacy can be linked to their past levels of success or failure in teaching students, researchers point out that this factor is not the whole story. For example, Goddard and Skrla (2006) looked at school characteristics reported by 1,981 teachers and correlated them with teachers' reported levels of efficacy. Less than half the difference in efficacy could be accounted for by factors such as the school's SES level, students' achievement level, and faculty experience. Based on this, they suggest that principals have the opportunity to build collective efficacy through the experiences they provide for teachers.

Hipp's (1996) study of the influence of principal leadership behaviors identified some behaviors as significantly related to efficacy. Teachers reporting high levels of efficacy were led by principals who modeled behaviors such as risk-taking and cooperation. In addition, these teachers perceived their principals as inspiring group purpose—as contributing to the development of a "shared vision which centered on creating a student-centered atmosphere" (Hipp, 1996, p. 18).

Building on such findings, Goddard et al. (2000) suggest that one way for school leaders to improve student achievement is by working to raise the collective efficacy beliefs of their faculties. Pointing to the impact of past teaching experiences on the development of a teacher's sense of efficacy, Hoy, Sweetland, and Smith (2002) suggest that school leaders should lead in ways that promote mastery experiences for teachers.

While Goddard et al. agree, they also recognize that, "Although mastery experiences are the most powerful efficacy changing forces, they may be the most difficult to deliver to a faculty with a low collective efficacy" (2000, p. 502). They continue this discussion by writing that this situation can be remedied if school leaders "provide efficacy-building mastery experiences" through "thoughtfully designed staff development activities and action research projects" (p. 502).

Pfaff (2000) studied elementary school teachers who participated in a study group that discussed issues related to instruction. Survey data found the participating teachers felt themselves to be more effective after the experience and that they had implemented "subtle but powerful," changes in their teaching styles and use of instructional strategies. The participating teachers were also significantly more likely than nonparticipants in the same school to maintain a high level of general teaching efficacy—the belief that teachers can make a difference regardless of a student's background—throughout the year.

> *"It is not enough to hire and retain the brightest teachers—they must also believe they can successfully meet the challenges of the task at hand."* *(Goddard et al., 2000, p. 165)*

In Summary

In this time when high standards for all students are emphasized, the concept of teacher efficacy—from the standpoint of individual teachers and of the faculty as a whole—is critically important. Teachers who believe they can teach all children in ways that enable them to meet these high standards are more likely to exhibit teaching behaviors that support this goal. On a positive note, school staff can work together to develop teachers' individual and collective sense of efficacy. As Goddard et al. remind us, "It is not enough to hire and retain the brightest teachers—they must also believe they can successfully meet the challenges of the task at hand" (2000, p. 165).

References

Bandura, A. (1977). Self-efficacy: Toward a unifying theory of behavioral change. *Psychological Review, 84*(2), 191-215.

Brinson, D., & Steiner, L. (2007). *Building collective efficacy: How leaders inspire teachers to achieve* (Issue Brief). Washington, DC: Center for Comprehensive School Reform and Improvement. Retrieved from http://www.centerforcsri.org/files/CenterIssueBriefOct07.pdf

Goddard, R. D., Hoy, W. K., & Hoy, A. W. (2000). Collective teacher efficacy: Its meaning, measure, and impact on student achievement. *American Educational Research Journal, 37*(2), 479-507.

Goddard, R. D., & Skrla, L. (2006). The influence of school social composition on teachers' collective efficacy beliefs. *Educational Administration Quarterly, 42*(2), 216-235.

Henson, R. K. (2001). *Teacher self-efficacy: Substantive implications and measurement dilemmas.* Paper presented at the Annual Meeting of the Educational Research Exchange in College Station, TX.

Hipp, K. A. (1996). *Teacher efficacy: Influence of principal leadership behavior.* Paper presented at the Annual Meeting of the American Educational Research Association in New York.

Hoy, A. W. (2000) *Changes in teacher efficacy during the early years of teaching.* Paper presented at the Annual Meeting of the American Educational Research Association in New Orleans, LA.

Hoy, W. K., Sweetland, S. R., & Smith, P. A. (2002). Toward an organizational model of achievement in high schools: The significance of collective efficacy. *Educational Administration Quarterly, 38*(1), 77-93.

Hoy, W. K., Tarter, C. J., & Hoy, A. W. (2006). Academic optimism for schools: A force for student achievement. *American Educational Research Journal, 43*(3), 425-446.

Jerald, C. D. (2007). *Believing and achieving (Issue Brief).* Washington, DC: Center for Comprehensive School Reform and Improvement. Retrieved from http://www.eric.ed.gov/ ERICDocs/data/ericdocs2sql/content_storage_01/0000019b/80/28/fe/93.pdf

Pfaff, M. E. (2000). *The effects on teacher efficacy of school-based collaborative activities structured as professional study groups.* Paper presented at the Annual Meeting of the American Educational Research Association in New Orleans, LA.

Shaughnessy, M. F. (2004). An interview with Anita Woolfolk: The educational psychology of teacher efficacy. *Educational Psychology Review, 16*(2), 153-175.

Implications for Our School: Questions for Discussion and Reflection

- Do we, as a staff, believe that through our efforts we can ensure that all students achieve? If so, what evidence would a visitor to our school see to show that we believe this?

- What kinds of staff development experiences (for example, study groups, action research projects) would help teachers in our school build a greater sense of efficacy?

- As a staff, do we send the message to both new and experienced teachers that it's okay to ask one another for help as a way of increasing our ability to work with all kinds of students?

- Have staff members respond to the questions in the Collective Efficacy Scale provided at http://www.waynekhoy.com/collective_efficacy.html. Then score and discuss the implications of the results.

Follow-up and Action Items

_____

_____

_____

_____

_____

_____

_____

_____

_____

_____

_____

_____

Chapter 10

Becoming Effective Data Users

Effective data-informed decision making requires well-organized processes as well as conditions that support data use.

The phrase "data-based decision making" has been widely used in the past decade's discussions about school improvement, with many research studies confirming the importance of the practice to school improvement (Brinson, Kowal, & Hassel, 2008; Datnow, Park, & Kennedy, 2008; Williams et al., 2005). Research also tells us that more effective schools typically use data *differently* than less effective ones. For example, one study compared schools with rapid improvement to schools that made less progress and found that a primary difference was:

> the extent of data use to *inform instruction*. [Staff members] from growth schools more elaborately discussed the use of data to inform collaboration, guide them in making needed instructional adjustments, adjust their alignment with standards, develop intervention strategies, assess individual student progress, and develop instructional modifications. (California Comprehensive Center and American Institutes for Research, 2006, p. 5)

The bottom line is that it makes sense to use data to help clarify decisions, identify alternative solutions to problems, and target resources more effectively. The real question should not be *whether* to integrate the use of data in school improvement, but *how*. Two key elements of this are establishing a process for data use and ensuring that conditions to support effective data use are present. Research conducted in schools that use data well provides helpful direction for both these elements.

- "School systems are awash in data. So much so, in fact, that some principals feel like they are drowning in it. Unfortunately, although most schools are data rich, they are also information poor." (Mills, 2006, p. 45)

- "Data are just the tip of the iceberg . . . reminding us that what lies beneath is what counts—the curriculum, instruction, assessment, and professional development practices." (Love, Stiles, Mundry, & DiRanna, 2008, p. 14)

- "The examination of data is not an end in itself but rather a means to improve decisions about instructional programs, placements, and methods." (U.S. Department of Education, 2008, p. 6)

- In essence, effective data use consists of two key elements: "asking the right questions and acting on the answers." (Protheroe, 2001)

Effective Data Use as a Process

In Love's view, data and results are, in too many schools, "two shores with an ocean in between.... What is often lacking is a process that enables schools to connect the data with the results they want" (2008, pp. 7-8). Perhaps the first step to developing a more effective process is shifting to a framework in which data are understood to *inform* decisions. Knapp, Swinnerton, Copland, and Monpas-Huber stress that this change in terminology away from data-driven decision making signals an important shift in the way data use should be viewed. In this new framework, data are not thought to "drive" decisions. Instead, data use explicitly acknowledges that educators bring "core values and insights" into the process (2006, p. 6).

Some schools have shifted to this view of data-informed leadership and have begun to use more effective processes. However, other schools are looking for guidance as to how to use data more and in ways that make efficient use of staff time. Gregory and Kuzmich (2004) find that more successful approaches often start small, and Johnson (2000) suggests that "a logical first step in using data is to begin making better use of existing data."

Depka has another suggestion in regard to data use; he advises schools to guard against a "the more, the merrier" approach to data use:

> Be selective about the data you choose . . . It is important to provide enough data so that participants can have a good degree of confidence that their observations are accurate. But too much information at one data delve can overwhelm, confuse, and exhaust people. (2006, p. 22)

Many "good data user" schools found that an important element of success involved expanding their definition of data beyond state assessment results and other more traditional indicators such as dropout statistics. Thus, a principal might intentionally use classroom observations to identify gaps in good teaching strategies that should be addressed by schoolwide teacher development. Or a school committee focusing on behavior and discipline issues might look closely at when and where problems in hallways tended to occur—with this data informing discussions about both problems and possible solutions.

Teachers in one middle school felt they needed a common understanding of students' literacy levels to inform their work around improving literacy. They decided to use an organized approach to sampling student work to do this:

> After much discussion, the teachers agreed that they should give a writing assignment that would allow them to collaboratively assess their students, using a rubric that they had developed. They developed the following assignment: "Teenagers on the street are reported to get into trouble, such as engaging in criminal behavior or getting involved in gang-related activities, after 10:00 p.m. Do you think it is a good idea for cities and towns to enforce curfews— times after which teenagers must be off the streets? Explain your reasons." (National Turning Points Center, n.d., p. 13)

The data collected through the work sampling provided information about the overall level of student proficiency and helped teachers focus their discussion on ways to improve instruction to better support student needs.

Finally, City, Kagle, and Teoh talk about some trade-offs schools may need to consider as they begin schoolwide data-use initiatives:

> If you examine instruction more quickly with limited data sources, you will get to designing and implementing solutions faster, but you may sacrifice some accuracy in understanding the teaching dimensions of the problem of practice. If you take your time and examine several data sources, you may be more accurate, but you may lose a sense of urgency and momentum for improvement…. If you have a few people do most of the examining instruction work, you may get it done more quickly and at greater depth, but you may not get the level of understanding and buy-in you'll want from the rest of the teachers whose practice you ultimately want to improve. (2005, p. 114)

Ultimately, your goal should be to embed the use of data in the day-to-day operations of your school as part of a continuous cycle of school improvement. Thornton and Perreault (2002) agree and describe the alignment of data use with a cycle of school improvement. Note how data collection and use are embedded in their description of the cycle:

- Develop a plan. The plan should focus data collection efforts on a specific systemic issue or issues. What data will be collected? How will we improve the system? What new instructional methods or procedure will be developed? What is the current baseline on critical measures? What staff development is needed?

- Implement the plan. Did we successfully implement the plan? How well is the plan working? Do staff members need further professional development? Regular assessments should be conducted. At this stage, it is crucial to monitor implementation, collect data, and provide feedback.

- Analyze the results. Are staff members working collaboratively? Are staff members exhibiting skills and confidence in data analysis? When determining whether the implementation is successful, criteria to consider are disaggregation of data, performance-based summaries, and open discussions.

- Take action. What have we learned? How can we improve the system? What adjustments in the system do the data suggest? (Excerpted from Thornton & Perreault, 2002, pp. 92-93.)

Thomas emphasizes the "take action" phase of data use as critical to school improvement. For example, he talks about a teacher team review of assessment and related data:

> Unless the team emerges from the data analysis process with a clear plan of action for identified students and for classroom instruction, it has wasted its time. The final step in the data analysis process is for the team to implement the enrichments and interventions within a definitive time frame, modify instructional or assessment practices, and collect data to determine the effectiveness of the changes. (Thomas, 2006, p. 42)

The Questions Are Key

Doug Reeves sees many educators as "drowning in data" and provides suggestions for "gaining control" of it. In his view, one of the most important elements of effective data use is developing "a clearly focused question" (2008/2009, p. 88). Lachat, Williams, and Smith agree. They stress the importance of organizing data use around "essential questions" and provide the following examples:

- Are specific reading and math interventions improving skills and reducing achievement gaps for selected groups of students?

- How do students' course grades compare to their results on state assessments and standardized tests?

- How do assessment results for students new to the district in grades 9 or 10 compare to the results of students who have been in the district for their middle school years? (2006, p. 20)

Supporting the Process

While studying schools making effective use of data, researchers Means, Padilla, DeBarger, and Bakia found a persistent pattern of what they called "prerequisites and supporting conditions" (2009, p. 2). Understanding such critically needed supporting conditions and then ensuring they are in place are important responsibilities for school leaders. Four such supporting conditions—a trusting environment, training for staff, opportunities for teachers to collaborate, and developing a culture of data use—are discussed briefly below.

A Trusting Environment

It's easy to see why some staff members might fear increased use of data since it can shine a brighter light on school problems or—even more worrisome—on their lack of success with some students. Thus, developing a trusting environment in which people feel comfortable and safe talking about and studying school- or classroom-based problems needs to begin even before the emphasis on data use is increased.

As an example of the importance of trust to data usage, Langer, Colton, and Goff talk about a group of teachers engaged in collaborative analysis of student work: "Trust in fellow group members allows [a teacher] to bring a struggling student's work to the group without fear of being judged or criticized" (2003, p. 46).

Training for Staff

Even in schools identified as good data users by researchers Means et al. (2009), teachers wanted more professional development related to data use. The following three topics were identified by more than half of the teachers in these schools as requested professional development topics:

- How to develop diagnostic assessments for my class;

- How to adjust the content and approach used in my class in light of student data; and,

- How to identify types of data that can help to monitor school progress against goals for improvement (2009, p. 30).

This need for teacher development has been addressed head-on by schools that have incorporated the effective use of data in their improvement efforts. Opportunities to learn how to analyze assessment data have typically been provided in a variety of ways, including:

- Staff development focused on how to "read" and analyze reports of assessment results;

- Presentations by central office staff or principals to school staff, followed by a discussion of possible next steps;

- One-on-one sessions of a principal, assistant principal, or lead teacher with a teacher to review and discuss results from his or her classes and students; and,

- Training of an in-school data expert, typically a teacher, who works with grade-level or subject-area teams to analyze the data.

However, Holcomb (2004) reminds us that effective data use requires more than number-crunching skills. Thus, training is often especially powerful when it is organized around an "authentic" task. For example, when a content-area team is guided through its initial efforts to take a more detailed view of achievement data for individual students, teachers on the team are simultaneously learning important skills. Finally, training for staff should include time spent on encouraging teachers and other school staff to recognize the data analysis skills they already have.

Opportunities for Teachers to Collaborate

Another key component of effective systems is the provision of time for teachers to discuss the data and to work together to develop solutions. Means et al. talk about this:

> The most sophisticated data warehouse in the world will have no effect on instruction if no one has—or takes—the time to look at the data, reflect on them, and draw inferences for instructional planning. Given that time is one of the most basic resources in any organization, there need to be strong expectations that educators will take the time to examine data and use those data to guide improvements in their programs and practices. (Means et al., 2009, p. 5)

Although teachers view such time for interaction as an opportunity both to develop their skills in data analysis and to brainstorm and share effective instructional strategies, they report that such opportunities are scarce in many schools (U.S. Department of Education, 2008). One study of high schools that effectively used data to inform improvement efforts found that "structured departmental and/or course-alike time for collaboration was essential for teachers to engage in data discussions" (Datnow, Park, & Kennedy, 2008, p. 80).

Harrison and Bryan talk about this as the critical next step many schools still need to take to make more effective use of data. In their view, data management systems may be in place but "the focus now needs to move to the structures and allocation of time that will allow teachers to engage in data conversations about student achievement and its implications for classroom planning and instruction" (2008, p. 15). Some of these "data conversations" may be whole-school, and include topics such as patterns of student achievement and needs for teacher development. However, another use of data may be to support student goal-setting conversations, with one teacher interacting with one student.

> *"Data by themselves are not very useful to principals and teachers for school improvement purposes. It's only when data have been turned into information, and that information is used to stimulate conversations about the future direction of the school, that data utilization is meaningful and important in school reform." (Williamson, in The Principals' Partnership, n.d.)*

Role of School Leaders

School leaders "play a major role in . . . setting expectations for staff participation in data-informed decision making, and making resources such as supported time available to support the enterprise" (Means et al., 2009, p. 5).

Thus, principal leadership is embedded in ensuring the "supporting conditions" described above are present. However, there are also other ways in which a principal can develop an environment supportive of data use. Thornton and Perreault talk about this:

> Demonstrating the utility of data is critical to gaining teachers' support and cooperation. In general, teachers need to become comfortable consumers; the data collected should become "their" data.... By engaging staff members in a meaningful project, the principal can identify and model the value of data-based decision making....To build teachers' confidence in data analysis, the principal should select an initial project that is likely to succeed. (2002, p. 90)

In Summary

Effective data use can be a powerful tool in improvement efforts from the classroom to the school level. Keys to this include both using data wisely and developing a school environment that supports its use. Finally, it's important that schools shift from the mindset of data-driven decision making to one of data-informed decision making since this rightfully recognizes the importance of educator experience and knowledge to the improvement process.

References

Boudett, K., & Moody, L. (2005). Organizing for collaborative work. In K. P. Boudett, E. A. City, & R. J. Murnane (Eds.). *Data wise: A step-by-step guide to using assessment results to improve teaching and learning.* Cambridge, MA: Harvard Education Press.

Brinson, D., Kowal, J., & Hassel, B. C. (2008). *School turnarounds: Actions and results.* Lincoln, IL: Center on Innovation & Improvement. Retrieved from http://www.centerii.org/survey/downloads/Turnaround%20Actions%20and%20Results%203%2024%2008%20with%20covers.pdf

California Comprehensive Center and American Institutes for Research. (2006). *Data-driven decision making based on curriculum-embedded assessment: Findings from recent California studies.* Sacramento, CA: California Comprehensive Center at WestEd.

City, E. A., Kagle, M., & Teoh, M. B. (2005). Examining instruction. In K. P. Boudett, E. A. City, & R. J. Murnane (Eds.). *Data wise: A step-by-step guide to using assessment results to improve teaching and learning.* Cambridge, MA: Harvard Education Press.

Datnow, A., Park, V., & Kennedy, V. (2008). *Acting on data: How urban high schools use data to improve instruction.* Los Angeles, CA: Center on Educational Governance, USC Rossier School of Education.

Depka, E. (2006). *The data guidebook for teachers and leaders: Tools for continuous improvement.* Thousand Oaks, CA: Corwin Press.

Gregory, G. H., & Kuzmich, L. (2004). *Data driven differentiation in the standards-based classroom.* Thousand Oaks, CA: Corwin Press.

Harrison, C., & Bryan, C. (2008, Fall). Data dialogue. *Journal of Staff Development,* 15-19.

Holcomb, E. (2004). *Getting excited about data* (2nd ed.). Thousand Oaks, CA: Corwin Press.

Johnson, J. H. (2000, Spring). Data-driven school improvement. *Journal of School Improvement.* Retrieved from http://www.ncacasi.org/jsi/2000v1i1/data_driven

Knapp, M. A., Swinnerton, J. A., Copland, M.A., & Monpas-Huber, J. (2006). *Data-informed leadership in education: A research report in collaboration with The Wallace Foundation.* Seattle, WA: Center for the Study of Teaching and Policy, University of Washington. Retrieved from http://depts.washington.edu/ctpmail/PDFs/DataInformed-Nov1.pdf

Lachat, M. A., Williams, M., & Smith S. C. (2006, October). Making sense of all your data. *Principal Leadership,* 16-21.

Langer, G. M., Colton, A. B., & Goff, L. (2003). *Collaborative analysis of student work: Improving teaching and learning.* Alexandria, VA: Association of Supervision and Curriculum Development.

Love, N. (2008). *Using data to improve learning for all: A collaborative inquiry approach.* Thousand Oaks, CA: Corwin Press.

Love, N., Stiles, K. E., Mundry, S., & DiRanna, K. (2008, Fall). Passion and principle ground effective data use. *Journal of Staff Development*, 14.

Means, B., Padilla, C., DeBarger, A., & Bakia, M. (2009). *Implementing data-informed decision making in schools—Teacher access, supports, and use.* Washington, DC: U.S. Department of Education, Office of Planning, Evaluation, and Policy Development. Retrieved from http://www.ed.gov/rschstat/eval/tech/data-informed-decision/data-informed-decision.doc

Mills, L. (2006, October). Transforming data into knowledge. *Principal Leadership*, 44-48.

National Turning Points Center. (n.d.). *Turning points—Transforming middle schools: Guide to data-based inquiry and decision making.* Boston, MA: Author.

The Principals' Partnership. (n.d.). *Research brief: Using data for school improvement.* Retrieved from http://www.principalspartnership.com/usingdata.pdf

Protheroe, N. (2001, Summer). Improving teaching and learning with data-based decisions: Asking the right questions and acting on the answers. *ERS Spectrum.* Retrieved from http://www.ers.org/spectrum/sum01a.htm

Reeves, D. (2008/2009, December/January). Looking deeper into the data. *Educational Leadership*, 88-89.

Thomas, R. S. (2006, October). How to survive data overload. *Principal Leadership*, 37-42.

Thornton, B., & Perreault, G. (2002, March). Becoming a data-based leader: An introduction. *NASSP Bulletin*, 86-96.

U.S. Department of Education. (2008). *Teachers' use of student data systems to improve instruction: 2005 to 2007.* Washington, DC: U.S. Department of Education, Office of Planning, Evaluation and Policy Development. Retrieved from http://www.ed.gov/rschstat/eval/tech/teachers-data-use-2005-2007/teachers-data-use-2005-2007.pdf

Williams, T., Perry, M., Studier, C., Brazil, N., Kirst, M., Haertel, E.,…Levine, R. (2005). *Similar students, different results: Why do some schools do better? A large-scale survey of California elementary schools serving low-income students.* Mountain View, CA: EdSource.

Implications for Our School: Questions for Discussion and Reflection

- Do we use data "to help clarify decisions, identify alternative solutions to problems, and target resources more effectively"? If not, what are some of the reasons why we don't?

- Do conditions in our school—such as opportunities for teachers to collaborate—support effective data use?

- Are there aspects of effective data use about which staff need development opportunities?

- Do we define data too narrowly—focusing mainly on results of state assessments? If so, what are some other sources of data we should begin to collect and analyze?

Follow-up and Action Items

_____

_____

_____

_____

_____

_____

_____

_____

_____

_____

_____

_____

Chapter 11

Differentiating Instruction in a Standards-Based Environment

Teachers who effectively differentiate instruction can enhance learning for all students.

On the surface, the standards-based expectations for today's schools seem to mandate a cookie-cutter approach to education. All students, regardless of abilities, background, and interests, are expected to learn a common set of standards. Both research and the experiences of educators, however, make it clear that a significant number of students will fail to learn the specified knowledge and skills unless focused attention is paid to the instructional needs of individual students.

One way in which many schools attempt to meet such needs is by differentiating instruction. But can these two seemingly incompatible orientations—one stressing common standards and one highlighting individual needs—work together? Tomlinson suggests they can: "There is no contradiction between effective standards-based instruction and differentiation. Curriculum tells us what to teach. Differentiation tells us how" (2000).

> *"All teachers differentiate instruction; it's natural, it's intuitive; we couldn't survive without differentiating. However, we can become more conscious and intentional in the ways we think about our students and in the ways we plan our lessons so that differentiation helps even more students succeed." (Campbell, 2009, p. 7)*

Differentiated instruction promotes a challenging curriculum for all students, but varies the level of teacher support, task complexity, pacing, and avenues to learning based on each student's readiness, interest, and learning profile.

Of course, good teachers have always differentiated. But to make classrooms more responsive to students and meet today's higher standards, teachers need to become more systematic in their approach to differentiation (Levy, 2008). Systematically planning for and implementing a differentiated classroom requires a new level of teacher skill. Bruce Campbell, a classroom teacher for over 30 years, talks about the need for teachers to explicitly integrate differentiation into their daily work: "If there is one thing I have learned, it is that I have to make that conscious and intentional effort to differentiate on a daily basis" (2009, p. 7).

The planning needed to differentiate is also complex and time-consuming. However, teachers who have developed a comprehensive approach to differentiation typically note that the process gets easier over time. One aspect of this is practice—practice with, for example, working with a multilevel plan of assignments for students. In addition, the learning activities needed to support a differentiated approach, once developed, are there to reuse the next time the unit is taught.

What Is Differentiated Instruction?

At its most basic, differentiated instruction means that teachers meet students where they are in the learning process and move them along as quickly and as far as possible in the context of a mixed-ability classroom. "Differentiated instruction is not a single strategy, but rather an approach to instruction that incorporates a variety of strategies" (The Access Center, n.d.).

Differentiating does not mean individualizing every assignment for every student every day (Fattig & Taylor, 2008). Nor does it mean simply assigning certain students more or less work (or different worksheets), asking high-achieving students more complex questions, or grading struggling students more leniently (Tomlinson, 2001). Rather, differentiated instruction is a complex mix of beliefs and instructional approaches, all directed toward increasing student success.

As an instructional orientation, differentiated instruction is based on the beliefs that students differ in their learning profiles; that students should be active learners, decision makers, and problem solvers in the classroom; and that the goal of instruction should be for students to understand material, not for the teacher to merely cover the curriculum (Sacramento City Unified School District, 2003).

What Does the Differentiated Instruction Classroom Look Like?

Classrooms in which differentiated instruction is the norm have the following characteristics:

- "Students are appreciated for the variety of abilities and experiences they bring to the group.

- Teachers recognize asynchronous development of their students and use information about readiness, interests, and learning styles as the basis of instruction.

- Learning options in content, process, and product are devised based on the gathered data, with materials varied according to challenge and purpose.

- All students participate in purposeful, valued learning activities.

- Essential skills are used to make sense of open-ended problems designed to teach key concepts and principles.

- Teachers present information in a variety of modalities to address individual needs.

- Students may have some choice of topics or modes of expression based on their own interests and learning styles.

- Homework extends individual understanding and ability level.

- There is flexibility in grouping and pacing.

- Assessment is varied and balanced, with grades reflecting individual growth." (Kapusnick & Hauslein, 2001, p. 157)

The last item—assessment—looks vastly different in a differentiated classroom than in a teacher-centered classroom. Effective differentiation depends on the teacher having accurate information about students' interests and needs. So in differentiated classrooms, ongoing assessment is built into the curriculum—not as an "end-of-lesson or end-of-unit phenomenon," but "at the beginning, at the end, and everywhere in between" (Brimijoin, Marquissee, & Tomlinson, 2003, p. 72).

For that reason, teachers in the differentiated classroom use a wide variety of pre-assessments at the beginning of new units of instruction and incorporate other measures—group discussions, exit cards, one-on-one oral questioning, written journal prompts, brainstorming sessions, objective tests or quizzes, quick-writes, essays, and so on—to continually monitor each student's understanding and then adjust instruction accordingly. They also use a variety of summative assessments, such as open-ended writing assignments, portfolios, visual creations, individual and group presentations, to give students many different kinds of opportunities to show what they have learned.

How to Differentiate Instruction

The First Priority: Knowing Your Students

A key to differentiating instruction is understanding the many ways in which each student is a unique learner. Here are some factors that are commonly identified as having the most influence on an individual's learning (Glass, 2009):

- *Academic readiness.* Every student comes to class with a level of academic readiness that is determined by a combination of individual aptitude, quality of previous instruction, early childhood experiences, home environment, temperament, and so on.

- *Cultural background and language proficiency.* The growing population of ELL students has increased the need for differentiation. It is important to recognize, however, that language minority students are not a homogeneous group. On the contrary, they vary greatly in educational background, family socioeconomic level, length of time they have lived in the United States, age, and level of English proficiency. It is also important not to assume that all members of one culture will learn in similar ways. But "it is the case that learning environments and procedures that are comfortable for many members of one cultural group may not be so to many members of other cultural groups. . . . In classrooms where varied cultural groups are represented, a single approach to teaching and learning is unlikely to serve all students well" (Dobush, n.d.).

- *Learning profile.* Researchers have developed a number of theories about the learning styles and preferences that determine how students learn best. For example, the theory of sensory-based differences points out that individuals differ in the extent to which they focus on auditory, visual, and kinesthetic sensory information. Thus, an auditory learner can more easily remember *what is said*, a visual/verbal learner remembers *what is read*, a visual/iconic learner remembers *what is seen*, and a kinesthetic learner remembers *what is manipulated or touched* (Howard & James, 2003). The well-known theory of multiple intelligences, introduced by Howard Gardner in *Frames of Mind: The Theory of Multiple Intelligences* (1983), proposed that people are smart in seven distinct ways: linguistic, logical/mathematical, spatial, musical, bodily/kinesthetic, inter-personal, and intrapersonal, with an eighth way—naturalist—added later. Ongoing observation and student choice (for example, allowing students to either listen to a book on tape or read it in print) gives the teacher clues as to student learning profiles.

- *Interest.* Obviously, students come to class with a wide range of interests, and they will be more engaged (and thus learn more) if they are allowed to pursue and share these interests as part of their learning. Becoming aware of students' interests can be as simple as talking with them or al-lowing them to choose their own subject for writing. Interest surveys may also be useful.

Deciding What to Differentiate

The literature on differentiated instruction commonly identifies three main classroom elements that teachers can differentiate to respond to individual student needs:

- **Content** (the knowledge and skills that are taught). Differentiation does *not* mean compromising the goal of having all students master the essential understandings that are determined by state and local standards, district curriculum guides, and the teacher's own judgment. "Differentiated instruction allows for variations in content without losing sight of the curriculum to which all children are entitled" (Levy, 2008, p. 162). Keeping this goal in mind, differentiation does allow for adjusting the pace and depth of content coverage. For example, pre-assessment of student knowledge and skills may determine that some students can skip more basic steps or are likely to move more quickly through material; these learners may be given opportunities to explore concepts in more depth or engage in enrichment activities that extend the topic under study. In contrast, some students may be found to lack background knowledge or needed skills and so need instruction and extra support in these before moving on.

- **Process** (activities through which students learn and make sense of key knowledge and skills). This may be the most complex aspect of differentiating instruction since it requires planning for and managing a range of activities, with instruction provided through a combination of whole-class, small-group, and single-student approaches.

- **Product** (how students demonstrate the knowledge and skills they have learned). Although all students should be expected to demonstrate mastery of core content, they can demonstrate their mastery in various ways.

Tomlinson and Strickland (2005) identify two additional elements that teachers should consider in meeting their students' needs:

- **Affect** (how students link thought and feelings in the classroom). For example, if struggling students are given too many worksheets and too much repetitive practice, they may feel that they are being treated as "dumb," leading to anger and resentment. At the same time, gifted students in the class may need enrichment activities; if they don't feel adequately challenged, these students are likely to become bored.

- **Learning environment** (both visible and invisible classroom conditions in which teaching and learning activities are embedded). The differentiated classroom makes flexible use of three aspects of the learning environment: (1) space (e.g., classroom furniture may be rearranged to allow for individual, small-group, and whole-group work); (2) materials (e.g., the teacher may make a variety of supplies freely available to students to use for individual and small-group projects); and (3) time (e.g., classroom routines may be established in which some students work independently while the teacher provides individual instruction to others who need extra help).

Putting Differentiation Into Action

Tobin talks about the essential first step for teachers who are developing a plan for differentiated instruction: "A DI approach calls for teachers to be crystal clear on the essential understandings first, and then to design opportunities to practice or engage in skills to support the essential understandings" (2008, p. 160). She goes on to describe what differentiated instruction is—and is not:

> Differentiating does not mean that a teacher is taking into account the individual interests, profiles, and readiness of the thirty students five hours per day in every curricular and instructional decision. To suggest that would be ludicrous. Rather, differentiating means that a teacher is approaching the . . . curriculum and her students with a responsive disposition—an orientation to planning, decision making, curriculum selection, and instructional flow that is flexile and opportunistic. (2008, p. 160)

Here are a few of the myriad of strategies that teachers can weave into daily instruction to respond to students' readiness levels, learning preferences, and interests (Fonville & Lewis, 2004; Glass, 2009; Tomlinson & Strickland, 2005):

- *Curriculum compacting.* Before beginning a particular unit of study, pre-assess to identify students who have already mastered the unit's essential learning or who need a shorter period of time to master the material. Then, compress instruction and provide curriculum enrichment for those students while others master the core material.

- *Tiered assignments.* Provide instruction on the core curriculum content using different levels of instructional complexity, open-endedness, and abstractness according to students' levels of readiness.

- *Instructional materials at various levels of difficulty.* Make a wide variety of reading materials available for topics under study, including textbook excerpts from different grade-level texts, articles, picture books, and so forth. Depending on the circumstances, assign groups and individuals text that is appropriate to their performance level or allow them to choose texts based on their desired level of challenge and their interests. Also have nontext materials available, such as videotapes, audiotapes, computer programs, live demonstrations, and manipulatives.

- *Flexible grouping.* Provide many different sizes and types of groups to match instruction to student readiness, interest, or learning profile. Because student performance varies, it is important to permit movement between groups. Provide a mixture of homogeneous groups that enable students to work with others at the same level, and heterogeneous groups that enable students to share different perspectives and abilities.

- *Peer teaching.* When a student needs one-on-one instruction but then masters the material after this extra help, designate that student as the "resident expert" for that concept or skill. By teaching the material to peers, the student not only gets more valuable practice but also has the opportunity to be a leader.

- *Independent study.* Work with individual students to identify topics of special interest to them, investigate those topics, and plan projects that will best express their learning. Such projects involve many kinds of differentiation.

- *Learning agendas.* To give students a more prominent role in differentiation, work with them to draw up a personalized list of learning tasks. Usually, a due date is provided, and students complete the tasks in any order. Learning agendas are a good way for teachers to manage the multiple layers of a personalized classroom. Teachers often choose to set aside a time for students to work on their agenda items.

Organizing these strategies and many others into a coherent system of instruction is more complicated than teaching in a traditional, teacher-centered classroom with uniform instructional and evaluation activities for all students. Differentiated instruction represents both planning and organizational challenges. Teachers need to consider the five elements of content, process, product, affect, and learning environment, and decide how differentiation can be realistically—and productively—incorporated into the classroom routine. That's why differentiated instruction is not a science, but an art.

A suggestion made repeatedly by teachers who have moved to a differentiated approach is start small! Initial changes might include:

- selecting a small group of students and differentiating content for one unit;

- adding several different learning activities to one unit lesson plan; or,

- offering students options for demonstrating competence (Wehrmann, 2000).

Planning for Differentiated Instruction

As a teacher begins to shift toward more explicitly differentiating instruction, it soon becomes clear that almost as much time is needed to *plan* instruction as actually provide it. While this is daunting—and rightfully so—two observations from teachers experienced with using a differentiated approach demonstrate that it is not an impossible task.

First, much of the time needed is spent on development of activities, instructional modules, and so on for students at different levels. Once these are developed, they become "a toolbox of instructional choices ready to go" (Center on Innovation & Improvement, 2008, p. 65), and, even more important, they can be used again and again. Second, in many situations, teachers working together in grade-level or content-area teams can share the development work. Ideally, this work begins with conversations about standards. The goal is to create three tiers for each objective:

- Target—for students ready to work on the objective but who have not yet mastered it;

- Enhanced—for students who have already mastered the objective and who should receive opportunities for related work to expand their understanding and knowledge; and,

- Prerequisite—for students who need additional instruction before moving on to the target objective (Center for Innovation & Improvement, 2008, p. 65).

Teachers then move on to talking about strategies to address the needs of students in each of the three groups. Since differentiation will also require a teacher to spend time with small groups of students, or even individual students, one aspect of this discussion will be to identify different modes of instruction (such as whole group, small student-directed groups, and independent work), some of which will go on simultaneously with teacher as manager. The Center for Innovation & Improvement (2008) suggests that teachers develop a Learning Plan Grid that integrates:

- A description of instructional content and approaches for students at each of three levels (enhanced, target, and prerequisite); and,

- Planning for different types of student work focused on the objective (independent work, computer-based, student-directed heterogeneous groups, teacher-directed group, and homework).

Learning Plan Grids—each focused on an objective—provide a roadmap for students at each of the three levels. Thus, this approach addresses the concern expressed by many teachers—"I can't develop 30 separate lessons for every class." Instead, a teacher goes to the grid and identifies one of the three levels, along with associated instructional strategies and content, for each student.

The Skills Teachers Need to Differentiate

The "heart and soul" of differentiated instruction lies with the classroom teacher. Most teachers believe in helping each child, but some lack the practical strategies necessary to accomplish this goal. Just as each student has a level of readiness, each teacher has a personal knowledge base and comfort level that will either help or hinder a move toward differentiated instruction (Gregory, 2003). As mentioned before, differentiating instruction calls for a high level of teacher skill in a number of areas. Teachers need:

- An understanding of what differentiation is and a broad repertoire of strategies to individualize instruction;

- Classroom management skills;

- Knowledge of the "power instructional strategies" in the content area being taught, including the most effective ways to sequence the content;

- Knowledge of best practices to support English Language Learners, special education students, and struggling students; and,

- Deep content knowledge, including what aspects of that content are essential and what rigorous understanding of the topic looks like (Waters & O'Meara, 2007).

This last need—deep mastery of the content being taught—is especially important, according to Tomlinson:

> If I understand a concept, there are all sorts of ways to help kids learn it. For example, instead of teaching facts about dinosaurs, teachers might approach dinosaurs according to the concept of classification: Is it a dinosaur that runs or walks? That eats animals or plants? That fights or hides? We could also study dinosaurs according to the concept of extinction—what it means to adapt or not adapt to the environment and what happens when something isn't well-suited to its environment. (in Association for Supervision and Curriculum Development, 2000)

To help teachers prepare to make the change, schools need to provide resources on differentiated instruction, as well as time for teachers to discuss them. Teachers need training in differentiation methods and in management of this more complex approach to instruction. They also need access to high-quality instructional materials and well-developed diagnostic and benchmark assessments with prompt reports of results (Waters & O'Meara, 2008).

Teachers also might find it useful to reflect on their own beliefs about teaching and learning. Individual teachers can do this through journal writing; or a group can do it in a study group or in a staff meeting. Questions for reflection might include: How do you know when your students are engaged in learning? Do all of your students learn the same way? As they begin making changes in their instruction, teachers may want to focus their reflections on what happened in the classroom each day. Which learners responded to which types of activities? What went well about the day (Gregory, 2003)?

> *Differentiated instruction "simply means thinking about our students differently and planning our lessons in more conscious and intentional ways." (Campbell, 2009, p. 9)*

In Summary

Differentiated instruction is not a new concept, but over the last 2 decades, it has grown more prevalent in classrooms and schools across the United States. More and more teachers are experiencing the power of intentionally planning for and using a variety of instructional strategies and models to organize classrooms around the success of all students. The increasing diversity of the student body and the continuing expectation for high achievement for all students make differentiation more crucial than ever today.

Make no mistake—systematic differentiation requires a high level of skill and a sizable investment of time and effort from teachers, as well as a commitment by district- and building-level leaders to nurture teachers and help them become expert teacher/managers. However, if we believe that we have a responsibility to make sure all students reach their highest potential, do we really have a choice?

References

The Access Center. (n.d.). *Differentiated instruction for reading.* Retrieved from http://www. k8accesscenter.org/training_resources/readingdifferentiation.asp

Association for Supervision and Curriculum Development. (2000, Spring). Viewpoint. *Curriculum Technology Quarterly.* Retrieved from http://www.ascd.org/handbook/demo/ctq/8spr00.html

Brimijoin, K., Marquissee, E., & Tomlinson, C. A. (2003). Using data to differentiate instruction. *Educational Leadership, 60*(5), 70-73.

Campbell, B. (2009). To-With-By: A three-tiered model for differentiated instruction. *The NERA Journal, 44*(2), 7-10.

Center on Innovation & Improvement. (2008). *Training for instructional leaders: Effective teaming, collegial learning, instructional planning, instructional delivery.* Lincoln, IL: Author.

Dobush, K. (n.d.). *Handbook of research-based instructional methods for teaching literacy to exceptional students*. Bridgewater, MA: Bridgewater State College. Retrieved from http://webhost.bridgew.edu/kdobush/strategies%20for%20teaching%20reading/handbook/Diff_Inst/Differentiated%20Instruction.htm

Fattig, M. L., & Taylor, M. T. (2008). *Co-teaching in the differentiated classroom.* San Francisco: Wiley & Sons.

Fonville, G., & Lewis, S. (2004, January/February). Helping each student succeed through differentiated instruction. *Today's School*, 24-28.

Gardner, H. (1983). *Frames of mind: The theory of multiple intelligences.* New York: Basic Books.

Glass, K. T. (2009). *Lesson design for differentiated instruction, grades 4-9.* Thousand Oaks, CA: Corwin Press, Inc.

Gregory, G. H. (2003). *Differentiated instructional strategies in practice: Training, implementation, and supervision.* Thousand Oaks, CA: Corwin Press, Inc..

Howard, L., & James, A. N. (2003). *What principals need to know about teaching: Differentiated instruction.* Alexandria, VA: Educational Research Service and National Association of Elementary School Principals.

Kapusnick, R. A. & Hauslein, C. M. (2001, Summer). The "silver cup" of differentiated instruction. *Kappa Delta Pi Record*, 156-159.

Levy, H. M. (2008, March/April). Meeting the needs of all students through differentiated instruction: Helping every child reach and exceed standards. *The Clearing House*, 161-164.

Sacramento City Unified School District. (2003). *What is differentiated instruction?* Sacramento, CA: Author. Retrieved from http://www.scusd.edu/gate_ext_learning/differentiated.htm

Tobin, R. (2008, Winter). Conundrums in the differentiated literacy classroom. *Reading Improvement*, 159-169.

Tomlinson, C. A. (2000, September). Reconcilable differences? Standards-based teaching and differentiation. *Educational Leadership*. Retrieved from http://www.ascd.org/ed_topics/el200009_tomlinson.html

Tomlinson, C. A. (2001). *How to differentiate instruction in mixed-ability classrooms* (2nd ed.). Alexandria, VA: Association for Supervision and Curriculum Development.

Tomlinson, C. A., & Strickland, C. A. (2005). *Differentiation in practice: A resource guide for differentiating curriculum, grades 9-12.* Alexandria, VA: Association for Supervision and Curriculum Development.

Waters, L. B., & O'Meara, K. W. (2007). Defining a comprehensive aligned instructional system: To ensure powerful teaching and learning for every student in every classroom. *ERS Spectrum, 25*(4), 23-31.

Wehrmann, K. S. (2000, September). Baby steps: A beginner's guide, the journey to a differentiated classroom starts with small steps. *Educational Leadership*, 20-23.

Implications for Our School: Questions for Discussion and Reflection

- Is differentiated instruction a schoolwide practice in our school, or does it depend on individual teachers' expertise and inclination?

- Has a focus on standards and accountability increased or decreased personalization and responsiveness to each student's individual needs in our school?

- Does lack of time limit our ability to differentiate? If so, what can we do about it?

- Does professional development in our school help teachers develop the knowledge and skills that support differentiation (such as an understanding of cognitive processes and developmental stages, deep subject-matter knowledge, and a repertoire of strategies for differentiation)? If not, how can we integrate such content into future professional development?

Follow-up and Action Items

_____

_____

_____

_____

_____

_____

_____

_____

_____

_____

_____

_____

Chapter 12
Effective Mathematics Instruction

Effective mathematics instruction requires attention to both content—what is taught—and how it is taught.

Research-based knowledge about good mathematics instruction, although not as extensive as that focused on reading instruction, has increased in recent years. It now provides a solid base of information for educators to use as they identify mathematics skills students need to develop as well as teaching strategies and instructional approaches that best support the development of these skills.

What Gets Taught

When considering content knowledge and skills, it is obvious that schools need to look first at state standards students are expected to master. Over the past decade, these standards have become more specific, "driven, in part, by increased accountability in the form of state-mandated testing and, not coincidentally, by a call from teachers asking for more guidance in what mathematics to focus on at particular grades" (Reys, Dingman, Sutter, & Teuscher, 2005, p. 2).

Those outside education might assume that what particular mathematical concepts are presented and when they are taught are fairly similar state to state—reflecting both some consistency of opinions about what students should learn as well as an understanding about the development of children's cognitive abilities. However, after analyzing information on current state standards, researchers Reys and Lappan (2007) found that "mathematics learning expectations vary across the states along several dimensions" (p. 677), with some grade-level placement of academic expectations "dramatically different" (p. 678).

In addition, research studies comparing math instruction in the United States and other countries point to an underlying problem with many of our standards-based systems. Typically, they address many standards at each grade level—encouraging the development of a curriculum that has been characterized as a mile wide but an inch deep.

The wide array of state standards impacts the content included in mathematics textbooks—and, so, instruction. In their analysis, Ginsburg, Leinwand, Anstrom, and Pollock found that, in their efforts to serve multiple state markets, textbook publishers:

> find it necessary to cover almost twice as many topics per grade so that all topics from many states' frameworks can be covered. Consequently, individual topic coverage in U.S. textbooks is much shorter and less comprehensive than what is found in Singaporean texts. (2005, pp. xii-xiii)

Goals of Effective Mathematics Instruction: Some Fundamental Principles

- Basic skills with numbers continue to be vitally important for a variety of everyday uses. They also provide crucial foundation for the higher-level mathematics essential for success in the workplace which must now also be part of a basic education. Although there may have been a time when being able to perform extensive paper-and-pencil computations mechanically was sufficient to function in the workplace, this is no longer true. Consequently, today's students need proficiency with computational procedures. Proficiency, as we use the term, includes both computational fluency and understanding of the underlying mathematical ideas and principles.

- Mathematics requires careful reasoning about precisely defined objects and concepts. Mathematics is communicated by means of a powerful language whose vocabulary must be learned. The ability to reason about and justify mathematical statements is fundamental, as is the ability to use terms and notation with appropriate degrees of precision. By precision, we mean the use of terms and symbols, consistent with mathematical definitions, in ways appropriate for students at particular grade levels. We do not mean formality for formality's sake.

- Students must be able to formulate and solve problems. Mathematical problem solving includes being able to (a) develop a clear understanding of the problem that is being posed; (b) translate the problem from everyday language into a precise mathematical question; (c) choose and use appropriate methods to answer the question; (d) interpret and evaluate the solution in terms of the original problem; and (e) understand that not all questions admit mathematical solutions and recognize problems that cannot be solved mathematically (Ball et al., 2005).

However, the researchers also identified areas of relative strength in U.S. mathematics instruction; specifically,

> The U.S. frameworks give greater emphasis . . . to developing important 21st century mathematical skills such as representation, reasoning, making connections, and communication.... [In addition], the U.S. places a greater emphasis on applied mathematics, including statistics, probability, and real-world problem analysis. (2005, p. xiv)

In recognition of the "mile high and inch deep" problem, the National Council of Teachers of Mathematics (NCTM) developed Curriculum Focal Points, a report that identifies three broad—but critical—mathematical concepts that should be addressed in each grade. NCTM describes the focal points as "major instructional goals and desirable learning expectations, not a list of objectives for students to master" (National Council of Teachers of Mathematics, 2006). As an example, these are focal points for second grade:

- *Number and Operations:* Developing an understanding of the base-ten numeration system and place-value concepts;

- *Number and Operations* and *Algebra:* Developing quick recall of addition facts and related subtraction facts and fluency with multidigit addition and subtraction; and,

- *Measurement:* Developing an understanding of linear measurement and facility in measuring lengths.

NCTM suggests that state boards of education and other groups developing standards use the focal points as a "clear organizational model for establishing a mathematics curriculum from prekindergarten through grade 8" (National Council of Teachers of Mathematics, 2006). At the local district and school levels, teacher conversations and staff development could be organized around the Focal Points. For example, a discussion group that includes teachers from several grades could help focus attention on needed linkages of math instruction from grade to grade.

The Debate About Skills- vs. Inquiry-Based Mathematics Instruction

"The discussion about math skills has persisted for many decades. One aspect of the debate is over how explicitly children must be taught skills based on formulas or algorithms (fixed, step-by-step procedures for solving math problems) versus a more inquiry-based approach in which students are exposed to real-world problems that help them develop fluency in number sense, reasoning, and problem-solving skills. In this latter approach, computational skills and correct answers are not the primary goals of instruction.

Those who disagree with the inquiry-based philosophy maintain that students must first develop computational skills before they can understand concepts of mathematics. These skills should be memorized and practiced until they become automatic. In this view, estimating answers is insufficient and, in fact, is considered to be dependent on strong foundational skills. Learning abstract concepts of mathematics is perceived to depend on a solid base of knowledge of the tools of the subject. Of course, teaching in very few classrooms would be characterized by the extremes of these philosophies. In reality, there is a mixing of approaches to instruction in the classroom, perhaps with one predominating." (National Mathematics Advisory Panel, 2007, pp. 1-2)

How Math Is Taught

During the reading wars between proponents of a whole language approach and those favoring skills-based instruction, educators found that a careful and intensive review of research revealed the importance of using a combination of both approaches. Similarly, there are at least two camps prominent in the discussion of how math should be taught. The two teaching approaches have clear differences.

In skills-based instruction, teachers focus on developing computational skills and recall of facts. In the second approach, teachers encourage students to explain how they arrived at a solution and to consider more than one way of solving a problem.

Ideally, teachers should strive for a balance between the two approaches. Doug Grouws, honored for his long-time contributions to mathematics education by his selection as an NCTM Lifetime Achievement Awardee, talks about this:

> Research suggests it is not necessary for teachers to focus first on skill development and then move on to problem solving. Both can be done together. Skills can be developed on an as-needed basis, or their development can be supplemented through the use of technology. In fact, there is evidence that if students are initially drilled too much on isolated skills, they have a harder time making sense of them later. (2004, p. 168)

> *"First and foremost, effective mathematics provides high-quality instruction focused on three important areas: teaching for conceptual understanding, developing children's procedural literacy, and promoting strategic competence through meaningful problem-solving investigations." (Shellard & Moyer, 2002, p. 8)*

Research can help inform discussion about other aspects of math instruction as well. Spear-Swerling talks about this:

> Less is known about the components of effective mathematics instruction than about the components of effective reading instruction, because research in math is less extensive than in reading. However, conclusions still can be drawn from some very good studies that do exist. (2005)

First, "…there is no single 'best' program for teaching mathematics" (Spear-Swerling 2005). Fuson, Kalchman, and Bransford (2005) used research-based principles presented by the National Research Council in *How People Learn* to develop three parallel principles for mathematics instruction. In their view,

- Mathematics instruction should build on students' existing knowledge and should also "engage students' preconceptions—particularly when they interfere with learning" (p. 219). As an example of a preconception that acts as a barrier for students, they highlight the belief held by some students that "some people have the ability to 'do math' and some don't" (p. 221).

- Instruction should foster the development of both "conceptual understanding and procedural fluency, as well as an effective organization of knowledge—in this case one that facilitates strategy development and adaptive reasoning" (p. 231).

- Instruction should include opportunities that support metacognition through helping students reflect on and discuss the ways they "do" math.

Hiebert and Grouws use research to link two critical mathematics goals—skill efficiency and conceptual understanding—with instructional practices that support these goals:

- *Skill efficiency.* Teaching effectiveness was associated with the following behavioral clusters: whole-class instruction with demonstrations by the teacher, a task-focused environment, faster-paced lessons and more homework, and classrooms relatively free of behavioral problems. More effective mathematics teachers asked more questions than less effective teachers did, with most of the questions lower-order product questions. The more effective teachers also ran well-organized classrooms focused on academic tasks and emphasized whole-class instruction with some time devoted to seat-work and practice. Mathematics teaching that facilitates skill efficiency is rapidly paced; includes modeling by the teacher with many teacher-directed, product type of questions; and displays a smooth transition from demonstration to substantial amounts of error-free practice. The teacher plays a central role in organizing, pacing, and presenting information to meet well-defined learning goals.

- *Conceptual understanding.* Two features of instruction emerge from the literature as especially likely to help students develop conceptual understanding of the mathematics topic they are studying: attending explicitly to connections among facts, procedures, and ideas; and encouraging students to wrestle with the important mathematical ideas in an intentional and conscious way (exerpted from Hiebert & Grouws, 2007, p. 1).

Studies comparing and contrasting math instruction in the United States with approaches used in other countries provide information about instruction in addition to curriculum. The American Educational Research Association summarizes some of the findings:

The 1999 Trends in International Mathematics and Science Study looked at the ways that mathematics instruction differs among seven countries. It found that although effective teaching varies from culture to culture, the key difference between instruction in the United States (the lowest performer in the study) and the other countries was the way teachers and students work on problems as a lesson unfolds.

While higher achieving countries did not use a larger percentage of high cognitive demand tasks compared to the United States, tasks here rarely were *enacted* at a high level of cognitive demand. High-performing countries avoided reducing mathematics tasks to mere procedural exercises involving basic computational skills, and they placed greater cognitive demands on students by encouraging them to focus on concepts and connections among those concepts in their problem-solving.

Other research found that in classrooms in which instructional tasks were set up and enacted at high levels of cognitive demand, students did better on measures of reasoning and problem-solving than did students in classrooms in which such tasks were set up at a high level but declined into merely "following the rules," usually with little understanding. In successful classrooms, task rigor was maintained when teachers or capable students modeled high-level performance or when teachers pressed for justifications, explanations and meaning through questioning or other feedback. (2006, p. 2)

"Because teaching and learning are two sides of the same coin and because effective teaching is defined primarily in terms of the learning it supports, we cannot talk about one without talking about the other." (Griffin, 2005, p. 258)

Good Teaching Is Key

Of course, effective mathematics instruction begins with effective teaching. No lesson, no matter how well planned, can be successful if the elements of effective teaching are not in place. Grouws discusses instructional practices that research has shown to have a positive impact on student learning—and then highlights the important role teachers play:

> The quality of the implementation of a teaching practice greatly influences its impact on student learning. The value of using manipulative materials to investigate a concept, for example, depends not only on whether manipulatives are used, but also on how they are used with the students. Similarly, small-group instruction will benefit students only if the teacher knows when and how to use this teaching practice. (2004, p. 162)

One team of researchers went directly to classrooms to observe the behaviors of exemplary mathematics teachers. They found:

> Good math teaching looks pretty much the same everywhere. These teachers know math well. But perhaps more importantly, they know how to teach it, employing a range of approaches: "holistic" instruction that integrates various ways of understanding concepts, connecting math concepts to the real world, relating to their students on a personal level, and creating a social environment where students talk about math. (Klupinski, 2007, p. 11)

For example, one of the observed teachers defined a "social environment" as not simply letting students work together. In her view, "Talking about mathematical ideas—that's what a good mathematics class is about" (Hallenbeck, in Klupinski, 2007, p. 14).

An Effective Mathematics Environment

Obviously, good math teachers must also exhibit some general characteristics of good teachers. They must exhibit good classroom management skills—especially in classrooms using differentiated instruction, actively engage their students, and make efficient use of instructional time. A mathematics lesson cannot succeed if the other elements of teaching—classroom management, a logical progression of lessons, an effective use of assessment, and time management—are not in place.

However, there are some additional teacher behaviors that "matter" in the teaching of mathematics. In effective classrooms, teachers:

- *Demonstrate acceptance of students' divergent ideas.* They challenge students to think deeply about the problems they are solving and ask them to explain the solutions. Such an approach helps students develop confidence in their own abilities to do mathematics and to gain an even firmer grasp of key concepts and processes.

- *Pose challenging and interesting questions.* They present questions that stimulate students' curiosity and encourage them to investigate further. Such questions encourage students to rely on themselves and their peers for ideas about mathematics and problem solving.

- *Use interdisciplinary connections to teach mathematics.* For example, using literature as a springboard for mathematical investigation is a useful way to introduce authentic problem-solving situations that may have "messy" results. This engages students in connecting the language of mathematical ideas with numerical representations and develops important skills that support students' abilities to solve word problems.

- *Project a positive attitude about mathematics and about students' ability to "do" mathematics.* This includes demonstrating enthusiasm for the content as well as a belief that all students are capable of learning the material, with lessons designed to encourage curiosity, interest, and skill building. (excerpted from Shellard & Moyer, 2002)

Their classrooms also display some specific characteristics:

- *Students are actively engaged in doing mathematics.* They are not sitting back watching other students solve problems.

- *Students are solving challenging problems.* Mathematics is a stimulating and interesting field generating new knowledge every day, and students should be exposed to this excitement and challenge, using real-world examples when possible.

- *Students are sharing their mathematical ideas while working in pairs and groups.* Such opportunities appeal to the social nature of most children, while thinking though problems collaboratively makes it less likely that a student will get caught in a procedural dead end.

- *Students are using a variety of approaches to communicate mathematically.* They may draw a picture to represent their ideas or write them in mathematics journals. Whole-class discussions are used to provide opportunities to hear about and perhaps challenge other students' ideas in an environment of respect and understanding.

- *Students are using manipulatives and other tools.* Both teacher demonstration and guided opportunities for practice are provided. (Excerpted from Shellard & Moyer, 2002.)

Special Support for Struggling Students

Helping students who might struggle with mathematics is another aspect of schoolwide effective mathematics instruction. Research can also help address this challenge. For example, researchers Gersten and Clark analyzed a large research base in an effort to identify "specific aspects of instruction that are consistently effective in teaching students who experience difficulties with mathematics.... Consistently strong effects were found for systematic, explicit instruction" (2007, p. 1), which was defined as teacher description/

demonstration of a specific strategy to solve a problem, with opportunities provided for students to apply and practice it. A similar finding was reported in a U.S. Department of Education practice guide that found strong evidence for explicit and systematic instruction embedded in interventions for struggling students. The authors elaborate:

> This includes providing models of proficient problem solving, verbalization of thought processes, guided practice, corrective feedback, and frequent cumulative review. (Gersten, et al., 2009, p. 6)

Another issue with relevance for teaching of struggling students is the use of a practice such as grouping. While the research on grouping and tracking for mathematics instruction is mixed, some studies suggest grouping can work if "membership" of groups is not kept static over long periods, but shifted intentionally and in response to ongoing assessments of student skills. Using this approach, the teacher makes intensive use of information gathered through formal and informal assessment—much of which is embedded in instruction—to decide which skills and knowledge individual students need at specific points in time to help them move toward competence in a particular standard. Although ability grouping is used in addition to whole-class instruction, the groups are fluid and membership changes often, depending on the specific instruction needed to move specific students to higher levels of learning.

Recommendations From the National Mathematics Advisory Panel

The essence of the panel's message is *to put first things first*.

- The mathematics curriculum in Grades PreK–8 should be streamlined and should emphasize a well-defined set of the most critical topics in the early grades.

- Use should be made of what is clearly known from rigorous research about how children learn, especially by recognizing (a) the advantages for children in having a strong start; (b) the mutually reinforcing benefits of conceptual understanding, procedural fluency, and automatic (i.e., quick and effortless) recall of facts; and (c) that effort, not just inherent talent, counts in mathematical achievement.

- Instructional practice should be informed by high-quality research, when available, and by the best professional judgment and experience of accomplished classroom teachers. High-quality research does not support the contention that instruction should be either entirely "student centered" or "teacher directed." Research indicates that some forms of particular instructional practices can have a positive impact under specified conditions.

Excerpted from National Mathematics Advisory Panel, 2008, pp. xiii-xiv.

In Summary

For teachers and others responsible for ensuring our students receive the best possible mathematics education, ongoing efforts to stay informed about current research findings—companioned with opportunities for teacher discussion about both the "what" and "how"—will be as important as the frameworks provided by state standards.

> For materials related to the work of the National Mathematics Advisory Panel, go to:
>
> http://www2.ed.gov/about/bdscomm/list/mathpanel/index.html
>
> Resources include the panel's final report as well as those from the panel's task forces, materials for parents, and a What Works section for teachers that discusses how to apply the panel's findings in the classroom.

References

American Educational Research Association. (2006, Fall). Do the math: Cognitive demand makes a difference. *Research Points*, 1-4.

Ball, D. L., Ferrini-Mundy, J., Kilpatrick, J., Milgram, R. J., Schmid, W., & Schaar, R. (2005). *Reaching for common ground in K-12 mathematics education*. Retrieved from http://www. maa.org/common-ground/cg-report2005.html

Fuson, K. C., Kalchman, M., & Bransford, J. D. (2005). Mathematical understanding: An introduction. In M. S. Donovan & J. D. Bransford (Eds.), *How students learn: History, mathematics, and science in the classroom* (pp. 217-256). Washington, DC: The National Academies Press.

Gersten, R., Beckmann, S., Clarke, B., Foegen, A., Marsh, L., & Star, J. R., et al. (2009). *Assisting students struggling with mathematics: Response to Intervention (RtI) for elementary and middle schools* (NCEE 2009-4060). Washington, DC: National Center for Education Evaluation and Regional Assistance, Institute of Education Sciences, U.S. Department of Education. Retrieved from http://ies.ed.gov/ncee/wwc/publications/practiceguides/

Gersten, R., & Clarke, B. S. (2007). *Effective strategies for teaching students with difficulties in mathematics* (Research Brief). Retrieved from www.nctm.org/uploadedFiles/Research_Issues_and_News/Briefs_and_Clips/research%20brief%2002%20-%20Effective%20Strategies(1).pdf

Ginsburg, A., Leinwand, S., Anstrom, T., & Pollock, E. (2005). *What the United States can learn from Singapore's world-class mathematics system (and what Singapore can learn from the United States): An exploratory study*. Washington, DC: American Institutes of Research. Retrieved from http://www.air.org/news/documents/Singapore%20Report%20(Bookmark%20Version).pdf

Griffin, S. (2005). Fostering the development of whole-number sense: Teaching mathematics in the primary grades. In M. S. Donovan & J. D. Bransford (Eds.), *How students learn: History, mathematics, and science in the classroom* (pp. 257-308). Washington, DC: The National Academies Press.

Grouws, D. A. (2004). Mathematics. In G. Cawelti (Ed.), *Handbook of research on improving student achievement* (3rd ed.) (pp. 162-181). Arlington, VA: Educational Research Service.

Hiebert, J., & Grouws, D. A. (2007). *Effective teaching for the development of skill and conceptual understanding of number: What is most effective?* (Research Brief). Retrieved from http://www.nctm.org/news/content.aspx?id=8448

Klupinski, S. (2007, February/March). Tips from effective teachers. *Catalyst Cleveland*, 11-14.

National Council of Teachers of Mathematics. (2006). *Curriculum focal points for prekindergarten through grade 8 mathematics*. Retrieved from http://www.nctm.org/focalpoints.aspx?ekmensel=c580fa7b_10_48_btnlink

National Mathematics Advisory Panel. (2007). *Preliminary report.* Washington, DC: U.S. Department of Education. Retrieved from http://www.ed.gov/about/bdscomm/list/mathpanel/pre-report.pdf

National Mathematics Advisory Panel. (2008). *Foundations for success: The final report of the National Mathematics Advisory Panel.* Washington, DC: U.S. Department of Education. Retrieved from http://www.ed.gov/about/bdscomm/list/mathpanel/report/final-report.pdf

Reys, B., & Lappan, G. (2007, May). Consensus or confusion? The intended math curriculum in state-level standards. *Phi Delta Kappan*, 676-680.

Reys, B. J., Dingman, S., Sutter, A., & Teuscher, D. (2005). *Development of state-level mathematics curriculum documents: Report of a survey.* Columbia, MO: Center for the Study of Mathematics Curriculum. Retrieved from http://mathcurriculumcenter.org/ASSM_report.pdf

Shellard, E., & Moyer, P. S. (2002). *What principals need to know about teaching math.* Alexandria, VA: National Association of Elementary School Principals and Educational Research Service.

Spear-Swerling, L. (2005). *Components of effective mathematics instruction.* Retrieved from http://www.ldonline.org/article/5588

Implications for Our School: Questions for Discussion and Reflection

- Has our mathematics curriculum been aligned to state standards? Are all teachers using this curriculum as a guide for what is taught?

- Does mathematics instruction in our school have an appropriate balance between skills- and inquiry-based instruction?

- Are teachers using the good teaching strategies discussed in the chapter?

- Is there a need for teachers to discuss mathematics instruction across grades? How would we make time for this?

Follow-up and Action Items

_____

_____

_____

_____

_____

_____

_____

_____

_____

_____

_____

_____

_____

_____

Chapter 13

Using Curriculum-Based Measurement to "Get a Handle" on Student Progress

Curriculum-based measurement offers a research-validated method of progress monitoring that can help gauge the impact of instruction while signaling trouble spots for some students.

One of the most urgent priorities facing schools today is raising the achievement of struggling students. Response to Intervention (RTI) is an approach to this challenge that is increasingly on the radar screen of many schools. One critical requirement at every tier of RTI is student progress monitoring. The most commonly used and well-researched method of progress monitoring is curriculum-based measurement (CBM), an approach with benefits even outside the RTI framework.

What Is CBM?

"CBM is a scientifically validated form of student progress monitoring that incorporates standard methods for test development, administration, scoring, and data utilization" (Stecker & Lembke, 2005, p. 1). It was originally defined as a "set of specific measurement procedures that can be applied to quantify student performance in reading, written expression, spelling, and arithmetic" (Deno, 1989, p. 15).

In contrast to standardized achievement tests, which do not provide immediate feedback, CBM tests are given frequently to track student progress toward annual goals, monitor the effectiveness of interventions, and make instructional changes as needed throughout the year. As Wright points out, "much of the power of CBM…seems to lie in its ability to predict in a short time whether an intervention is working or needs to be altered" (n.d., pp. 1-3). In an RTI context, CBM can help identify students in need of intervention, decide which level of intervention is most appropriate, and help determine whether an intervention is successful (Mellard & Johnson, 2008).

> *"Much of the power of CBM…seems to lie in its ability to predict in a short time whether an intervention is working or needs to be altered." (Wright, n.d., p. 1-3)*

Unlike classroom assessments that test mastery of a single skill, each CBM test samples the year-long curriculum and, therefore, measures small student gains toward long-term goals (Deno, Fuchs, Marston, & Shin, 2001; Stecker, Fuchs, & Fuchs, 2005). For example, a third-grade teacher may traditionally test students on their mastery of multiplication immediately after completing a multiplication unit. The math CBM test, in contrast, would include problems that test each skill that students are expected to master by the end of third grade (e.g., addition, subtraction, multiplication, and division problems). The data gathered from CBM serve as "vital signs of student educational health" (Deno, 1985, p. 230). In other words, CBM provides educators with an overall indicator of student competence and progress in the curriculum.

In addition to being an assessment tool that allows educators to frequently measure student progress in the year-long curriculum, CBM provides some additional benefits:

- It can provide documentation of student progress for accountability purposes, including AYP and IEPs.

- It can facilitate communication about student progress with other professionals and with parents.

- Its use may result in fewer special education referrals.

- It allows teachers to compare students against other students in the classroom, rather than against national norms.

- It helps schools and districts develop local norms that can then guide teachers when interpreting data (Holland-Coviello, n.d.; National Center on Student Progress Monitoring, n.d.)

What Does the Research Say?

Nearly 30 years of empirical evidence tells us that CBM provides a valid and reliable indicator of student progress in basic academic areas, especially reading, math, and writing, and that it can have a positive impact on student achievement (Foegen, Jiban, & Deno, 2007; McMaster & Espin, 2007). Studies have shown that teachers who use CBM to monitor progress, adjust instruction, and determine the effectiveness of interventions have higher rates of student achievement and student learning than teachers who do not use CBM (Bowman, 2003; Mellard & Johnson, 2008). Hosp and Hosp state that "CBM stands out as one of the best measures to efficiently accomplish" the requirements for monitoring student progress and informing parents of how their child is performing and progressing in school (2003, p. 11).

Research has also shown that the data gathered from CBM can be used in numerous educational decisions, such as screening, determining eligibility for special education, and reintegration. More recently, researchers have been examining the effectiveness of CBM in other areas as well, such as predicting performance on high-stakes tests and measuring growth in content areas (Deno, 2003).

Even with decades of research-based evidence, CBM was not commonly used by teachers, particularly in the general education classroom, until the inclusion of RTI in the 2004 amendment of the Individuals with Disabilities Education Act (Ardoin et al., 2004; Hosp & Hosp, 2003). Mellard and Johnson discuss the use of CBM from an RTI perspective:

> Within an RTI model, the types of decisions that a system of progress monitoring can inform include whether a student is making adequate progress in the general classroom, whether a student requires a more intensive level of intervention, and whether a student has responded successfully to an intervention and, therefore, can be returned to the general classroom. (2008, p. 59)

> *Even with decades of research-based evidence, CBM was not commonly used by teachers, particularly in the general education classroom, until the advent of RTI.*

The link between CBM and RTI means that most of the research on CBM has been conducted at the elementary level. However, as interest in using CBM has grown and as RTI expands from the elementary grades upwards, the body of literature is expanding as well. For example, researchers have begun to look at using CBM to measure growth in content-area learning and to assess English Language Learners (Deno, 2003).

How Is It Done?

One of the key aspects of CBM is that the "mechanics"—how the test is administered, the directions given to students, the procedures for scoring—are standardized (Deno & Fuchs, 1987). Standardization is important because it (1) ensures that the data are valid and reliable indicators of a student's proficiency, (2) allows for individual and group data to be compared across time, and (3) facilitates the development of local norms (Deno, 2003; Wright, n.d.).

CBM *probes,* or tests, are quick and easy to administer and are generally given once or twice per week. Each test is different, but of equivalent difficulty. "Because CBM converts student academic behaviors into numbers (e.g., number of words read correctly per minute), teachers can easily chart the resulting data over time" (Wright, n.d., p. 3-1) and visually see when instructional changes need to be made. The oral reading fluency (ORF) probe, for example, has students read aloud from a passage for 1 minute as the teacher follows along marking words that are read incorrectly. After 1 minute, the number of words read correctly is recorded and graphed. It takes approximately 5 minutes to administer, score, and graph the result.

Decision rules are used to interpret the data points on a CBM graph. Baseline data indicate a student's initial level of proficiency. A goal line is drawn connecting the baseline data to the desired year-end proficiency level. Following each CBM test, teachers plot a student's score on the graph, look to see whether the student is scoring above or below the goal line, and then apply a predetermined decision rule to decide if instruction needs to be modified. The four-point rule, for example, says that once six data points have been collected, look at the four most recent points and, if all four fall above the goal line, raise the goal; if all four fall below the goal line, implement an instructional change; if the four points fall both above and below the goal line, keep collecting data (Stecker, Fuchs, & Fuchs, 1999).

Researchers have proposed several decision rules, in addition to the four-point rule, that educators can use to determine if a teaching change should be implemented. While it may be less important which rule educators choose to use, it is critical that one is chosen and then applied consistently across time and among all students being monitored. For instance, in one elementary school's RTI model, the following decision rule is used: If a student receiving Tier 2 interventions scores below the goal line three times, the intervention is modified. If the student continues to score below the goal line, the student is considered for Tier 3 intervention (Mellard & Johnson, 2008).

Making CBM Work: A Few Guidelines

According to a recent review of the research, student achievement can be improved through the use of CBM. The studies that looked at the effects of CBM on the achievement of students who have disabilities suggest the following:

- Teachers need to examine the student data and modify their instruction based on what the data indicate.

- Data-based decision rules should be used by teachers to make necessary modifications to their instruction.

- Computer applications facilitate the use of decision rules and contribute to teacher satisfaction with CBM.

- Lack of opportunities to consult with other professionals about instructional recommendations makes it more difficult for teachers to use CBM to plan instructional programs.

- Ongoing teacher support is needed so that teachers can use CBM to meet the individual needs of students.

Sources: National Center on Student Progress Monitoring, n.d.; Stecker et al., 2005.

Providing Teacher Support and Training

Obviously school use of CBM should be preceded by opportunities for teachers to learn about the process. So, what factors should your school address from the perspective of preparing and supporting teachers to use CBM?

Research that examined the effect of CBM on the achievement of students with learning disabilities concluded the following:

- Progress monitoring alone will not have a significant impact on student achievement. Teachers need to modify their instruction based on what the data indicate.

- The use of data-based decision rules is important and they should be used by teachers to make necessary instructional changes.

- Computer applications that collect, store, manage, and analyze data make using CBM more efficient and contribute to teacher satisfaction.

- Ongoing teacher support, including a system that provides teachers with instructional recommendations, may be needed (Stecker et al., 2005).

For many teachers, using CBM regularly to modify instruction will be a change. One of the largest, or perhaps most contentious, issues that schools may face is the issue of time. While CBM is designed to be time efficient for teachers, it is still important to note that time is cited as the biggest barrier to its implementation. Teacher training and practice are therefore imperative to counter many of the apprehensions teachers may have. Teachers will need training and practice in all aspects of CBM, such as how to administer the various probes, how to set annual performance goals, and how to analyze graphs.

> *While CBM is designed to be efficient for teachers, it is important to note that time is cited as the biggest barrier to its implementation.*

Actually using the data to make instructional changes may be one of the most difficult steps for teachers. To assist teachers with implementing instructional changes, Wesson (1991) looked at the process of follow-up consultations. She found that students made more progress when teachers met with one another—as opposed to meeting with a university expert—to consult about their students. Based on these findings, Wesson (1991) suggests that, as districts train teachers to use CBM, they should encourage teachers to meet regularly to discuss what they are finding.

In Summary

Although a "seamless and flexible system of progress monitoring" (Wallace, Espin, McMaster, Deno, & Foegen, 2007, p. 66) remains a goal of researchers, three decades of study has produced a significant research base of reliable and valid CBM measures that schools can use to monitor student progress—either with or without implementation of RTI.

References

Ardoin, S. P., Witt, J. C., Suldo, S. M., Connell, J. E., Koenig, J. L., Resetar, J. L., et al. (2004). Examining the incremental benefits of administering a maze and three versus one curriculum-based measurement reading probes when conducting universal screening. *School Psychology Review, 33*(2), 218-233.

Bowman, L. J. (2003). *Secondary educators promoting student success: Curriculum-based measurement*. Retrieved from http://coe.ksu.edu/esl/lasestrellas/presentations/Lisa_CBM.ppt

Deno, S. L. (1985). Curriculum-based measurement: The emerging alternative. *Exceptional Children, 52*(3), 219-232.

Deno, S. L. (1989). Curriculum-based measurement and special education services: A fundamental and direct relationship. In M. R. Shinn (Ed.), *Curriculum-based measurement: Assessing special children* (pp. 1-17). New York: Guilford Press.

Deno, S. L. (2003). Developments in curriculum-based measurement. *The Journal of Special Education, 37*(3), 184-192.

Deno, S. L., & Fuchs, L. S. (1987). Developing curriculum-based measurement systems for data-based special education problem solving. *Focus on Exceptional Children, 19*(8), 1-16.

Deno, S. L., Fuchs, L. S., Marston, D., & Shin, J. (2001). Using curriculum-based measurement to establish growth standards for students with learning disabilities. *School Psychology Review, 30*(4), 507-524.

Foegen, A., Jiban, C., & Deno, S. (2007). Progress monitoring measures in mathematics. *The Journal of Special Education, 41*(2), 121-139.

Holland-Coviello, R. (n.d.). *Using curriculum-based measurement (CBM) for student progress monitoring*. Retrieved from http://www.studentprogress.org/player/playershell.swf

Hosp, M. K., & Hosp, J. L. (2003). Curriculum-based measurement for reading, spelling, and math: How to do it and why. *Preventing School Failure, 48*(1), 10-17.

McMaster, K., & Espin, C. (2007). Technical features of curriculum-based measurement in writing: A literature review. *The Journal of Special Education, 41*(2), 68-84.

Mellard, D. F., & Johnson, E. (2008). *RTI: A practitioner's guide to implementing Response to Intervention*. Thousand Oaks, CA: Corwin Press and National Association of Elementary School Principals.

National Center on Student Progress Monitoring. (n.d.). *Common questions for progress monitoring*. Retrieved from http://www.studentprogress.org/progresmon.asp#2

Stecker, P. M., Fuchs, L. S., & Fuchs, D. (1999). *Using curriculum-based measurement for assessing reading progress and for making instruction decisions*. Retrieved from http://www. onlineacademy.org/modules/a300/lesson/lesson_3/xpages/a300c3_40200.html

Stecker, P. M., Fuchs, L. S., & Fuchs, D. (2005). Using curriculum-based measurement to improve student achievement: Review of research. *Psychology in the Schools, 42*(8), 795-819.

Stecker, P. M., & Lembke, E. S. (2005). *Advanced applications of CBM in reading: Instructional decision-making strategies manual*. Washington, DC: National Center on Student Progress Monitoring.

Wallace, T., Espin, C. A., McMaster, K., Deno, S. L., & Foegen, A. (2007). CBM progress monitoring within a standards-based system. *The Journal of Special Education, 41*(2), 66-67.

Wesson, C. L. (1991). Curriculum-based measurement and two models of follow-up consultation. *Exceptional Children, 57*(3), 246-256.

Wright, J. (n.d.). *Curriculum-based measurement: A manual for teachers*. Retrieved from http://www.jimwrightonline.com/pdfdocs/cbaManual.pdf

Implications for Our School: Questions for Discussion and Reflection

- How does our school currently monitor student progress? Is it working for us?

- Would curriculum-based measurement improve our ability to keep track of our students' growth in language and math skills?

- Are we doing the best job possible of identifying struggling students in time to give them the interventions—or changes in instructional strategies—they need?

- What steps would we need to take to implement curriculum-based measurement schoolwide? What possible barriers should we anticipate?

Follow-up and Action Items

_____

_____

_____

_____

_____

_____

_____

_____

_____

_____

_____

_____

_____

Section III

Implementing Effective Schoolwide Practices

Chapter 14

Using Professional Learning Communities to Support Teaching and Learning

Creating and sustaining professional learning communities is one powerful way your school can improve professional practice and student learning.

The norm of closed-door teaching is changing in many schools. As the potential power of teacher collaboration and reflective dialogue to improve both teaching and learning becomes ever more obvious, educators are asking what these ways of interacting look like and how they can be developed.

One form of collaboration that has been growing in popularity in recent years is professional learning communities. According to Hargreaves (2007) the increased acceptance of professional learning communities is evidenced by their being given a nickname, "PLCs." In addition, the focus of the literature on PLCs has shifted away from the rationale behind them and toward creating and sustaining them.

What Is a Professional Learning Community?

Defining the concept of "professional learning community" is not easy, and use of the term spread before its meaning was fully understood. "Thus, we have many examples of superficial PLCs—educators simply calling what they are doing professional learning communities without going very deep into learning and without realizing they are not going deep" (Fullan, 2006). According to DuFour "...the term has been used so ubiquitously that it is in danger of losing all meaning" (2004). Despite varied and complex definitions, some researchers have reviewed the literature and highlighted ideas and principles they believe reflect the nature of true professional learning communities.

Professional learning communities should not be considered new "initiatives" or "programs." Although they often include explicit structures, such as teacher study groups, they are more basic than any structure. A school characterized as a professional learning community has a *culture* that recognizes and capitalizes on the collective strengths and talents of staff.

When a professional learning community culture is in place, teachers more often participate in collaborative activities and take collective responsibility for student learning. Lieberman provides the following description of what such a school might look like:

> You would hear lots of discussion about data and the work of students, particularly students who are having difficulty. Teachers are talking about what they are learning from their students, from other people in the school, and from sources outside the school…. Teachers feel comfortable enough to admit that they need help and others feel empowered to help when they can. (in Sparks, 1999)

In DuFour's view, the staff members within a school that can be characterized as a learning community:

> have a clear sense of the mission they are to accomplish and a shared vision of the conditions they must create to achieve their mission. They work together in collaborative teams that engage in collective inquiry into both best practices for accomplishing their aims and the current reality of the conditions in their organization. (2003, p. 15)

What You'll See in an Effective PLC

- A focus on learning

- A collaborative culture with a focus on learning for all

- Collective inquiry into best practices and current reality

- Action orientation—learning by doing

- A commitment to continuous improvement

- Results orientation

Source: DuFour, DuFour, Eaker, & Many, 2006, p. 3

Hord (1997) has identified the following five "defining characteristics" of professional learning communities:

- supportive and shared leadership (specifically, a principal who invites staff input in decision making and who facilitates participation);

- collective learning and application of learning to solutions that address students' needs;

- shared vision and values, including an unwavering focus on student learning;

- the presence of supportive physical conditions (such as the time to meet and talk), as well as supportive personal conditions (such as respect and trust among colleagues); and,

- shared professional practice (such as observations of each other's teaching and discussion of these observations).

A principal of a Virginia elementary school sums up what professional learning communities are like. In her view, a PLC is a school "…that emphasizes what students are learning instead of what teachers have taught." She continues, "In a traditional setting, teachers will say 'I taught it, they just did not learn it.' More importantly, teachers take ownership of the successes and failures of their students, and the school makes instructional decisions based on analysis of data" (Jesse, in Cromer, 2006).

The Benefits of Professional Learning Communities

Implicit in the discussion of what a professional learning community looks like are some of the benefits. These fall into three major categories of impact: as a support for school improvement efforts, a mechanism for teacher professional development, and, ultimately, a factor that contributes to higher student learning.

Support for School Improvement Efforts

Morrissey talks about the role of professional learning communities in school improvement efforts. In her view:

> Rather than becoming a reform initiative itself, a professional learning community becomes the supporting structure for schools to continuously transform themselves through their own internal capacity. (2000, p. 10)

For example, researchers from the Southwest Educational Development Laboratory found "few to no avenues for problem solving or collaboration among staff" in low-performing schools they studied. In contrast, schools with well-developed professional learning communities provided time for staff to engage in "substantive work and learning together" (Morrissey, 2000, p. 14).

As more is learned about the potential power of PLCs for improving teaching and learning, researchers have begun to include indicators of the existence of effective PLCs in their studies of factors that impact student achievement and have found some positive relationships. For example, in a study of the Children Achieving program in Philadelphia elementary schools, researchers found higher fourth-grade reading scores in schools with a "greater sense of Teacher Professional Community" (Tighe, Wang, & Foley, 2002, p. 21), as measured by survey responses from teachers.

Support for Teacher Development

Today there is increasing recognition that opportunities to collaborate with other teachers represent valuable, although often untapped, resources that should be considered an important element of professional development. Professional development of this type occurs on a daily basis in schools that have developed the culture of a professional learning community. Teacher learning is no longer reserved for after-school workshops or inservice days. Rather, it occurs every day in activities such as the sharing of good practice and model lessons, cross-disciplinary teaching, cross-grade activities, and the sharing of subject matter expertise.

Hord (1997) summed up the following benefits for staff in schools with professional learning communities:

- reduced isolation of teachers

- increased commitment to the mission and goals of the school and increased vigor in working to strengthen the mission

- shared responsibility for the total development of students and collective responsibility for students' success

- powerful learning that defines good teaching and classroom practice and that creates new knowledge and beliefs about teaching and learners

- increased meaning and understanding of the content that teachers teach and the roles that they play in helping all students achieve expectations

- higher likelihood that teachers will be well informed, professionally renewed, and inspired to inspire students

- more satisfaction, higher morale, and lower rates of absenteeism

- significant advances into making teaching adaptations for students, and changes for learners made more quickly than in traditional schools

- commitment to making significant and lasting changes

- higher likelihood of undertaking fundamental, systemic change

Support for Student Learning

A review of the literature on PLCs identifies "two characteristics . . . as having the most significant influence on student outcomes: cultural norms around learning and the collective responsibility of teachers for learning of all students" (National Alliance on the American High School, 2003, p. 1). Researchers have also looked at the link between PLCs and student achievement:

- Lee, Smith, and Croninger (1995) report on a study of 820 secondary schools. In those schools characterized as professional learning communities, teachers had collaborated to improve classroom pedagogy. In addition, teachers were found to see themselves both individually and collectively responsible for all students. Students in these schools demonstrated higher levels of learning in math, reading, science, and history than in other schools. In addition, the achievement gap was smaller.

- Reyes, Scribner, and Paredes-Scribner (1999) describe the impact of professional learning communities in previously low-performing schools serving populations of Hispanic students. In these schools, staff members identified the development of PLCs as essential to their improvement efforts, and their schools experienced higher levels of student achievement.

- A Charles A. Dana Center study of nine urban elementary schools that attained higher-than-expected levels of student learning found all nine schools were characterized by a positive culture and led by principals who actively sought to provide opportunities within the school day for teachers to "work, plan, and learn together around instructional issues" (1999, p. ix).

Developing a Professional Learning Community

While they can be very effective tools for improving student learning and teacher practice, it is important to recognize that "…PLCs are at the early stages of being pursued seriously" (Fullan, 2006). The transformation of a school into a PLC can be challenging (Wells & Feun, 2007). "What is frequently not communicated in the hype for professional learning communities is how difficult it is to build and sustain them within a school's unique culture, shaped by limited time, inflexible structures, and unrealistic expectations" (Donaldson, 2001, in Moller, 2006, p. 524).

PLCs require a shift from the norms of traditional teaching, away from working in isolation. Some teachers "…view collaboration as an invasion of their academic freedom or in conflict with the union contract" (White & McIntosh, 2007, p. 34). Others feel that time spent working in professional learning communities could be spent in the classroom. Professional learning communities also require different types of shared leadership, which has its own challenges. Graham and Ferriter talk about this:

> Building a commitment to a common purpose in a PLC depends on the work of . . . teacher leaders. Struggling schools leave vision building in the hands of administrators. In successful schools, accomplished teachers step forward to lead, understanding that the key figures in any successful change effort are influential practitioners who can help colleagues to embrace new patterns of behavior. (2010, p. 15)

However, some teachers may be reluctant to take on leadership roles and so will need encouragement and support (Moller, 2006). Thus, building a PLC might require first developing a firmer foundation of teacher leadership. Finally, there are the logistical problems. Full school schedules can provide little wiggle room for teacher collaboration.

According to researchers at the Southwest Educational Development Laboratory (SEDL), strategies and factors that contribute to a school's success in transitioning to a professional learning community include the following:

- There must be some factor or purpose around which the staff rallies its interest and energy to join the community, and that factor must ultimately benefit students.

- In combination, an external force (such as a new curriculum) and an internal force (the leadership of the principal) often provide the needed structure for the initial development of a community of professional learners.

- A climate of democratic participation (in matters of authority and decision making) by all constituents in the school—administrators, teachers, other staff, students, and parents—generates energy and enthusiasm for everyone to work together to reach goals.

- An undeviating schoolwide focus on students is the compelling motivator of a successful professional learning community (Hord & Rutherford, 1998).

Because of the many challenges associated with the implementation of PLCs, school leaders play a crucial role in establishing the conditions that will allow teachers' collaborative efforts to thrive. Here are two things on which leaders should focus: developing an environment of trust and developing structures for teacher collaboration.

Develop an Environment of Trust

Leaders must understand the importance of school culture and the role they play in establishing it. Through daily activities, language, and behavior, they continuously contribute—in a positive or negative way—to the development of the environment in which staff work.

For some teachers used to closed-door teaching, the move to routinely observe and evaluate each other's work and to share ideas can be uncomfortable or even threatening at first. For this reason, the literature on professional learning communities repeatedly talks about the importance of building a foundation of trust.

To support the development of a PLC, schools should include opportunities to gauge and—if trust levels are low—improve trust among staff members in their planning process for PLCs. Gordon (2002) lists the four "vital signs" of relational trust identified by Anthony Bryk and Barbara Schneider, two University of Chicago researchers who have conducted extensive research in 400 Chicago elementary schools over a 6-year period. He also provides questions that can be used to begin assessing the level of trust currently present in a school:

- "Respect. Do we acknowledge one another's dignity and ideas? Do we interact in a courteous way? Do we genuinely talk and listen to each other?

- Competence. Do we believe in each other's ability and willingness to fulfill our responsibilities effectively?

- Personal regard. Do we care about each other both professionally and personally? Are we willing to go beyond our formal roles and responsibilities if needed—to go the extra mile?

- Integrity. Can we trust each other to put the interests of children first, especially when tough decisions have to be made? Do we keep our word?" (Gordon, 2002, p. 2)

Once PLCs begin to function in the school, it is important to help teachers develop team norms of trust. According to DuFour et al., "When individuals work through a process to create explicitly stated norms, and then commit to honor those norms, they increase the likelihood they will begin to function as a collaborative team rather than as a loose collection of people working together" (2006, p. 103). Hirsh, Delehant, and Sparks (in DuFour et al., 2006) suggest addressing the following when developing norms:

- What will the rules be regarding meeting times?

- How will listening be fostered and interruptions discouraged?

- What will the rules be about confidentiality?

- How will decision making take place?

- What will the expectations be regarding attendance and participation?

- What rules or norms do we need regarding expectations from members?

> *"The levels of trust on our team are high because we've got an extensive base of shared experiences with one another. When conflict comes, it's productive, built on the belief that everyone on our team is working towards a shared mission even when we see alternative routes to the same end point. We've learned to listen to one another, to approach collaborative work as an experiment, and to embrace struggles as learning experiences." (Bill Ferriter, in Teacher Leader Network, 2009)*

Developing Structures for Teacher Collaboration

By providing time and structure for teachers to talk about instruction, problem solve, and act as resources for one another, schools can develop an environment supportive of the development of a professional learning community. To facilitate teacher collaboration, DuFour (2001) suggests principals take the lead by:

- providing time for collaboration in the school day and school year;

- identifying critical questions to guide the work of collaborative teams;

- asking teams to create products as a result of their collaboration;

- insisting that teams identify and pursue specific student achievement goals; and,

- providing teams with relevant data and information.

However, DuFour and his fellow authors also provide this thought about collaboration—one which schools working to develop PLCs should address in their discussions and planning:

One of the most common mistakes we have seen educators make as they attempt to implement the PLC concepts is to regard collaboration as the end itself, rather than as a means to an end. Collaboration will impact student achievement in a positive way only if the "co-laboring" and collective inquiry focus on the *right* work. (DuFour, DuFour, Eaker, & Karhanek, 2010, p. 33)

Strategies to Create Time for Collaboration

- **Provide common preparation time.**

- **Use parallel scheduling,** for instance, schedule all special classes for an entire grade level at the same time, freeing up some teachers.

- **Adjust start and end times.**

- **Share classes** to free up one teacher.

- **Schedule group activities, events, and testing** supervised by nonteaching staff, freeing up teachers.

- **Bank time** so that instruction can end early some days, creating time for collaboration.

- **Use inservice and faculty meeting time wisely** by allowing the time to be used for collaboration.

Source: DuFour et al., 2006, p. 97

There are many ways to organize teachers for collaboration. Dufour et al. (2006) believe that interdisciplinary teams can work if they are given guidelines for how to stay focused on the topic of student learning expectations, but that the best team structure is one where all members teach the same grade or subject. They offer three suggestions for creating working teams:

(1) *Vertical teams* link teachers with those who teach content above or below their students. (2) *Electronic teams* use technology to create powerful partnerships with colleagues across the district, the state, or the world. (3) *Logical links* puts teachers together in teams that are pursuing outcomes linked to their areas of expertise. (2006, p. 95)

For instance, specialist teachers can join content-area teams to identify and discuss ways to integrate instructional concepts.

> *"The first (and biggest) of the big ideas that drive the work of schools and districts that operate PLCs is straightforward: the fundamental purpose of the school is to ensure that all students learn rather than to see to it that all students are taught—an enormous distinction." (DuFour et al., 2010, p. 7)*

In Summary

The research shows that PLCs can support school efforts to maximize student learning. By helping teachers learn new ways to exchange ideas and collaborate—and by keeping the focus on student learning—the intellectual talents and energies of school staff can be harnessed to move teaching and learning to higher levels of productivity. When implemented properly, and sustained over time, PLCs have great potential to improve student achievement.

References

Charles A. Dana Center. (1999). *Hope for urban education: A study of nine high-performing, high-poverty, urban elementary schools*. Washington, DC: Planning and Evaluation Service, U.S. Department of Education.

Cromer, I. (2006). *Vaughan elementary principal tapped for consultant post* [Press release]. Manassas, VA: Prince William County Public Schools. Retrieved from http://www.pwcs.edu/admin/news/NR.asp?NRnum=157&NRdate=12/7/2006

DuFour, R. (2001). In the right context. *Journal of Staff Development*. Retrieved from http://www.nsdc.org/library/jsd/dufour221.pdf

DuFour, R. (2003, May). Building a professional learning community. *The School Administrator*. Retrieved from http://www.aasa.org/publications/sa/2003_05/DuFour.htm

DuFour, R. (2004). Schools as learning communities. *Educational Leadership* [Electronic version], *61*(8), 6-11.

DuFour, R., DuFour, R., Eaker, R., & Karhanek, G. (2010). *Raising the bar and closing the gap: Whatever it takes.* Bloomington, IN: Solution Tree.

DuFour, R., DuFour, R., Eaker, R., & Many, T. (2006). *Learning by doing: A handbook for professional learning communities at work.* Bloomington, IN: Solution Tree.

Fullan, M. (2006). Leading professional learning [Electronic version]. *The School Administrator*, *10*(63), 10-14.

Gordon, D. T. (2002, July/August). Fuel for reform: The importance of trust in changing schools. Are good social relationships key to school improvement? *Harvard Education Letter*, 1-4.

Graham, P., & Ferriter, W. M. (2010). *Building a professional learning community at work: A guide to the first year.* Bloomington, IN: Solution Tree.

Hargreaves, A. (2007). Sustainable professional learning communities. In I. Goodson & A. Hargreaves (Series Eds.) & L. Stoll & K. S. Louis. (Vol. Eds.). *Professional learning communities: Divergence, depth, and dilemmas* (pp. 181-195). Berkshire, England: Open University Press.

Hord, S. M. (1997). *Professional learning communities: Communities of continuous inquiry and improvement.* Austin, TX: Southwest Educational Development Laboratory. Retrieved from http://www.sedl.org/pubs/change34/

Hord, S. M., & Rutherford, W. L. (1998). *Creating a professional learning community: Cottonwood Creek School: Issues about change.* Austin, TX: Southwest Educational Development Laboratory.

Lee, V. E., Smith, J. B., & Croninger, R. G. (1995). Another look at high school restructuring. *Issues in restructuring schools.* Madison, WI: Center on Organization and Restructuring of Schools, School of Education, University of Wisconsin-Madison.

Moller, G. (2006). Teacher leadership emerges within professional learning communities. *Journal of School Leadership*, *16*, 520-533.

Morrissey, M. S. (2000). *Professional learning communities: An ongoing exploration.* Austin, TX: Southwest Educational Development Laboratory. Retrieved from http://www.sedl.org/pubs/change45/plc-ongoing.pdf

National Alliance on the American High School. (2003). *Brief overview of literature on professional learning communities.* Retrieved from http://www.hsalliance.org/Litreview.pdf

Reyes, P., Scribner, J.D., & Paredes-Scribner, A. (Eds.). (1999). *Lessons from high-performing Hispanic schools: Creating learning communities.* New York: Teachers College Press.

Sparks, D. (1999, Fall). Real-life view: An interview with Ann Lieberman. *Journal of Staff Development.* Retrieved from http://www.nsdc.org/library/jsd/lieberman204.html

Teacher Leader Network. (2009). *PLCs at work: An interview with teacher-author Bill Ferriter.* Retrieved from http://teacherleaders.typepad.com/tln_teacher_voices/2009/12/bill-ferriter-interview.html

Tighe, E., Wang, A., & Foley, E. (2002). *An analysis of the effect of Children Achieving on student achievement in Philadelphia elementary schools.* Philadelphia: Consortium for Policy Research in Education.

Wells, C., & Feun, L. (2007). Implementation of learning community principles: A study of six high schools [Electronic version]. *NASSP Bulletin, 91*(2), 141-160.

White, S. H., & McIntosh, J. (2007). Data delivers a wake-up call: 5-year plan unites teachers into a collaborative culture. *Journal of Staff Development, 28*(2), 30-35.

Implications for Our School: Questions for Discussion and Reflection

- What student achievement goals would be the best focus for the work of PLCs in our school?

- What PLC structures would work best for our school? Should teachers meet in grade-level groups, in subject matter groups, in interdisciplinary groups, or in some other grouping?

- What difficulties would we have opening up classroom practice to one another? Would the benefits be worth it?

- What strategies can we use to find time for teacher teams to work together?

Follow-up and Action Items

_____

_____

_____

_____

_____

_____

_____

_____

_____

_____

_____

_____

_____

_____

Chapter 15
Making Homework Work for Your School

Your school's homework practices can help—or hinder— student learning as well as home-school communication.

Homework is often a hot-button issue for schools. As American family life has become more complex, with adults working long days and children participating in an array of sports and other after-school activities, debates over the purpose and value of homework assignments have sometimes become heated. Thus, it is critically important that the message about the good purposes that homework can support be communicated through good homework practices as well as words. Rowell and Hong (2002) put the burden for ensuring that homework "works" squarely on schools. In their view, homework assignments that are inappropriate or aren't used to provide constructive feedback can impact students' attitudes toward homework and school, as well as parents' feelings about the school in general.

Thus, a school's homework policy and practices are worthy topics for discussion. A good place to start is with research dealing with two important questions: does homework support higher levels of student learning, and what are characteristics of effective homework practices?

What Does Research Say About Homework and Student Learning?

As with many of the school-related variables that could impact student learning, it is difficult to isolate a connection between homework and student learning. Many additional factors—quality of the homework, student motivation, family support, and so on are always part of the equation. While some researchers attempt to control for such factors, much of the research that has been conducted "simply correlates homework and achievement, with no attempt to account for student differences" (Cooper, 2006). Looking at the body of research as a whole, "the link between homework and achievement is far from clear. There is no conclusive evidence that homework increases student achievement across the board" (Center for Public Education, 2007).

Harris Cooper (2007), the most widely cited researcher on homework, agrees. However, he also points to the few carefully controlled studies that have found positive links between homework and student scores on end-of-class tests. For example, one study found that second-grade students assigned math homework did better on math tests than comparable students who were not assigned homework.

Unfortunately, only a few such carefully controlled studies exist. Thus, some researchers use an approach called meta-analysis to attempt to identify themes from the larger body of homework research, using even those studies that simply correlated homework and student achievement. Using this approach, Cooper, Robinson, and Patall (2006) found "generally consistent evidence for a positive influence of homework on achievement." Marzano and Pickering agree. Their review of the homework research found that "with only rare exceptions, the relationship between the amount of homework students do and their achievement outcomes was found to be positive and statistically significant" (2007a, p.76).

Syntheses of homework research have also identified differences in the effects of homework by grade level. Typically, the correlation between homework and achievement appears to be stronger in grades 7-12 than in K-6 (Cooper, Robinson, & Patall, 2006; Marzano & Pickering, 2007a). Such research, however, is generally talking only about a direct link between homework and achievement. Cooper (2001) suggests that educators should look more broadly at possible benefits of homework that can ultimately impact student learning, highlighting three of these:

- long-term academic benefits such as better study habits and skills;

- nonacademic benefits including greater self-direction, greater self-discipline, better time organization, and more independent problem solving; and,

- greater parental appreciation of, and involvement in, schooling.

> *"The impact of homework on academic achievement is mediated by factors such as appropriateness of the design of the homework, student learning abilities, student attitudes, and parent and peer support." (Lee, 2005, p. 252)*

Effective Homework Practices

If the homework research only addressed the homework-achievement link, educators might reasonably feel that little guidance has been provided for them. However, researchers have also addressed an important question: What practices help to increase the benefits of homework while minimizing potential problems?

Marzano and Pickering provide a good starting point to the discussion about effective homework practices. "Homework should not be assigned simply as a matter of routine" (2007b, p. 513), but instead only when there is a clear purpose in regard to student learning. In essence, good homework practices are consistent with good teaching.

Marzano, Gaddy, and Dean (2000) emphasize that teachers should make sure the purpose of homework assignments is clear. Students should leave the classroom with no confusion about either what they are being asked to do or how to do it.

The research is especially clear about one point in relation to homework: It should not be used to teach new material (Cooper, 2001). Preparation homework assignments may be appropriate to introduce concepts that will be taught in future lessons (such as gathering current newspaper articles on a specific science topic or interviewing grandparents for their first-hand account of historical events). Tasks assigned for preparation purposes, however, should be discussed and expanded on, with explicit connections made to material presented in class.

Five Major Reasons Why Students May Fail to Complete Homework

1. **Academic**—Task is too hard or too lengthy for the student's working speed.

2. **Organizational**—Getting it home, getting it done, and getting it back is difficult.

3. **Motivational**—Burnout, overload, too much experience with failure, or frustration with the specific task.

4. **Situational**—Unable to do work at home, too many other activities vying for time, or no materials available to complete the assignment at home.

5. **Personal**—Depression, anxiety, family problems, or other personal issues.

Source: Vatterott, 2009

Marzano and Pickering highlight another characteristic of effective homework: It "should be structured in a way the students can accomplish it with relatively high success rates" (2007b, p. 513). Teachers should make sure their students fully understand concepts and possess the skills needed to complete any homework assigned. For example, requiring students to practice math problems at home that they do not fully understand in class will only discourage and frustrate them. Further, practicing a skill that is either not well understood or—worse—misunderstood "might also serve to habituate errors or misconceptions" (Marzano, Pickering, & Pollock, 2001, p. 63).

"Homework should not be assigned simply as a matter of routine, but instead only when there is a clear purpose in regard to student learning." (Marzano & Pickering, 2007b, p. 513)

Paulu suggests that use of a consistent homework schedule "helps students remember to do assignments. A consistent schedule can also help busy parents remember when their children's assignments are due" (1998). Vaughn and her research colleagues synthesized the research on students' perceptions related to homework. Their findings provide additional good practice suggestions; students found it helpful when teachers:

- assigned homework toward the beginning of class;

- explained how to do the homework, including providing examples and writing directions on the chalkboard;

- gave students time to start the homework in class, then checked for understanding and/or provided assistance before the end of the class period;

- explicitly related the homework to class work; and,

- permitted students to work together on homework while they were in class (in ERIC Clearinghouse on Disabilities and Gifted Education, 2001).

Walberg and Paik (2004) identify teacher feedback to homework as having a powerful positive effect on student learning. Specifically, "students learn more when they complete homework that is graded, commented upon, and discussed by their teachers" (2004, p. 28), with these researchers also suggesting that it is especially important to reinforce what has been done correctly and to reteach the concepts and skills homework has demonstrated students still have not mastered. Marzano, Gaddy, and Dean (2000) suggest that not all this feedback needs to be in the form of teacher notes on the top of every assignment. For example, student discussion of homework can provide helpful feedback, as long as the teacher also monitors the work of individual students to ensure that a student who has struggled with the homework is not overlooked.

Finally, teachers should never give homework as punishment. Cooper warns, "It implies you think schoolwork is aversive. Kids will pick up this message" (in Silvis, 2002).

> *"The quality of homework assignments is more important than the quantity of work a student is to complete or the amount of time a student must put in to complete the work at home." (Oliver, 2009, p. 3)*

Designing Good Homework

Homework should never be assigned without a purpose in mind. A helpful place to begin when planning homework is by thinking of "categories" of homework—practice, preparation, extension, or integration.

Practice assignments are meant to reinforce understanding and help students master what was taught in class. Preparation assignments introduce students to material that will be presented in future lessons, giving them the background knowledge necessary to help with comprehension (Cooper, 2006). Practice and preparation homework often includes worksheets, problems from textbooks, and reading assignments; they are not necessarily interesting or intriguing (Oliver, 2009). Extension homework involves the transfer of previously learned skills, such as abstract principles, to new situations not covered in class. Another type of homework is integration or creative homework, which requires the student to apply a number of separately learned skills to produce a single product, such as a science project, book report, or performance (Cooper, 2006; Oliver, 2009). While this category is likely to be challenging for some students, it may also be easier to design as a high-interest assignment.

Something as simple as when homework is assigned during a class can also affect its potential impact. For example, if assignment of homework is left until the last few minutes of class, it can limit the homework's effectiveness. There should be enough time for teachers to clearly explain the assignment and to provide examples if the assignment type or the skills involved are new to students—and then for students to ask questions.

The most effective homework appears to be assignments that contain content that either covers several lessons or asks students to practice past lessons as well as prepare for future lessons. This type of homework that distributes content helps to assess both long- and short-term retention (Cooper, 2007). Research also shows that distributing study time over several sessions generally leads to better retention of information than a single study session (Willingham, 2002). This phenomenon is called the spacing effect, and it basically works on the premise that asking students to study math facts for 5 minutes each night is better than asking students to study math facts for 25 minutes one night a week.

If the purpose is to give students practice with a new skill, teachers will want to design homework around a rule or principle that will ultimately help students solve the problem independently. They should ask themselves: Do the students possess the background knowledge and prior experiences necessary to understand this new or novel situation (Fisher & Frey, 2008)?

Finally, just as effective teachers adapt instruction to meet the individual needs of their students, they also adapt homework assignments. For example, if a student is a slow worker, the teacher may tell him to stop working after a certain amount of time, whether the student has completed the assignment or not (Bailey, 2008). To verify this, the teacher may ask the student to write on the top of the homework the time when he or she started the assignment and the time when he stopped working. Or, the student could be instructed to answer every other or every third question, provided the chosen questions will show an understanding of concepts (Bailey, 2008). Students who struggle with writing could be allowed to dictate their answers to a parent who writes them down verbatim, or they could be allowed to record their answers and hand in the recording rather than a written assignment (Bailey, 2008). Another option would be to allow students to complete an essay assignment as a visual presentation instead of a written one (Pasi, 2006).

> *"Well-designed homework helps students learn; it also offers parents opportunities to see what students are learning, talk with children about their learning, and interact with teachers…about ways to support student learning." (Walker, Hoover-Dempsey, Whetsel, & Green, 2004)*

Taking a Schoolwide Approach

A school policy regarding homework, along with clear expectations for teachers as to what constitutes good homework, can help to strengthen the benefits of homework for student learning while decreasing potential problems. As one element, the policy might define the role of homework in learning at each grade level. Cooper talks about this.

> [H]omework should help young children develop good study habits, promote positive attitudes toward school, and communicate to students that learning takes place outside as well as inside school. Thus, assignments to elementary students should be brief, should involve materials commonly found in the home, and should not be too demanding. (Cooper, 1994)

The Center on Innovation & Improvement sees "Homework [as] a primary point of interface between the school and the home [with parents better able] to support the school's purposes for homework when they understand what is expected of their students and their role in monitoring their children's homework" (2009, p. 18).

Marzano, Gaddy, and Dean (2000) suggest that schools use the school's homework policy be used to address questions parents often have about homework. For example, the homework policy could specify some responsibilities of teachers, parents, and students (Cooper, 1994). The homework policy used by one Massachusetts elementary school—and developed through collaboration of teachers, parents, and other school staff—delineated some specific responsibilities for teachers. These included communicating clear expectations for each assignment; assigning developmentally appropriate homework, not busy work; limiting the amount of homework given to allow for independent reading time; acknowledging an assignment's importance with corrections and feedback; and periodically soliciting feedback on assignment difficulty and completion time from parents and students (Shellard & Turner 2004).

What to Include in Schoolwide Homework Policies

- The percentage of a student's grade that will be affected by homework, if at all

- The rubrics that will be used to grade homework that is to be considered in the student's final grade

- How feedback will be provided on homework that is not graded

- The strategies and resources to be offered to students who may not have the support necessary to complete homework at home

- The amount of time students are expected to spend on homework each night

- The degree to which assignments can be altered to meet individual student's needs

Source: Pasi, 2006.

Another role for schools—and teachers should also be sensitive to this potential problem—involves recognizing limitations students' home environments may place on their ability to do homework well, or even to do homework at all. Vatterott cautions that "used improperly, homework disproportionately causes students who are academically or situationally challenged to fail" (2003, p. 64) and so may increase achievement gaps. For some students, an after-school program that provides homework assistance may be almost a necessity.

In Summary

At its best, homework can enhance learning, provide feedback to help teachers strengthen individual student's knowledge, improve organizational skills and study habits, teach responsibility and time management, and ultimately increase academic achievement. At its worst, homework can be a source of frustration for students, a burden on parents, an inaccurate reflection of student ability, and a deterrent to engaging students in learning.

This brief overview of the current research and practice related to homework highlights the complexity of the issue. Your school's homework policy can help make homework a more effective part of the instructional program—one that is carefully planned to support specific educational goals, takes into account the specific abilities and needs of students, and strengthens the link between home and school.

References

Bailey, E. (2008). *Classroom strategies for dyslexia: Modifying tests and homework assignments help LD students*. Retrieved from http://specialneedseducation.suite101.com/article.cfm/classroom_strategies_for_dyslexia

Center for Public Education. (2007). *What research say about the value of homework: At a glance*. Retrieved from http://www.centerforpubliceducation.org/site/c.kjJXJ5MPIwE/b.2480699/k.D9C5/Homework.htm

Center on Innovation & Improvement. (2009). *Training for instructional leaders: Session four—Instructional delivery*. Lincoln, IL: Author.

Cooper, H. (1994, Summer). Homework research and policy: A review of the literature. *Research/Practices Newsletter*. Retrieved from http://cehd.umn.edu/CAREI/Reports/Rpractice/Summer94/homework.html

Cooper, H. (2001). *The battle over homework: Common ground for administrators, teachers, and parents* (2nd ed.). Thousand Oaks, CA: Corwin Press, Inc.

Cooper, H. (2006). *Does homework improve academic achievement?* Retrieved from http://news.duke.edu/2006/09/homework_oped.html

Cooper, H. (2007). *The battle over homework: Common ground for administrators, teachers, and parents* (3rd ed.). Thousand Oaks, CA: Corwin Press.

Cooper, H., Robinson, J. C., & Patall, E. A. (2006). Does homework improve academic achievement? A synthesis of research, 1987-2003. *Review of Educational Research, 76*(1), 1-62

ERIC Clearinghouse on Disabilities and Gifted Education. (2001, Spring). Views from the field. *Research Connections in Special Education*, 6-7.

Fisher, D., & Frey, N. (2008). Homework and the gradual release of responsibility: Making "responsibility" possible. *English Journal, 98*(2), 40–45.

Lee, S. W. (2005). *Encyclopedia of school psychology.* Thousand Oaks, CA: Sage Publications.

Marzano, R. J., Gaddy, B. B., & Dean, C. (2000). *What works in classroom instruction?* Aurora, CO: McReL.

Marzano, R. J., Pickering, D. J., & Pollock, J. E. (2001). *Classroom instruction that works: Research-based strategies for increasing student achievement.* Alexandria, VA: Association for Supervision and Curriculum Development.

Marzano, R. J., & Pickering, D. J. (2007a). The case for and against homework. *Educational Leadership, 64*(6), 74-79

Marzano, R. J., & Pickering. D. J. (2007b). Errors and allegations about research on homework. *Phi Delta Kappan 88*(7), 507-513.

Oliver, B. (2009). The homework dilemma. *Just for the Asking!, 6*(4). Retrieved from http://www.justaskpublications.com/images/stories/ask/pdf/newsletters/jfta/2009/jfta_april_2009.pdf

Pasi, R. (2006). Homework that helps. *Principal Leadership, 7*(1), 8–9.

Paulu, N. (1998). *Helping your students with homework: A guide for teachers.* Washington, DC: Office of Educational Research and Improvement, U.S. Department of Education. Retrieved from http://www.ed.gov/PDFDocs/hyc.pdf

Rowell, L., & Hong, E. (2002). The role of school counselors in homework intervention. *Professional School Counseling.* Retrieved from http://findarticles.com/p/articles/mi_m0KOC/is_4_5/ai_86059889/

Shellard, E. G., & Turner, J. R. (2004). *ERS focus on: Homework—Research and best practice.* Arlington, VA: Educational Research Service.

Silvis, H. (2002, Summer). Take-home lessons. *Northwest Education Magazine.* Retrieved from http://www.nwrel.org/nwedu/2002sum/take-home.html

Vatterott, C. (2003, January/February). There's something wrong about homework. *Principal,* 64.

Vatterott, C. (2009). *Rethinking homework: Best practices that support diverse needs.* Alexandria, VA: ASCD.

Walberg, H., & Paik, S. (2004). Effective general practices. In G. Cawelti (Ed.), *Handbook of research on improving student achievement* (3rd ed.) (pp. 25-38). Arlington, VA: Educational Research Service.

Walker, J., Hoover-Dempsey, K., Whetsel, D., & Green, C. (2004). Parental involvement in homework: A review of current research and its implications for teachers, after school program staff, and parent leaders. *Harvard Family Research Project*. Retrieved from http://www.hfrp.org/publications-resources/browse-our-publications/parental-involvement-in-homework-a-review-of-current-research-and-its-implications-for-teachers-after-school-program-staff-and-parent-leaders

Willingham, D. (2002). Allocating student study time. *American Educator*. Retrieved from http://www.aft.org/pubs-reports/american_educator/summer2002/askcognitivescientist.html

Implications for Our School: Questions for Discussion and Reflection

- What best practices related to the amount, type, and grading of homework are important for teachers in our school to use? Do all teachers in our school consistently use these practices?

- Do we know how parents feel about the amounts and kinds of homework their children bring home? How can we gain insight from parents on this topic? How can we involve parents more positively in supporting the school's homework practices?

- What supports do we have in place for students who have trouble completing homework? Are these supports responsive to students' actual needs? How do we know?

Follow-up and Action Items

_____

_____

_____

_____

_____

_____

_____

_____

_____

_____

_____

Chapter 16
Teachers Working With Teachers to Improve Instruction

Teacher development needs to move beyond traditional sit-and-get sessions to harness the potential of teacher-to-teacher sharing.

As recently as 15 years ago, staff development opportunities for teachers were defined almost exclusively as workshops, typically lasting no more than one day and presented by outside "experts." Teachers interested in implementing the newly presented approaches would go back to their classrooms and practice on their own, with little to no continuing support provided. Today, however, there is increasing recognition that opportunities to collaborate with other teachers represent a valuable, although often untapped, resource and should be considered an essential element of staff development.

The growing research base on effective school districts provides strong support for the importance of this type of approach to professional development:

> Recent findings about top-performing school systems in the world support the notion that learning improves when teacher learning happens in the classroom, teacher leadership receives consistent support, and teachers have opportunities to learn from one another. It is critical for teachers to have a familiarity with one another's work that comes with frequent conversations of a professional nature centered on the work, access to each other's classrooms, and collaborative planning time. It is also very clear that as self-reflective as a teacher may be, receiving constructive feedback from one's peers is imperative in order to improve teaching. (Friesen, 2009, p. 6)

In Sparks and Hirsh's "vision" for professional development, they describe the "learning school" as one in which

> all staff members…[are] engaged in sustained, intellectually rigorous study of what they teach and how they teach it. …[The] traditional model of isolated "adult pull-out programs" [is replaced by] an entire school focused on increasing learning collaboratively. Teachers learn better when they learn together and support one another in planning more advanced lessons, improving the quality of students' work, and solving the day-to-day problems of teaching and learning. Such a school embeds staff development into all of its daily activities. (2000, p. 11)

Even when schools do not provide formal structures that encourage collaboration, teachers often create opportunities to learn from each other. In response to his survey of a sample of Michigan teachers, Follo found that teachers valued conversations with colleagues and that these were most often focused on how to teach, followed by concerns such as meeting individual students' needs. The conversations took place in the teachers' lounge, classrooms, hallways, and the lunchroom, as well as in the parking lot and in lavatories. When asked what support they needed to increase their use of this important resource to improve their own teaching, teachers overwhelmingly asked for more time (1999).

> *"Continuous improvement of each teacher's skills is achieved through a variety of means including whole-faculty workshops, consultations with Instructional Teams, the principal's work with individual teachers and with teams, and through collegial learning—teacher to teacher (including peer observations, study groups, coaching, and mentoring)." (Redding, 2007, p. 109)*

Teacher Collaboration in Effective Schools

Observations of effective schools provide support for the value of increased opportunities for teacher collaboration as a tool to increase levels of student learning. The culture in many of these effective schools explicitly supports teacher-to-teacher sharing. For example, a study of nine urban elementary schools that have attained higher than expected levels of student achievement discusses some similarities among the schools regarding strategies used to improve academic achievement. According to researchers, the schools were similar in that school leaders actively sought to provide opportunities within the school day for teachers to "work, plan, and learn together around instructional issues" (Charles A. Dana Center, 1999, p. ix).

In her study of eight schools recognized for the effectiveness of their professional development programs, Killion found that:

Teachers valued more opportunities for "informal" learning. Informal learning is job-embedded, job-related, teacher-directed, more spontaneous, and is continuous and unbound by rigorous time schedules. Informal learning includes teacher planning, grade-level or department meetings, conversations about students, reflection on students' and teachers' work, problem solving, assisting each other, classroom-based action research, coaching and supporting one another, making school-based decisions, developing assessments, curriculum, and instructional resources, etc. In informal learning, teachers largely determine what and how much they will learn and how much effort they will invest in learning. "Every conversation between two professionals is professional development," said one teacher. In the award-winning schools, more informal learning occurred than "formal" learning. (1999)

A study of Maryland "outlier" schools, some doing significantly better than expected on statewide tests and some doing less well than expected, discussed some of the characteristics found in these two groups of schools. In the more effective schools, researchers found:

> [a] team mentality of working together to improve the abilities of students. ...Collaboration occurs with respect to the way in which the mission that guides instruction gets carried out, as well as the processes used to craft it initially. ...In schools where collaboration is high, time is allowed for working together, and the principal supports experimentation and risk taking on the teacher's part to remove barriers to learning. Collaboration occurs among classroom teachers, special education teachers, and education support staff as well. Team teaching in classrooms occurs frequently with special educators and classroom teachers and with the reading specialist. ...As collaboration develops, so does collegiality, with teachers willing to share instruction and work with particular children. (Schafer et al., 1997)

In contrast, in the less successful schools,

> a collaborative problem solving process [was] not in place to remove barriers to learning. Teachers, administration and education support personnel each appear to be waiting for one of the parties to take the lead; no one fully takes responsibility in improving the school. Some schools have a number of teacher cliques which make it difficult for collaboration as they work against each other and at cross purposes. Territoriality [concerns for one's own grade level or subject area] appears to be a factor that prevents teachers from coming together. (Schafer et al., 1997)

Characteristics of Effective Staff Development

- Begins with a clear sense of what students need to learn and be able to do

- Is based on standards for student learning, teaching, and staff development

- Focuses on schoolwide goals for student learning that are based on the unique strengths and challenges faced by that particular school community

- Is job-embedded and team based

- Is built on a core set of ideas and beliefs

- Is matched to the instructional processes desired in the school

- Is focused to a large extent on content and content-specific pedagogy

- Changes the organization's structure and culture at the same time individual teachers and administrators are acquiring new knowledge and skills

- Provides a great deal of follow-up support in the classroom over a sustained period of time if training is the learning mode being used

- Provides generous amounts of time for collaborative work and various learning activities

Source: Sparks, 2004.

Creating Opportunities for Teacher Collaboration

While teacher-to-teacher sharing and support to improve student learning happens informally every day in schools across the country, many schools and districts have developed more formal approaches that capitalize on the expertise of their own teachers. Several of these are briefly described below.

"Grow Your Own" Trainers

A twist on the traditional model of inservice expert training is for schools and districts to develop "in-house experts"—teachers who are expected to serve as resources for other teachers in the school. These teachers may have been identified as already expert in the use of particular strategies or instructional approaches, or they may be provided with time and opportunity to work with external experts to become proficient in the application of a new skill. In either case, they not only provide the initial training to their peers; they are also available on a continuing basis to provide support for teachers as they introduce the "new" strategies in their classrooms. In-house experts can:

- work with teachers in small groups or even one-to-one as needed;

- make a connection between theory and classroom practice that is specific to the needs of a particular school or classroom rather than general in nature;

- observe classroom lessons and work with colleagues over a period of time to help teachers improve their grasp and use of the new skills after the initial presentations; and,

- help teachers design ways to measure the impact of the new approach on student learning.

Teacher Mentoring

Learning to teach is a process that only begins in teacher preparation programs. Mentoring provides a systematic induction and learning process for new teachers, and a means of instructional renewal and improvement for experienced teachers who serve as mentors. Essentially, "a mentor serves as a role model, sponsor, encourager, counselor, and friend to a less skilled or less experienced person for the purposes of promoting the latter's professional and/or personal growth" (Janas, 1996, p. 3). These responsibilities vary at times throughout the relationship, as the new teacher's personal and professional needs change (Bey, 1995).

The mentor has a multifaceted role in the relationship. He or she:

- promotes the new teacher's professional competence and personal growth;

- serves as an instructional advisor (for instance, helping the new teacher plan lessons, organize instruction, or evaluate student learning);

- provides information about research on teaching and learning and is available to suggest innovative and/or alternative approaches;

- observes the new teacher during instruction and offers feedback for improvement (however, the literature strongly suggests that the mentor not play a part in the formal evaluation process);

- is a caring and concerned friend; and,

- may choose to be an advocate for the new teacher (Blank & Sindelar, 1992; Weeks, 1992).

Not all experienced teachers will be good mentors. Effective mentors are both excellent instructors and team players, have an even temper and a good sense of humor, are people-oriented and nurturing, and have engaged in reflective practice and inquiry themselves throughout their career.

Alternatively, teachers arranged in a team configuration might be able to act as an "academic mentoring team." In this scenario, inexperienced teachers receive the collegial support they need and experienced teachers share the responsibility of mentoring (Turk, 1999).

To effectively assist beginning teachers as well as those with less experience in a particular curriculum area or instructional strategy, mentors ought to have an understanding of:

- the principles and practices of adult development and adult learning;

- the stages of teacher development (from concerns about survival to a focus on impact on students);

- teaching as a complicated job conducted in a complex setting;

- how to model the behaviors and attitudes that are characteristic of a professional; and,

- innovative approaches to curriculum design and teaching strategies (Ganser, 1996b).

Ganser (1996a) also suggests that good mentors need to be skilled in conferencing, problem-solving, goal-setting, teacher observation, and role-playing.

Peer Coaching

While peer coaching is similar in some ways to mentoring in that two teachers are paired, peer coaching typically involves two more experienced teachers who observe and learn from each other's teaching (Ackland, 1991). Collegial interaction, rather than supervisory evaluation, is the emphasis as teachers are encouraged to reflect on their current practices and expand their instructional repertoire. Says one teacher, "[peer coaching] encourages you to sit down and talk with someone and not go back to your room and into your own little world. You get ideas or get reassured that you're doing okay" (Delany & Arredondo, 2001, p. 154). Another teacher writes:

> There is no competition, no superstars, because everyone is a star teacher. Everyone helps everyone else. Teachers teach for each other, share all ideas and strategies, give advice, listen, and mentor new people. It makes no difference what your role, support is always available. There are no boundaries when we work together. Everyone depends on each other. Some of the most effective staff development is what is learned from colleagues just by asking for help. (WestEd, 2000)

Through a careful pairing of appropriate personalities and expertise, as well as some initial training in critical observation, data collection and analysis, and peer conferencing, peer coaching can promote:

- reduced isolation among teachers;

- the establishment of collaborative norms that enable teachers to give and receive ideas and assistance;

- the creation of a forum for addressing instructional problems;

- teacher sharing of successful practices;

- the transfer of training from workshop to workplace;

- the concept of teachers as researchers; and,

- reflective practice (Robbins, 1991).

In some peer coaching models, coaching partners provide "technical" feedback—suggestions for improving teaching—in the post-observation conference. Peer coaching should not be a tool for teacher evaluation, and when these evaluative undertones creep into teacher feedback, instructional innovation can be stifled. In a model described by Showers and Joyce, the person teaching is considered the coach, and the observer is considered the person being coached. "Teachers who are observing do so in order to learn from their colleague," and both teachers are provided with opportunities to observe (1996, p. 15).

Knight (2007) stresses the importance of teachers experiencing the peer coaching relationship as a partnership where dialogue is confidential and respectful communication is valued. Several other elements have been identified as contributing to a successful peer coaching experience, including:

- a specific focus for observation during the lesson;

- the accurate collection of data during observation; and,

- objectivity in the presentation of observation feedback (Robbins, 1991; Speck & Krovetz, 1996).

Teachers involved in a reciprocal coaching arrangement can benefit from training focused on the skills they need to be effective in conferences and during observation. Training can help the partner teachers learn to:

- *wait* while partners think and reflect

- *actively listen*, and repeat or paraphrase what their partner has said

- *clarify* partners' statements

- *request* more specific information from their partners

- *reframe* the issues when partners get off track

- *design* and suggest ways that data may be collected during observation

- *collect* data during observation

- *offer* neutral comments (Robbins, 1991; Speck & Krovetz, 1996).

Study Groups and Collaborative Action Research

While study groups and collaborative action research are typically described separately in the literature, they have many similarities from the perspective of what participating teachers do, the knowledge they can take away from the process, and the impact the activities can have on school improvement efforts. When teachers collaborate with peers in study groups or on an action research project, they work together to improve learning for students in the school, and simultaneously foster growth in their own and their peers' understanding of effective teaching strategies (Cramer, Hurst, & Wilson, 1996).

Kutz questions the assumption that effective classroom research must begin with a "big question" that is teased out of heavy research tomes. In reality, valuable classroom research often originates from "small questions, with the wonderings of individual teachers" (1992, p. 193). For example, a team might decide to study how a regular and special education teacher can effectively co-teach. Or the teachers might ask, "Why do some students fail to participate in cooperative learning groups?" or, "Which approach to teaching eighth-graders to problem solve works best?"

Kochendorfer (1997) makes the connection between collaborative approaches to research and study and teacher-to-teacher learning. In his view, these activities provide opportunities for teacher colleagues to provide each other with new ideas and insights and to help clarify one another's thinking. However, in some schools, time, patience, and efforts to build trust may be needed before this collaborative approach to study and problem-solving can be used successfully. For example, Allen and Calhoun found that some teachers were reluctant to open their classrooms to schoolwide action research, since "it was much less threatening to gather information about student behavior in the lunchroom than to study individual classroom instructional practices for their effects on student achievement" (1998, p. 707). Thus, the school leader has a role to play in nurturing such efforts.

Murphy and Lick (2004) suggest that study groups can perform the following functions, all of which support efforts to raise the level of student learning while providing a host of opportunities for teachers to learn from each other:

- *They support the implementation of curricular and instructional innovations.* Group members may help each other design lessons, and report to one another on the success of the instructional innovation in the classroom. Murphy relates the experience of a school whose new heterogeneous (across grade level) study groups of teachers decided that the use of long-neglected math manipulatives would be the first focus of group study and innovation. "For two months (eight study group meetings), teachers came to the study group meetings with a lesson that they either had taught or were going to teach, shared videos of their teaching, and visited each other's classrooms to see how the students were responding to the activities" (1995, p. 38).

- *They integrate and give coherence to a school's instructional practices and programs.* Every year new "innovations" are introduced to schools; every year a number of them are abandoned. Study groups help teachers connect these new instructional strategies to their actual teaching, "bringing coherence to disjointed efforts, by exploring the theoretical and research base of the various instructional models that routinely confront faculties" (Murphy, 1995, p. 38).

- *They target an identified schoolwide need.* After careful study of relevant whole-school data, faculty members may collaboratively determine that there are several areas of curriculum or instruction that need attention if increased schoolwide learning is to occur. Study groups focus in-depth on these areas of need.

- *They study research on teaching and learning.* Study groups can review the professional literature available on a particular innovation or strategy. "Study groups help teachers take more seriously what other districts are discovering about general improvement strategies and be more actively involved in collecting and analyzing the data that comes from their own classrooms and schools" (Murphy, 1995, p. 39).

- *They monitor the impact of innovations on students and on changes in the workplace.* Study groups promote action research—identifying a student need, taking action to meet that need, and monitoring and measuring the effectiveness of the action taken—among group members (Murphy, 1995).

Barriers to Teacher-to-Teacher Sharing

- Lack of time

- Tradition of closed door teaching

- General lack of trust across the school

- Teacher concern that asking for help sends a message of incompetence

- Worry that "data" collected from mentoring or peer classroom visits will be used in developing teacher evaluations

- Lack of comfort with providing—or accepting—advice from peers

---

Building a Culture of Collaboration

Support for teachers talking, studying, and working together should be an indelible part of a school's culture—what DuFour describes as the norm that shapes "how its people think, feel, and act" (1998, p. 58). Nurturing a culture in which teachers feel like professionals—people who possess a shared vision for student improvement, good ideas, and important skills—is a primary responsibility of school leaders.

School leaders can help to create a community of learning, and encourage teacher reflection and collaboration, by fostering conditions that the professional literature cites as vital to the success of any good staff development effort. These include:

- *Authenticity.* Professional development that encourages teachers to focus on real students' needs and practical issues in the school and classroom has the power to engage teachers in reflective practice—and, by extension, to improve student learning (Hannay, 1994, p. 23).

- *Time.* DuFour (1998) suggests that schools implementing new programs and practices should build time for collaboration into the regular school day and year, thus sending a message about the importance of collaboration to efforts to improve teaching. Specifically, a community of collaborative learners needs:

  - *Time to plan.* Discrete blocks of time are needed to plan what sort of effort will be undertaken, what it will look like, who will be involved, what the goals of the training will be, how progress will be assessed, etc. Once that is done, teachers need time together to discuss how they intend to implement the program in their classrooms.

  - *Time to implement.* Teachers need time to practice and become comfortable with the new approach in practice before they feel they are required to demonstrate mastery. Often, this involves more time for discussion as teachers experiment and desire feedback from colleagues.

  - *Time to assess.* Teachers need time to plan how the impact of the new approach or program will be assessed—and then to do the assessment. Time for further collaboration at this step allows the teachers to talk about the results and develop improvements based on the data (Smith, Babu, & Sullivan, 1996; Sparks, 1995).

- *A willing and confident staff.* Teachers who are eager to expand their repertoire of teaching strategies, implement their new learning in the classroom with their students, examine and refine their current practice, and encourage their colleagues to improve their own instruction are key to a successful staff development program.

- *Supportive leadership.* Principals should see themselves as "learning leaders," and their schools and districts as communities of learning—both for students and for teachers (Lashway, 1998). A supportive principal will work to provide teachers with the environment and resources they need to foster opportunities for teachers to collaborate professionally.

> *"Improving teachers' learning—and, in turn, their own practice and their students' learning—requires professional development that is closely and explicitly tied to teachers' ongoing work." (Neufeld & Roper, 2003, p. 1)*

Summary

Research and experience indicate that teacher collaboration can support efforts to raise the level of student learning in schools across the country. Gordon Cawelti goes to the heart of the issue when he states that, within a culture that encourages teachers to exercise their professional competence, explore promising practices, and share information among themselves, "much of the best staff development goes on teacher-to-teacher every day" (1995, p. 4).

Given the opportunity, most teachers are eager to work together and to learn from each other, with the ultimate goal of helping their students succeed. But in order to create a culture in which teacher collaboration flourishes, schools must provide adequate time and build structures that support collaboration. By doing so, schools can become true communities of learning, which support all of their members in achieving their full potential.

References

Ackland, R. (1991, Winter). A review of the peer coaching literature. *Journal of Staff Development*, 22-26.

Allen, L., & Calhoun, E. F. (1998, May). Schoolwide action research: Findings from six years of study. *Phi Delta Kappan*, 706-710.

Bey, T. M. (1995, November). Mentorships: Transferable transactions among teachers. *Education and Urban Society*, 11-19.

Blank, M. A., & Sindelar, N. (1992, September/October). Mentoring as professional development: From theory to practice. *The Clearing House*, 22-26.

Cawelti, G. (1995). Using the knowledge base to improve student achievement. In G. Calweti (Ed.), *Handbook of research on improving student achievement* (3rd ed.). Arlington, VA: Educational Research Service.

Charles A. Dana Center. (1999). *Hope for urban education: A study of nine high-performing, high-poverty, urban elementary schools*. Washington, DC: U.S. Department of Education, Planning and Evaluation Service.

Cramer, G., Hurst, B., & Wilson, C. (1996). *Teacher study groups for professional development*. Bloomington, IN: Phi Delta Kappa Educational Foundation.

Delany, J. C., & Arredondo, D. E. (2001, Spring). Collegial coaching and reflection as mechanisms for changing middle school cultures. *Research in Middle Level Education Annual*, 143-158.

DuFour, R. (1998, Winter). Learning-centered schools grow from strong cultures. *Journal of Staff Development*, 58-59.

Follo, E. J. (1999, Summer). What are teachers talking about? Peer conversations as professional dialogue. *ERS Spectrum*, 16-22.

Friesen, S. (2009). Teaching effectiveness: A framework and a rubric. Toronto, ON: Canadian Education Association. Retrieved from http://www.cea-ace.ca/media/en/WDYDIST_Teaching_EN.pdf

Ganser, T. (1996a, Summer). What do mentors say about mentoring? *Journal of Staff Development*, 36-39.

Ganser, T. (1996b, Fall). Preparing mentors of beginning teachers: An overview for staff developers. *Journal of Staff Development*, 8-11.

Hannay, L. M. (1994, Summer). Strategies for facilitating reflective practice: The role of staff developers. *Journal of Staff Development*, 22-26.

Janas, M. (1996, Fall). Mentoring the mentor: A challenge for staff development. *Journal of Staff Development*, 2-5.

Killion, J. (1999, December/January). Exemplary schools model quality staff development. *Results*, 3.

Knight, J. (2007). *Instructional coaching: A partnership approach to improving instruction.* Thousand Oaks, CA: Corwin Press.

Kochendorfer, L. (1997, Winter). Active voice: Types of classroom teacher action research. *Teaching and Change*, 157-173.

Kutz, E. (1992, March). Teacher research: Myths and realities. *Language Arts*, 193-197.

Lashway, L. (1998). Creating a learning organization. *ERIC Digest,* Number 121. Eugene, OR: ERIC Clearinghouse on Educational Management.

Murphy, C. (1995, Summer). Whole-faculty study groups: Doing the seemingly undoable. *Journal of Staff Development*, 37-44.

Murphy, C. U., & Lick, D. W. (2004). *Whole-faculty study groups: A powerful way to change schools and enhance learning* (3rd ed.). Thousand Oaks, CA: Corwin Press.

Neufeld, B., & Roper, D. (2003). *Coaching: A strategy for developing instructional capacity.* Washington, DC: Aspen Institute. Retrieved from http://www.edmatters.org/webreports/CoachingPaperfinal.pdf

Redding, S. (2007). Handbook on restructuring and substantial school improvement. Lincoln, IL: Academic Development Institute.

Robbins, P. (1991). *How to plan and implement a peer coaching program.* Alexandria, VA: Association for Supervision and Curriculum Development.

Schafer, W. D., Hultgren, F. H., Hawley, W.D., Abrams, A. L., Seubert, C. C., & Mazzoni, S. (1997). *Study of higher-success and lower-success elementary schools.* College Park, MD: University of Maryland. Retrieved from www.mdk12.org/practices/benchmark/improve/study/phasefour/index.html.

Showers, B., & Joyce, B. (1996, March). The evolution of peer coaching. *Educational Leadership*, 12-16.

Smith, G. B., Babu, S., & Sullivan, P. (1996). *Measuring the effect of staff development training on school effectiveness in large-city school districts*. Dallas, TX: Dallas Public Schools. Retrieved from http://www.dallasisd.org/eval/research/articles/Smith-Measuring-The-Effects-of-Staff-Development-Training-in-Large-City-School-Districts.pdf

Sparks, D. (2004). Focusing staff development on improving the learning of all students. In G. Calweti (Ed.), *Handbook of research on improving student achievement* (3rd ed.). Arlington, VA: Educational Research Service.

Sparks, D., & Hirsh, S. (2000). *A national plan for improving professional development*. Retrieved from http://www.eric.ed.gov/ERICDocs/data/ericdocs2sql/content_storage_01/0000019b/80/16/48/5b.pdf

Speck, M., & Krovetz, M. (1996, Winter). Developing effective peer coaching experiences for school administrators. *ERS Spectrum*, 37-42.

Turk, R. L. (1999). Get on the team: An alternative mentoring model. In M. Scherer (Ed.), *A Better Beginning: Supporting and Mentoring New Teachers*. Alexandria, VA: Association for Supervision and Curriculum Development.

Weeks, P. V. (1992, May). A mentor's point of view. *Intervention in School and Clinic*, 303-306.

WestEd. (2000). *Teachers who learn, kids who achieve*. San Francisco: Author. Retrieved from http://www.WestEd.org/online_pubs/teachers_who_learn/TeachLearn.pdf

Implications for Our School: Questions for Discussion and Reflection

- Review Sparks's list of characteristics of effective staff development on p. 173. Do our school practices align with these?

- Now look at Barriers to Teacher-to-Teacher Sharing on p. 178. Does our school need to address any of these concerns?

- Are there any peer coaching teams—whether formal or informal—in place in our school? If yes, how are they implemented? If no, how could we facilitate their development?

- Is our system for mentoring new teachers effective? What are its strong points and weaknesses?

Follow-up and Action Items

_____

_____

_____

_____

_____

_____

_____

_____

_____

_____

_____

_____

_____

Chapter 17

Single-Sex Education

Would single-sex education provide the solution some students in your school need to focus on learning?

Single-sex education, once the norm in the United States, has been largely confined to private schools ever since public schools adopted a coeducational approach in the 19th century. More recently, however, interest in single-sex education among educators, policymakers, and parents was revived with the introduction of the final version of the so-called "single-sex regulations," announced in October 2006.

From a legal standpoint, public schools and districts now have more flexibility in regard to single-sex programs. However, it is obvious that more than legal issues will impact school staff thinking about the possibility of offering such programs.

Anecdotal evidence from schools that have implemented single-sex education suggests that it can have a positive impact on achievement and student learning. However, opponents of the approach contend that research-based evidence is lacking and inconclusive and that single-sex classes might impose gender inequity and stereotypes. The following discussion briefly outlines the legal guidance for implementing single-sex programs and, more importantly, provides research findings that could help make a decision about whether this approach might be right for your school.

> *The National Association for Single Sex Public Education (2009) reported that, as of Fall 2009, there were almost 550 public schools offering single-sex education opportunities. The majority of these schools are coed and offer single-sex classes in various subjects, although about 90 are single-sex schools.*

The New Title IX Regulations

In October 2006, the U.S. Department of Education announced the release of the final version of the single-sex regulations of Title IX, legislation originally part of the Education Amendments of 1972. Although the new regulations only apply to education programs or activities receiving federal financial assistance, they represent a fundamental shift in the interpretation of the law as it applies to public schools.

Prior to publication of the new regulations, single-sex classes were generally prohibited except in limited circumstances, such as sex education or physical education. The new regulations state that districts are permitted to establish a single-sex class if the single-sex nature of the class is "substantially related" to the achievement of an "important governmental or educational objective." The two objectives identified are:

- "to provide a diversity of educational options to parents and students; and

- to meet the particular, identified educational needs of students" (U.S. Department of Education 2006, p. 62,530).

Male and female students must be treated in an "evenhanded manner" and a "substantially equal" coeducational class must always be provided. (U.S. Department of Education, 2006, p. 62,530). In addition, enrollment in the single-sex class must be voluntary.

> *The Federal Register posting of the single-sex regulations can be found online at http://www.ed.gov/legislation/FedRegister/finrule/2006-4/102506a.pdf.*

Why Offer Single-Sex Programs?

Proponents of single-sex education offer a variety of reasons why such classes or schools would be an improvement over the almost solely coeducational settings we now have. Their views are sometimes driven by personal experiences, sometimes by data, and sometimes by ideological beliefs. Here are a few justifications heard frequently.

Addressing the "Boy Crisis." While for years concerns had been expressed that education might be shortchanging female students, attention began to shift in the late 1990s towards problems boys might experience in "typical" classrooms (Viadero, 2006). Those concerned about the existence of a "boy crisis" point to lower scores by male students on assessments such as the National Assessment of Educational Progress (National Center for Education Statistics, 2005); higher dropout, retention, and suspension rates for male students; higher incidence of classification of learning disabilities and behavior disorders; and lower test-taking rates on assessments such as the SAT, ACT, and AP (Mead, 2006; Sadker, 2002).

Accommodating Biological Differences. Other advocates argue that brain-based research shows that males and females are "wired" differently, and so should receive educational experiences designed to meet their special needs (see Sax, n.d.). Although most researchers agree that the differences within one sex are greater than the differences between girls and boys (Campbell and Sanders 2002), the idea that boys and girls learn differently is certainly part of the everyday lore of schools, with some of the perceptions supported by "data" and others by years of teacher observation and experience. For example, some common perceptions include: boys read less and have less enthusiasm for reading; males prefer competition while girls prefer collaboration; and boys are naturally more active.

Addressing Gaps. Another impetus to consider single-sex programs relates to suggestions they might provide a way to address achievement gaps—either gaps between the performance of boys and girls, or more narrowly, to provide focused attention on the educational needs of a group such as African American male students. Mead points out that achievement gaps are much larger along race and class lines than gender lines, and noted that "[t]here are groups of boys for whom 'crisis' is not too strong a term. When racial and economic gaps combine with gender achievement gaps in reading, the result is disturbingly low achievement for poor, black, and Hispanic boys" (2006, p. 9). Barnett and Rivers agree with Mead's assessment stating that "the alarming statistics on which the notion of a crisis is based are rarely broken out by race or class. When they are, the whole picture changes. It becomes clear that if there is a crisis, it's among inner-city and rural boys" (2006).

Removing Distractions. Some parents—as well as some educators—ask whether dividing the sexes could remove distractions and/or help teachers more effectively teach by providing a single-sex environment. For example, Gurian and Henley (2001) asked teachers to comment on their experiences with single-sex exercises or classes. In response, they heard that "putting boys in the position of working only with boys resulted in fewer discipline problems" and that, in an all-boys' class, boys work better together and have fewer problems (2001, p. 210).

Concerns About Single-Sex Education

One argument often provided against single-sex education is the finding from *Brown v. Board of Education* that separate is "inherently unequal." Marcia Greenberger, copresident of the National Women's Law Center, characterizes the new regulations as "an invitation to discriminate," and the organization's vice president Jocelyn Samuels suggests that educational agencies that develop single-sex programs do so "at their peril" and may face legal challenges (in Green, 2006).

The National Coalition for Women and Girls in Education (NCWGE) also expressed opposition to the proposed changes in the regulations. In addition, NCWGE stated its belief that:

> single-sex education does not guarantee improved schools. Rather, the elements that enable children to succeed in single-sex education can be replicated in coeducational settings. These elements include a focus on core academics, small class size, qualified teachers, sufficient funding, and parental involvement. (2002)

Another commonly voiced objection to single-sex schooling is the fact that, although gender differences do exist,

> we actually know very little about why these differences exist or how important they are. There are many things—including biological, developmental, cultural, and educational factors—that affect how boys and girls do in school. But untangling these differences is incredibly difficult. (Mead, 2006, p. 14)

A concern sometimes expressed about single-sex programs is the limit they place on opportunities for male and female students to work together and to socialize. For this reason, some single-sex programs are limited to certain core courses, with students attending some coeducational classes. While a more difficult problem to address if the program is a single-sex school, supporters point out that students will still have opportunities to interact during community activities.

A final objection is the concern that single-sex classrooms may reinforce stereotypes. A study conducted of California's single-sex education pilot program, which was implemented in six districts, found that,

> Because boys were perceived to be talkative and active, they were likely to be taught in traditional classroom environments that were characterized by stricter discipline, a competitive atmosphere, and more physical activities. This compared strikingly to the kinder, gentler environment offered the girls who were viewed as more studious, collaborative, and well-behaved. (Datnow, Hubbard, & Woody, 2001, p. 7)

Are Boys and Girls Really Different?

Most researchers agree that boys and girls are more similar than they are different and that there is considerable overlap in cognitive processes (Campbell & Sanders, 2002). As Kafer describes it, average intelligence for males and females is the same, with far greater "variability in cognitive ability between individuals than between sexes" (2007, p. 8).

Hyde (2005), who supports the gender similarities hypothesis, asserts that males and females are similar on most, although not all, psychological variables. In her meta-analysis on psychological gender differences, she found that 78% of gender differences were small or close-to-zero in magnitude. She acknowledges that there are some exceptions, such as motor performance, where the magnitude of difference is moderate or large. However, she cautions that magnitude can fluctuate with age and that differences are dependent on context, which, as she notes, counters the idea that gender differences are large and stable.

> *"Males and females are overwhelmingly alike in their cognitive abilities."*
> *(Halpern, 2000, p. 128)*

Findings from the first wave of the National Institutes of Health (NIH) MRI Study of Normal Brain Development indicate that:

> Sex predicted few aspects of cognitive function, with gender effects less prevalent than in some previous studies. Boys performed better on perceptual analysis, and girls performed better on processing speed and motor dexterity. Girls also showed a slight advantage on verbal learning, but by adolescence, this advantage had disappeared. (Children's Hospital Boston, 2007)

Making causal links between boy-girl differences and ability is difficult as Halpern discusses:

> Very few true experiments with humans are ever conducted in the area of sex differences. A paradox in sex differences research is that the major variable of interest—being female or male—is never assigned at random.... There are many variables that covary (or go along) with biological indicators of sex in our society.... Given that so many variables are confounded with sex and that sex is never randomly assigned, causal attributions for any between-sex difference are difficult to support.... Researchers can never be certain if any between-sex differences are due to the biological aspects of sex, psychosocial concomitants of sex, the interaction between them, or some unidentified factor. (2000, p. 45)

Gender Differences and Generalizations

"Although it's possible and appropriate to report general observations about male/female differences, it's inappropriate to stereotype—to use a general observation about a group to predict the properties, capabilities, and behavior of any individual male or female within the group" (Sylwester, 2005).

James agrees that the cognitive differences between boys and girls are far less than the cognitive differences within each gender. However, she adds that there are differences between boys and girls in other areas and that these differences

> can be magnified in a school setting. Stereotyping, peer pressure, social expectations, and environmental influences from families, peers, and teachers, as well as the media and entertainment industry, all work together to intensify the importance placed on gender differences. (2007, p. 5)

What is perhaps most significant when thinking about gender differences and their relevance in the classroom is that "generalization about gender *at best* can only describe tendencies and patterns—not deterministic limitations" (Newkirk, 2002, p. 22).

> *"There are typical patterns of behavior to which many boys conform." (Younger & Warrington, 2005, p. 19)*

What Does Research Tell Us About Single-Sex Education?

One of the first efforts to review studies of single-sex education focused on the impact on female students and was conducted on behalf of the U.S. Department of Education. While characterizing the body of research as inconclusive, researchers Moore, Piper, and Schaefer (1993) also stated that there was "sufficient evidence" to suggest that single-sex educational opportunities may positively impact female students and that the "countervailing evidence" was not sufficiently convincing.

Another overview of the research, this one conducted by the American Association of University Women, also focused on the achievement of female students but contained different findings. *Separated by Sex: A Critical Look at Single-Sex Education for Girls* reports on some "points of consensus" (1998, p. 2) that emerged from a discussion of experts around the single-sex literature:

> There is no evidence that single-sex education in general "works" or is "better" than co-education.... Single-sex educational programs produce positive results for some students in some settings. However, researchers do not know for certain whether the benefits derive from factors unique to single-sex programs, or whether these factors also exist or can be reproduced in coeducational settings. (1998, p. 2)

Mael, Alonso, Gibson, Rogers, and Smith conducted a "systematic review of single-sex education" research on behalf of the U.S. Department of Education (2005, p. ix). Based on 40 quantitative studies of single-sex schools, the researchers characterized the results from their analysis of the research base as "equivocal," stating that:

> There is some support for the premise that single-sex schooling can be helpful, especially for certain outcomes related to academic achievement and more positive academic aspirations. For many outcomes, there is no evidence of either benefit or harm. (2005, p. x)

Smithers and Robinson (2006) conducted a review of studies that looked at educating girls and boys together and separately, either in different schools or in different classes. They looked at studies from Australia, the U.S., Canada, New Zealand, Ireland, and the U.K., and concluded that there were no consistent findings that single-sex education is either advantageous or disadvantageous. They also note that "the influences of gender are far outweighed by ability, social background, and race" (2006, p. 28). Overall, they concluded that there are excellent coeducational schools and excellent single-sex schools and that "they are excellent for reasons other than that they separate, or bring together, the sexes for their education" (2006, p. 31).

One study that Smithers and Robinson reviewed was conducted by Younger and Warrington (2005). These researchers studied the effects of single-sex classes in a coeducational school and found some positive effect. Smithers and Robinson talk about the findings:

> [B]oys and girls can feel more at ease in single-sex classes, feel more able to interact with learning and feel free to show real interest without inhibition. There can be positive effects on achievement particularly for boys in modern languages and English, and girls in the sciences and maths. (2006, p. 19)

However, some teachers in this same study characterized teaching in all-boy classes as challenging and found that some boys felt less comfortable in the single-sex environment (Smithers & Robinson, 2006).

Some researchers have looked at the literature more narrowly to identify potential impacts of single-sex education on groups such as disadvantaged male students. In Riordan's view:

> the research is "exceedingly persuasive" in demonstrating that single-sex schools are effective in terms of providing both greater equality and greater achievement, especially for low-income and working-class students, most particularly for African Americans and Hispanic American boys *and* girls. (2002, p. 13)

However, he also postulated that the "key explanatory variable" in these situations could be the pro-academic choice made by parents and students to attend a single-sex school (2002, p. 19).

Planning for a Single-Sex Program

As with the introduction of any other new educational program, careful planning and implementation are important in successful implementation of single-sex education. Obviously, any program will need to satisfy the guidelines implicit in the 2006 version of the regulations. However, any school considering a single-sex program should also engage in an intensive study of both "why" and "how" issues before implementation.

The most important question to address might be, "why a single-sex program?" For example, a look at assessment data disaggregated by gender might indicate a gender gap in a particular grade. Teacher discussions, as well as collection of classroom data on topics such as class participation and disciplinary actions, can also be informative.

> *Any school considering a single-sex program also should engage in an intensive study of both "why" and "how" issues before implementation.*

If analysis of available information reveals particular problems, consider a single-sex program as only one of the options, with others including more staff development for teachers on ways to differentiate instruction (Salomone, 2006b). Sadker and Zittleman support this approach by noting:

> [w]hat we applauded in private single-sex schools was not their gender uniformity, but their educational practices. Many educators, including us, attribute much of the academic successes of these private schools to their smaller class sizes, engaged parents, well-trained teachers, and strong academic emphasis. (2004)

Chadwell (2006) recommends doing some homework by reading the literature on the differences that may exist between how boys and girls learn differently and how single-sex education can potentially impact this.

Other areas of study and consideration might involve the grade levels or subject areas where a single-sex program might do the most good. In regard to grade level, Smithers and Robinson (2006) refer to a "diamond" pattern, where students are coeducated during their early and later years, but separated during the middle years, as one possibility for a single-sex education program. Gurian and Henley feel such an approach may help to reduce "unnecessary stressors" (2001, p. 207) thought to be present during the middle school years. In their view:

> This one environment [the school] can be relatively free of the gender stresses that [middle school children] encounter in the media, at home with siblings, on the street, on the Internet, and in other activities. It can be gender-safe; well-mentored; and focused not on mating, romance, and psychosocial challenges related to hidden hormonal flows but instead on learning. (2001, p. 209)

Salomone sees the decision about grade level as more complex. For example, she characterizes the elementary years as a "critical point . . . when maturational differences create in students the misperception that they are not programmed to succeed in certain subjects." For other students, the critical point may be during middle or secondary years "when social pressures inhibit some students from succeeding academically or finding a constructive source for developing a positive sense of self" (2006a). Single-sex education could help to address both these concerns.

Bell suggests that for certain subjects, such as poetry class, "it might do better to separate [boys and girls] for a specific unit instead of the whole school year" because, for example, research indicates that boys are not as likely to participate in a poetry class if girls are there (in Leech, 2005). Some teachers are finding that even small classroom exercises that divide the students according to sex provide successful learning opportunities.

Obviously, there is also the teacher variable to consider. For example, how will teachers be assigned to single-sex or coeducational programs (Chadwell, 2006)? Will they be permitted to opt out of teaching single-sex classes if they feel the concept is unsound (Gurian & Stevens, 2005)? Teachers who do participate in the program should receive adequate staff development—for example, opportunities to read about and discuss some boy/girl differences that might impact learning. In addition, Datnow, Hubbard, and Woody (2001) suggest that a single-sex environment might encourage students to talk more openly about sensitive issues such as gender and racial bias or sexuality. Teachers should be prepared for these discussions.

An examination of California's experiment with single-sex public education during the 1990s, which was largely viewed as unsuccessful, provides useful information on barriers to successful implementation. For example, Datnow, Hubbard, and Woody (2001) found schools had insufficient time to plan, gain the support of their constituencies, recruit and train teachers, and so on.

Salomone talks about another less-than-successful implementation of a single-sex program. Although test scores improved, there were also findings that the needs of boys and girls were not fully addressed because of "inadequate staff development, inexperienced teachers, and a school mission that was more focused on raising standardized test scores than consciously addressing the specific educational needs of girls and boys" (2003, p. 233).

Careful efforts to work with parents and others involved are critical. For example, schools must take special care when responding to requests for or against single-sex programs that, while couched in educational terms, may have as much or more to do with ideology. Thus, for community relations as well as educational reasons, a single-sex program should have a clearly articulated rationale and specific program goals before implementation efforts begin (Salomone, 2006b). Buy-in from teachers, parents, and students is also important, and Chadwell (2006) stresses the importance of communication with each of these groups while the plan is being considered, as well as during the planning phase.

Critical Questions to Address

- What are the goals of the program?

- Are single-sex schools or classes the *best* way to accomplish the goals?

- What might be lost if coeducation were generally abandoned? What are the costs and tradeoffs of establishing a single-sex school or class?

- When single-sex schools have been found to be effective, what factors produce that effectiveness? Does the proposal take these factors into account?

- What policy obstacles lie in the way of or conflict with the stated goals? Is sex segregation a means of reaching gender equity or a tool for increasing test scores?

- What are the rationales for the program? Gender equity? Differential brain function? Recruitment of girls into curriculum areas historically avoided?

- Has the program been well thought through?

- Will a program of professional development built around the goals of the program be provided for administration and faculty?

- Is there a sound plan to evaluate the outcomes of the program?

Excerpted from Bracey, 2006, p. 39.

In Summary

In considering single-sex classes, you should be aware that many factors affect whether such an approach is right for your school. Successful implementation of single-sex opportunities is complex. A single-sex class or school may provide the solution some students need to focus on learning and excel academically. For other students, coeducation may be where they will flourish. However, Chadwell cautions against expectations that single-sex education will be the "silver bullet" (2006) in regard to behavioral issues. Obviously, expectations should also be realistic in regard to students' academic progress.

It is also important to keep legal issues in mind. While the 2006 Title IX regulations establish some parameters for single-sex education, there is obviously still room for interpretation—as well as legal challenges to both the regulations or specific implementations of single-sex programs by public schools.

References

American Association of University Women. (1998). *Separated by sex: A critical look at single-sex education for girls*. Washington, DC: Author.

Barnett, R., & Rivers, C. (2006, October 2). The boy crisis—Fact or myth? *Teachers College Record*. Retrieved from http://www.tcrecord.org/Content.asp?ContentID=12750

Bracey, G. W. (2006, November). *Separate but superior? A review of issues and data bearing on single-sex education* (EPSL-0611-221-EPRU). Tempe, AZ: Arizona State University, Education Policy Research Unit.

Campbell, P. B., & Sanders, J. (2002). Challenging the system: Assumptions and data behind the push for single-sex schooling. In A. Datnow & L. Hubbard (Eds.), *Gender in policy and practice* (pp. 31-46). New York: Routledge.

Chadwell, D. (2006, October 14). *Introducing single sex classrooms in a coed middle school*. Presented at the National Association for Single Sex Public Education Midwest Regional Conference. Retrieved from http://www2.richland2.org/dm/DMS/Academics/SingleGender/SGE%20Resources/SGE%20into%20COED.pdf

Children's Hospital Boston. (2007). *A first glimpse at healthy brain and behavioral development*. Boston: Author. Retrieved from http://www.childrenshospital.org/newsroom/Site1339/mainpageS1339P1sublevel307.html

Datnow, A., Hubbard, L., & Woody, E. (2001). *Is single gender schooling viable in the public sector? Lessons from California's pilot program*. Retrieved from http://www.oise.utoronto.ca/depts/tps/adatnow/final.pdf

Green, E. (2006, October 27). Are single-sex classrooms legal? *U.S. News and World Report*. Retrieved from http://www.usnews.com/usnews/news/articles/061027/27singlesex.htm

Gurian, M., & Henley, P. (2001). *Boys and girls learn differently! A guide for teachers and parents*. San Francisco: Jossey-Bass.

Gurian, M., & Stevens, K. (2005). *The mind of boys: Saving our sons from falling behind in school and life*. San Francisco: Jossey-Bass.

Halpern, D. F. (2000). *Sex differences in cognitive abilities* (3rd ed.). Mahwah, NJ: Lawrence Erlbaum Associates.

Hyde, J. S. (2005). The gender similarities hypothesis. *American Psychologist, 60*(6), 581-592.

Kafer, K. (2007, April). *Taking the boy crisis in education seriously: How school choice can boost achievement among boys and girls* (Position Paper No. 604). Washington, DC: Women for School Choice: Independent Women's Forum.

James, A. N. (2007). *Teaching the male brain: How boys think, feel, and learn in school*. Thousand Oaks, CA: Corwin Press.

Leech, M. (2005, November 21). Shelby considers same-sex classes. *The Birmingham News*, 1A.

Mael, F., Alonso, A., Gibson, D., Rogers, K., & Smith, M. (2005). *Single-sex versus coeducational schooling: A systematic review*. Washington, DC: U.S. Department of Education, Office of Planning, Evaluation and Policy Development, Policy and Program Studies Service.

Mead, S. (2006, June). *The truth about boys and girls*. Washington, DC: Education Sector.

Moore, M., Piper, V., & Schaefer, E. (1993). Single-sex schooling and educational effectiveness: A research overview. In D. K. Hollinger (Ed.), *Single-sex schooling: Perspectives from practice and research* (pp. 7-68). Washington, DC: U.S. Department of Education.

National Association for Single Sex Public Education. (2009). *Single-sex schools/Single sex classrooms: What's the difference?* Retrieved from http://www.singlesexschools.org/schools-classrooms.htm

National Center for Education Statistics. (2005). *The nation's report card: NAEP 2004 trends in academic progress*. Washington, DC: U.S. Department of Education. Retrieved from http://nces.ed.gov/nationsreportcard/pdf/main2005/2005464.pdf

National Coalition for Women and Girls in Education. (2002). *Single-sex notice of intent comments*. Retrieved from http://www.ncwge.org/PDF/SingleSex-7-11-02.pdf

Newkirk, T. (2002). *Misreading masculinity: Boys, literacy, and popular culture*. Portsmouth, NH: Heinemann.

Riordan, C. (2002). What do we know about the effects of single-sex schools in the private sector?: Implications for public schools. In A. Datnow & L. Hubbard (Eds.), *Gender in policy and practice* (pp. 10-30). New York: Routledge.

Sadker, D. (2002). An educator's primer on the gender war. *Phi Delta Kappan, 84*(3), 235-240, 244.

Sadker, D., & Zittleman, K. (2004, April 8). Single-sex schools: A good idea gone wrong? *The Christian Science Monitor*. Retrieved from http://www.csmonitor.com/2004/0408/p09s02-coop.html

Salomone, R. C. (2003). *Same, different, equal: Rethinking single-sex schooling*. New Haven, CT: Yale University Press.

Salomone, R. C. (2006a). Putting single-sex schooling back on course. *Education Week, 26*(14), 32-33, 44.

Salomone, R. C. (2006b). Single-sex programs: Resolving the research conundrum. *Teachers College Record, 108*(4), 778-802.

Sax, L. (n.d.). *Department of Education study is "seriously flawed."* Retrieved 2007, from http://www.singlesexschools.org/EdDeptStudy.htm

Smithers, A., & Robinson, P. (2006). *The paradox of single-sex and co-educational schooling*. University of Buckingham, Center for Education and Employment Research. Retrieved from http://www.buckingham.ac.uk/education/research/ceer/pdfs/hmcsscd.pdf

Sylwester, R. (2005). *Single-sex classrooms*. Retrieved from http://www.yece.org/
Single%20sex%20classroom.htm

U.S. Department of Education. (2006). *Nondiscrimination on the basis of sex in education programs
or activities receiving federal financial assistance*. Washington, DC: U.S. Department
of Education, Office for Civil Rights. Retrieved from http://www.ed.gov/legislation/
FedRegister/finrule/2006-4/102506a.html

Viadero, D. (2006, March 15). Concern over gender gaps shifting to boys. *Education Week, 25*(27),
1, 16-17.

Younger, M. & Warrington, M. (2005). *Raising boys' achievement*. Retrieved from http://www.dfes.
gov.uk/research/data/uploadfiles/RR636.pdf

Implications for Our School: Questions for Discussion and Reflection

- Would single-sex classrooms be an effective way to address the following challenges in our school: (1) differing learning styles of male and female students; (2) behavior problems; (3) lagging achievement by boys; or (4) girls' difficulties taking leadership roles in classrooms?

- For what classes or grade levels in our school might single-sex classes be the most appropriate and beneficial?

- What training might teachers need to implement single-sex classes most effectively?

- As an alternative, would it be helpful for teachers to have development/discussion opportunities focused on diversifying instruction to better meet the learning needs of a wide range of students?

Follow-up and Action Items

_____

_____

_____

_____

_____

_____

_____

_____

_____

_____

_____

_____

_____

Section IV

Providing Effective Principal Leadership

Chapter 18

Using Classroom Walkthroughs to Improve Instruction

Frequent classroom visits focused on specific "look-fors"
can provide valuable information about what's working—
or not working—in your school.

A program of brief but frequent classroom walkthroughs has become an increasingly popular strategy in recent years. While the practice typically began with principals routinely visiting classrooms to observe teaching, it has expanded to include opportunities for teachers to be part of teams that visit classrooms. These visits—and the "data" collected from them through discussions after the walkthroughs—are not meant to impact the evaluations of individual teachers. Instead, they are intended to help school staff get a sense of how instruction is happening throughout the building.

But what is it about walkthroughs that can help improve a school's instructional program? And, are there elements of the process that should receive special attention in order to maximize their effectiveness? While there has not been extensive research done on walkthroughs, the experiences of schools that have introduced the practice help to address both these questions.

Why Use Classroom Walkthroughs?

What is the purpose of classroom walkthroughs? Cervone and Martinez-Miller (2007) talk about classroom walkthroughs as a tool to "drive a cycle of continuous improvement by *focusing on the effects of instruction.*" Principal John Skretta, who uses walkthroughs, sees their greatest value is in the collection of data that "can be used to prompt and provoke dialogue about instruction" (2007, p. 17). Ginsberg and Murphy talk about some specific benefits for principals, but also note that administrator-teacher walkthrough teams provide similar benefits for staff in general:

- "Administrators become more familiar with the school's curriculum and teachers' instructional practices.

- Administrators can gauge the climate of a school: Are students engaged? Are cross-curricular concepts a part of everyday teaching? Are new teachers catching on?

- A team atmosphere develops as teachers and administrators examine instruction and student motivation and achievement together. …

- Students see that both administrators and teachers value instruction and learning" (2002, p. 35).

What Do Walkthroughs Look Like?

Perry describes the approach as different from an observation that focuses on one classroom because its intent is to create "a schoolwide picture made up of many small snapshots . . . It's a strategy for providing a school, not an individual teacher, with feedback about what it's doing or not doing" (in Richardson, 2001). Teams at one school with which Perry works go through the building about once a week; teams include the principal and an assistant principal, plus three or four teachers who rotate on and off the team.

These walkthroughs follow a specific protocol, with time spent before the walkthrough to identify and discuss the focus of the observations and followed up by a "debriefing" discussion among team members to identify elements that should be shared with teachers. Perry describes the process:

> Preparing for a walkthrough to gauge the school's progress on that goal, the visitors would assemble in the principal's office for about 30 minutes and discuss what they would expect to find…. Before going into the classroom, visitors would be assigned a specific task. For example, one visitor might be assigned to note whether and what types of student writing are displayed in the room, another to write down what is written on the chalkboard, and another to pull aside one or two students to learn what they understand about the writing process…. After leaving each classroom, the team of visitors goes down the hall a short way and spends about five minutes comparing notes. After visiting all of the classrooms for that day, the visitors assemble and spend about 45 minutes going over the evidence they have collected. (in Richardson, 2001)

Key Elements of the Process

Perry's description makes it clear that observers—whether they are principals, teachers, or people from outside the school—are not simply wandering from classroom to classroom to gather general perceptions of what is going on. The carefully planned nature of the process is critical to its success, with three elements—identifying a focus for the observations, short but frequent visits to classrooms, and data analysis and reflection after the walkthrough—especially important.

Identifying the Focus of the Observations

Effective walkthroughs have a purpose. One principal talks about the quick but purposeful walks that target "specific things that we are looking for" (Miller, in Hopkins, 2008). For example, "one week they might be looking to learn *Is the objective of the lesson clear to the students?*…. The following week they might [ask] *What instructional strategy is the teacher using? Is this an appropriate strategy to use with the lesson?*" (Hopkins, 2008).

One approach to walkarounds calls the focus of the observation "look-fors"—"specific descriptors of conditions that when present in classrooms enable students to improve their achievement and learning levels" (Graf & Werlinich, n.d.a, pp. 4-5). Identifying them can provide a powerful—and collaborative—

opportunity for teachers and school leaders to address questions such as: "When we visit classrooms, what should we see that makes an important difference in student success? Is there something that we should see in every classroom?" (Graf & Werlinich, n.d.a, p. 15).

Preparing for a Walkthrough—One Approach

- What is the *focus* of the walkthrough?

- What are two *primary* questions that will be addressed?

- Five *clarifying* questions (to be answered in relation to the focus)

  —What will you expect to see on the walls and around the learning areas?
  —What will you expect to see adults doing?
  —What will you expect to see students doing?
  —What language do you expect to hear adults using?
  —What language do you expect to hear students using? (Baltimore Achievement First Schools, n.d.).

Visits to Classrooms

Many of the walkthrough protocols involve very short—as short as 5 minutes and typically no longer than 15 minutes—visits to the classroom. In Johnston's view, they should be a "scheduled part of the daily routine" (2003). Downey, Steffy, English, Frase, and Poston (2004) have developed a "3-minute classroom walk-through" model that includes five steps:

- Notice whether students appear to be oriented to the work.

- Review the curricular objectives being taught.

- Observe instructional practices.

- "Walk the walls" to look for information on what has been taught previously or may be taught in the future.

- Note the existence of any safety or health issues.

Other models have observers spending more time in each classroom and so provide "to-do's" for participants that may include, for example, time to talk with students.

Reflection After the Walkthrough

Love (2009) talks about opportunities for collaborative inquiry by school staff—especially among teachers—as a structure that helps develop a focus on what is working and what is not in terms of teaching and learning. Reflection after walkthroughs is built around that concept. Principal John Skretta talks about this:

The best walkthroughs give teachers relevant, real-time data on their instruction.... Feedback on the walkthroughs should be specific to observed behaviors, focused, and descriptive of the level of performance observed. (2007, p. 18)

One organization promoting the use of classroom walkthroughs discusses the type of reflective practice needed if classroom walkthroughs are to significantly impact teaching. It requires:

- A deliberate pause in the often-hurried pace of teachers and school leaders;

- Establishing a purposeful time for a close look at the "data" that have been collected;

- A willingness to be open to other points of view;

- An effort to consciously process your own thoughts—not simply leaving the classroom with general impressions;

- An intentional effort to gain new insights and understandings from both the observation and the analysis of data; and,

- Action based on the findings of the observations (Teachscape, 2007).

Four Debriefing Tools for Sharing Observations From Walkthoughs

- **Oral Feedback.** Provide verbal feedback to teachers about something observed during the walkthrough. Be specific and connect the feedback to "look-fors" or elements of effective instruction.

- **Written Feedback.** Write a general narrative about what was observed during the walk-through and distribute the information to the entire staff. The narrative includes specific examples (without identifying the specific teacher or classroom) and evidence of how "look-fors" are present in the school. Short email notes to individual teachers can be very effective also.

- **Faculty Meeting.** Conduct a short meeting to debrief the faculty immediately after completing the walkthrough. ...This meeting begins with a general overview of effective practices observed during the walkthrough and specific evidence of "look-fors" employed in classrooms. Feedback is focused on what is present in the school and not on individual teachers.

- **Study Groups.** Form small learning communities. Provide the time and resources for teachers to meet and discuss instruction and learning. Study groups can explore new strategies/research, share best practices and engage in action research projects in classrooms.

Excerpted from Graf & Werlinich, n.d.a, p. 12.

Experiences of Schools Using Walkthroughs

Rossi (2007) and Keruskin (2005) each used the walkthrough observation process developed by Graf and Werlinich (n.d.b) as the basis for their dissertation research. At the elementary school level, Rossi (2007) found staff members believed the walkthroughs conducted in their schools had affected instruction. Positive outcomes included:

- Teacher sharing of best practices;

- Increased principal awareness of what is happening in classrooms;

- Increase in teacher time on task;

- Better principal understanding of curriculum gaps and inconsistencies;

- Better principal understanding of professional development needs;

- Improvement in the quality of student work;

- Improved quality of conversations about instruction; and,

- Development of a common language around instruction.

Keruskin (2005) found similar opinions among high school staff:

- Look-fors improve instruction. Walkthroughs are a tool to make sure teachers are focusing on the look-fors.

- The habit (look-fors) starts to permeate the classrooms and the school.

- Teachers are practicing the look-fors defined at the beginning of the year.

- Last year's look-fors are old news; they have become habits.

- Current data collected in classrooms helps principals to focus on professional development days.

- There is collaboration of best practices and observing of those practices throughout the school.

- Change in student achievement is dramatic (p. 107).

One Kentucky school instituted a plan to conduct an ambitious program of classroom walkthroughs and was pleased with its impact on teaching; specifically, "every 'look for' item . . . showed growth from the first quarter through the fourth quarter" (Granada & Vriesenga, 2008, p. 27).

Skretta and Fisher talk about the impact of walkthroughs in their high school: "Informal classroom observations translate to improved student achievement by using the observations as opportunities to develop a common language for instruction and to promote meaningful dialogue about instruction" (2002, p. 39). They elaborate on this:

At Northeast, the anecdotal feedback enabled us to discuss what we consistently observed in classrooms, thus informing school improvement efforts. For example, walkthrough observations provided evidence that instructional practice was highly auditory in nature with little shift in modalities to increase engagement for different learning styles. Teachers seldom mixed small group activities or visual components with straight lecture formats. Observers also noted that assigned readings were typically short, silent passages followed by textbook questions to confirm comprehension. After these observations, efforts to identify appropriate staff development were seen through a new lens, the lens of an instructionally focused administrative team. The results included staff development in questioning strategies, learning modalities, and the use of graphic organizers to promote reading comprehension. (2002, p. 41)

Finally, one of the elementary school principals interviewed by Rossi was very specific about a benefit to him personally of using walkthroughs in his school:

The more opportunities I have to get into the classrooms, the more information I have to talk with teachers about and the more that we collectively research good practice and talk about good practice and tap in on each others' experiences and practices. ...They [don't just] come to talk with me about discipline problems, they come to talk about instruction. (Rossi, 2007, p. 96)

In Summary

Graf and Werlinich have these suggestions for principals in schools that are considering implementing a program of walkthroughs:

- Conduct a preliminary walkthrough to begin collecting baseline data around a wide spectrum of effective instructional practices.

- Conduct a walkthrough meeting with the staff. This meeting sets the stage for the walkthrough and helps to establish clear expectations for the staff related to the purpose and process of a walkthrough.

- Establish a focus for subsequent walkthroughs. Work collaboratively with teachers to identify the specific elements of effective instruction or guiding principles of learning that you wish to target for implementation—the "look-fors." This step creates clear expectations for the teachers and helps build commitment to the process.

- Connect the "look-fors" to established standards. This is an important step with respect to developing a common language for staff and for establishing a matching set of indicators around instruction and learning. (Excerpted from Graf & Werlinich, n.d.a, p. 8.)

Finally, be sure when beginning a program of walkthroughs to recognize the importance of trust and to making teachers feel comfortable during the classroom visits (Salter & Walker, 2008, p. 4). It needs to be clear that the walkthroughs are meant to provide a general picture of instruction schoolwide, not gather data for teacher evaluation.

References

Baltimore Achievement First. (n.d.). *The walkthrough: A strategy for providing instructional leadership*. Retrieved from http://www.schools.utah.gov/charterschools/training/2008-2009/PovidingLeadershipWalkthrough.pdf

Cervone, L., & Martinez-Miller, P. (2007, Summer). Classroom walkthroughs as a catalyst for school improvement. *Leadership Compass*. Retrieved from http://www.naesp.org/resources/2/Leadership_Compass/2007/LC2007v4n4a2.pdf

Downey, C. J., Steffy, B. E., English, F. W., Frase, L. E., & Poston, W. K. (2004). *The three-minute classroom walkthrough: Changing school supervisory practice one teacher at a time*. Thousand Oaks, CA: Corwin Press.

Ginsberg, M. B., & Murphy, D. (2002, May). How walkthroughs open doors. *Educational Leadership*, 34-36.

Graf, O., & Werlinich, J. (n.d.a). *Observation frustrations. Is there another way?: The walkthrough observation tool*. Retrieved from https://qcc.wikispaces.com/file/view/Walkthroughs+-Observation+Frustrations.pdf

Graf, O., & Werlinich, J. (n.d.b). *Walkthroughs: One vehicle to promote student learning*. Retrieved from http://www.iu1.k12.pa.us/iss/files/walkthrough/walkthrough_31.pps

Granada, J., & Vriesenga, M. (2008, March). Web-based walk-throughs. *Principal Leadership, 24-27.*

Hopkins, G. (2008). Walk-throughs are on the move. *Education World*. Retrieved from http://www.education-world.com/a_admin/admin/admin405.shtml

Johnston, H. (2003). Leadership by walking around: Walkthroughs and instructional improvement. *The Principals' Partnership*. Retrieved from http://www.principalspartnership.com/feature203.html

Keruskin, T. E. (2005). *The perceptions of high school principals on student achievement by conducting walkthroughs* (Doctoral dissertation. University of Pittsburgh). Retrieved from http://etd.library.pitt.edu/ETD/available/etd-09022005-081109/unrestricted/KeruskinToddAugust2005.pdf

Love, N. (Ed.). (2009). *Using data to improve learning: A collaborative inquiry approach*. Thousand Oaks, CA: Corwin Press.

Richardson, J. (2001, October/November). Seeing through new eyes. *Tools for Schools*. Retrieved from http://www.nsdc.org/library/publications/tools/tools10-01rich.cfm

Rossi, G.A. (2007). *The classroom walkthrough: The perceptions of elementary school principals on its impact on student achievement* (Doctoral dissertation. University of Pittsburgh). Retrieved from http://etd.library.pitt.edu/ETD/available/etd-07292007-140309/unrestricted/Rossi_ETD_7-29-07.pdf

Salter, S., & Walker, M. (2008). *Leading staff renewal through instructional leadership strategies of Looking at Student Work protocols and principal-led walkthroughs*. Retrieved from http://www.acel.org.au/fileadmin/user_upload/documents/conference_2008/papers/Salter-Walker.doc

Skretta, J. (2007, May). Using walkthroughs to gather data for school improvement. *Principal Leadership*, 16-23.

Skretta, J., & Fisher, V. (2002, November). The walk-through crew. *Principal Leadership*, 39-41.

Teachscape. (2007). *Classroom walkthrough with reflective practice*. A presentation to the Florida School Leaders.

Implications for Our School: Questions for Discussion and Reflection

- How could we integrate time into the schedule to conduct regular classroom walkthroughs in our school? What current activity would these replace or what additional resources would we need?

- Who should be involved in classroom walkthroughs? How would such an activity fit into our current professional learning programs?

- What instructional practices are important "look-fors" in our classroom walkthroughs? Do we believe that we use these practices consistently in our classrooms?

- How will we share the observations from the walkthroughs? And how will we use the findings to impact teacher development?

Follow-up and Action Items

_____

_____

_____

_____

_____

_____

_____

_____

_____

_____

_____

_____

Chapter 19
The School-Family Connection

Increasing diversity of student backgrounds makes building a strong school-family connection more challenging—but also more important—for today's schools than those of a decade ago.

Research on family connections with schools has demonstrated that parents are interested in their children's academic success regardless of ethnicity, culture, or economic status. When this interest is translated into support such as talking about school at the dinner table or encouraging their children to do well in school, students benefit. It is also clear that, when families are actively involved in schools, teachers learn more about students in their classes and are better able to provide appropriate educational services for them. Working together, educators and families can ensure students are ready and able to learn—and thus more likely to benefit from high-quality learning experiences (Caplan, 2001).

What Do We Know About Family Involvement?

It is clear family support for the academic side of students' lives is important. But has research demonstrated a link between family involvement with schools and academic achievement? While reviews of the research present the link as both direct and positive, the answer to the question needs to be more than a simple yes or no. As with much research focused on educational issues, it is difficult to isolate the variables related to student achievement. There is also a problem with definition of variables such as involvement. For example, how should they be defined and measured?

Henderson has conducted periodic reviews of research on parent involvement and student achievement. In 2002, she partnered with Mapp to develop an updated overview. Their analysis found:

> Taken as a whole, these studies found a positive and convincing relationship between family involvement and benefits for students, including improved academic achievement. This relationship holds across families of all economic, racial/ethnic, and educational backgrounds and for students at all ages…. [However,] while the effect sizes in many of these studies are statistically significant, they are small to moderate. A number of studies found that some forms of parent involvement with the school (communications with school, volunteering, attending school events, parent-parent connections) appeared to have little effect on student achievement, especially in high school. (Henderson & Mapp, 2002, p. 24)

Walberg and Paik, in their review of practices that research has identified as positively connected with improved student achievement, include this finding: "Learning is enhanced when schools encourage parents to stimulate their children's intellectual achievement" (2004, p. 27). Family practices identified as important include such things as:

> parent-child conversations about school and everyday events; encouragement and discussion of leisure reading; monitoring and critical review of television viewing and peer activities; deferral of immediate gratification to accomplish long-term goals; expressions of affection and interest in the child's academic and other progress as a person; and, perhaps, among such other unremitting efforts, laughter, caprice, and serendipity. In the years before school, reading to and with the child and animated discussion of everyday events prepare children for academic activities in school. (p. 27)

Redding conducted a similar review of the research, although with a more narrow focus on the home-school connection, and also identified contributions the "curriculum of the home" can make to student achievement. His conclusions highlight information important to all schools—but particularly to schools working with students typically considered to be more at risk of school-related problems:

> Research on the family's influence on school learning has a substantial history, and we can settle upon basic premises with great confidence. *With reasonable certainty we can state that poverty may statistically predict lower school performance, yet families that provide a stimulating, language-rich, supportive environment defy the odds of socioeconomic circumstance* [emphasis added]. In other words, an alterable "curriculum of the home"—including the family's relationships, practices and patterns of life—is a more powerful predictor of academic learning than the family's status. Schools can work with families to improve the curriculum of the home, regardless of the family's economic situation. This, then, is a message of great hope. (2000, p. 5)

> *"Research shows that schools can improve their students' learning by engaging parents in ways that directly relate to their children's academic progress, maintaining a consistent message of what is expected of parents, and reaching parents directly, personally, and with a trusting approach." (Perlman & Redding, 2009, p. 185)*

The Role Schools and Teachers Play

The research already discussed has highlighted both the positive relationship found between some types of parent involvement and student achievement. Research also links this information to the role teachers and other educators can play in encouraging parent involvement and in providing parents with knowledge and skills demonstrated to provide academic support for students.

For example, research repeatedly has identified the importance of a positive, welcoming school climate—and, in particular, the role of the principal in establishing such a climate—to providing a strong foundation for family involvement. In their summary of research about factors affecting parent involvement, Hoover-Dempsey et al. report on Griffith's finding that this is "especially important in schools serving families of children at higher risk for poor educational outcomes" (2005, p. 111).

Findings from a study conducted by EdSource found a relationship between school efforts to involve parents and student achievement and also identified some school practices that seemed to make a difference. Specifically, "practices that correlated positively with school performance were the frequency of special subject area (like math or English language arts) events held at a school and the frequency with which parents provide instructional support in classrooms" (2005). These efforts to involve parents more directly with their children's education correlated more strongly with achievement than other efforts to involve parents with the school. The study also found "a positive correlation also emerged for schools whose teachers reported most strongly that . . . their principal builds strong relationships with parents" (2005).

Henderson and Mapp's review of research also addressed the role of schools in helping parents involve themselves productively with their children's education. They found parent involvement:

> that is linked to student learning has a greater effect on achievement than more general forms of involvement. To be effective, the form of involvement should be focused on improving achievement and be designed to engage families and students in developing specific knowledge and skills. (2002, p. 38)

Henderson and Mapp also found schools could help prepare parents to better fill these roles. For example, workshops for Title I parents in one elementary school included updates on children's progress, distribution of reading and math learning packets plus training in how to use them, and training for parents on topics such as increasing a child's vocabulary.

> *"Family engagement has the most impact when it is directly linked to learning." (Westmoreland, Rosenberg, Lopez, & Weiss, 2009, p. 2)*

Teacher Impact on Parent Involvement

To many parents, their children's teacher—the person with whom they have the most direct contact—plays a critical role in establishing the nature of the home-school connection. In an overview of research on the topic of parent involvement, Hoover-Dempsey et al. found:

> Teacher invitations are especially powerful because they are responsive to many parents' expressed wishes to know more about *how* to support children's learning . . . [They] also enhance parents' sense of being welcome to participate in school processes, knowledge of

their children's learning, and confidence that their involvement efforts are useful and valued . . . [In addition, they] contribute to the development of trust in the parent-teacher relationship, a quality of an effective parent school partnership. (2005, p. 111)

Henderson and Mapp report on a study conducted by Westat and Policy Studies Associates that found students made "greater and more consistent gains when teachers were 'especially active' in outreach to parents" (Henderson & Mapp, 2002, pp. 38-39). This included teacher behaviors such as "meeting with parents face to face, sending materials on ways to help their child at home, and telephoning both routinely and when their child is having problems" (p. 39).

Further evidence that teacher efforts to involve parents can have a positive impact on student learning was found in a U.S. Department of Education study of 71 high-poverty schools. In the study, students were followed as they moved from third though fifth grades. For both reading and math, growth in scores of low-achieving students increased substantially more—50% higher in reading and 40% higher in math—for students with third-grade teachers reporting high levels of parental outreach through third grade, especially early in the year, than those with teachers reporting average levels of effort. The researchers working on the project hypothesized that "when teachers involved low-achieving students' parents early on, students were able to resolve their learning difficulties before they multiplied" (Westat and Policy Studies Associates, 2001, p. 13).

The Importance of Two-Way Communication

"Students do best when parents and teachers understand each other's expectations and stay in touch with one another regarding the child's learning habits, attitudes toward school, social interactions and academic progress. ...Communication between the school and the home is most effective when it flows in both directions, and schools should distinguish between efforts to inform parents and opportunities to communicate with parents." (Redding, 2000, p. 17)

What Should Family Involvement Look Like?

Both research and the day-to-day experiences of teachers support the belief that close connections between schools and students' families support student learning. For many educators, this connection and the accompanying parent involvement with schools often have been defined in traditional terms. Thus, "good" parents come to parent-teacher conferences, help their children with homework, and attend PTA meetings.

The term "family involvement" with schools and schooling, however, can refer to many additional forms of activity. Cotton and Wikelund describe some forms family involvement can take:

Parents can support their children's schooling by attending school functions and responding to school obligations (parent-teacher conferences, for example). They can become more involved in helping their children improve their schoolwork—providing encouragement, arranging for appropriate study time and space, modeling desired behavior (such as reading for pleasure), monitoring homework, and actively tutoring their children at home.

Outside the home, parents can serve as advocates for the school. They can volunteer to help out with school activities or work in the classroom. Or they can take an active role in the governance and decision making necessary for planning, developing, and providing an education for the community's children. (2001)

Research already discussed has identified some actions and attitudes parents can take that are linked with high student achievement. For example, expressing high expectations for their children and setting aside time and a place to do homework both have correlational relationships with student achievement. The Prichard Committee for Academic Excellence has identified some important out-of-school ways families can effectively support student learning:

- establish a daily routine;

- monitor their children's out-of-school activities;

- model the value of learning, self-discipline, and hard work;

- encourage their learning and progress in school and stay in touch with their teachers;

- read, write, and have frequent conversations; and,

- use community resources like libraries, recreation centers, after-school programs, family resource centers, clinics, etc. (2002).

Barriers to Family Involvement

While the benefits of family involvement in education are well recognized, school-home relationships can be fraught with tensions and challenges. Teachers and family members may share a desire to educate children, but they do not always agree on how best to accomplish that goal. While parents believe schools see them as important partners, they also express the opinion that schools need to learn ways to involve them more effectively (National Opinion Research Center, 1997).

Clearly, there are factors that significantly affect parents' ability or willingness to forge close bonds with schools. For example:

- "Some parents can't read or are functionally illiterate. Or, they can't communicate in English. They are embarrassed to come to school and interact with educators because they lack, or may believe they lack, these necessary communication skills.... Parents may be intimidated by new, unfamiliar course content, higher expectations for learning and computer technology. Their response may be to do nothing" (U.S. Department of Education and U.S. Department of Health and Human Services, 1999, pp. 10-11).

- Parents "who have bad memories about their own experiences in school may have trouble helping their children with schoolwork, especially in subject areas that they themselves did not master" (Funkhouser & Gonzales, 1997).

- Some parents are already overwhelmed by other day-to-day realities of their families' lives. Such parents feel they can't do another thing, or they may lack time, child care, and transportation (American Association of School Administrators, 1998).

Some families may care deeply about their children's educational success and—from their perspective—be actively supportive and involved, but seem to teachers and other educators to remain detached from the school community. For example, Lopez, Scribner, and Mahitivanichcha suggest that when educators define parent involvement in traditional ways—attendance at PTA meetings or helping with math homework—this can lead to the assumption that parents who are not involved in these ways "lack the capacity to provide adequate home learning environments for their children" (2001, pp. 256-257).

But this assumption often is inaccurate. Garcia-Coll talks about her findings from her study of Dominican, Cambodian, and Portuguese parents. In all three groups:

> A majority of the parents reported high aspirations for their children's future and recognized the importance of education in meeting those aspirations. (in Cole, n.d)

Often, these aspirations are backed up with substantial support—although the support might not fit many educators' definition of parent involvement. For example, Lopez interviewed immigrant families with children whom school personnel identified as highly successful in school and found these families viewed involvement as "teaching their children to appreciate the value of education through the medium of hard work" (2001, p. 422). However, he also found that "seen through a traditional academic lens, [such families] appear to be largely 'uninvolved' in their children's education" (2001, pp. 425-426).

Schoolwide Approaches to Strengthening the Home-School Connection

Although it is obvious that interaction with a teacher who is perceived as welcoming and supportive can encourage parents to make an active connection with a school, Funkhouser and Gonzales make an important point:

> Developing a successful school-family partnership must be a whole school endeavor, not the work of a single person or program. (1997)

Ferguson summarizes themes found in recent research on the school-family connection and identifies some school characteristics and actions that support effective connections:

- *Sense of Welcome.* When school-family partnerships are characterized by a sense of welcome, they incorporate processes that foster relationships between educators and noneducators, allowing all involved to discover that each family member, no matter the background or ability, can engage in supporting a child's education in meaningful ways.

- *Misconceptions Among Stakeholders.* Effective efforts to engage families use strategies that reveal and confront misconceptions that blind both school staff and families to the roles families can play in ensuring that all children reach their full potential academically, emotionally, physically, and socially.

- *Use of and Issues Related to Resources.* As those involved target their resources and identify additional resources to support student learning, they will increase involvement and create opportunities for effective engagement for family members.

- *Home Context and Student Performance.* Effective school-family connections prepare educators and noneducators to engage in two-way partnerships that uncover contextual barriers to purposeful family involvement while simultaneously creating opportunities to encourage and maintain family support for student learning.

- *Program Structures.* Structures that effectively support school-family connections avoid isolated family involvement events by adopting a systemic approach to preparing both educators and noneducators to take on roles that ensure that the academic, emotional, physical, and social needs of all students are met.

- *Roles of Those Involved in School-Family Connections.* By building the self-efficacy of those involved in these efforts for the roles they need to take on, effective school-family programs create a groundswell of support to meet student needs as well as create the foundation for long-term, systemic improvements. (Excerpted from Ferguson, 2008, pp. 23-24.)

This list makes it clear that educators are likely to find they will need to do more than simply increase the intensity of their current efforts to involve families. McCollum speaks of the need to focus on "valuing, not changing parents." He expands on this:

> Most programs for parent involvement are centered upon the premise that parents need to be changed in order to teach them how to work successfully with their own children. Unfortunately, this approach is a deficit approach that ignores that parents from culturally diverse backgrounds, as well as working-class parents, may have ways of interacting with their children that support learning, yet differ from the patterns exhibited by U.S. middle-class parents. (1996)

Redding suggests that many of these seemingly noninvolved parents—especially those from different cultures—will need more than programs. They must first be "engaged within a nonthreatening, positive, and supportive social context" (Redding, 2000, pp. 24-25). Successful school efforts to build family-school partnerships "are not stand-alone, add-on programs. Instead, they are well integrated with the school's overall mission" (Center for Comprehensive School Reform and Improvement, 2005).

The Teacher's Role in Building Relationships

Research identifying the important role teachers play in strengthening the home-school link has already been highlighted here. It is simply human nature for parents to feel more comfortable with teachers they view as welcoming, supportive of their children, and appreciative of the role parents play in children's education. But establishing and maintaining this relationship is often complicated and requires skill as well as perseverance.

So what are some concrete ways teachers can work to strengthen home-school connections within the framework of already jam-packed days? The most important component for success may be attitude, and ensuring that at least some of the school-to-home communication includes "good news" may play a key role. Because research has identified a tendency in schools serving low-income students to make more contacts with families about problems children are having, it is especially important for teachers in such schools to create opportunities for positive communication (Epstein, 1995).

> *"Communicating with parents regularly is an important way to engage them in the life of a school. But too often contact with a parent occurs only when a student is in trouble or does poorly in class." (KSA-Plus Communications, 2000, p. 9)*

Boethel addresses another critical issue—that of some parents' lack of familiarity with schools that may be accompanied by a lack of comfort when dealing with teachers and other school personnel. To help address this potential problem, she advises teachers to "think of school as a small country, with its own patterns of behavior and unwritten, as well as formal, rules and expectations" (2003). The problem for many families may be that these patterns of behavior, rules, and expectations are foreign to them. By keeping this in mind—and by taking advantage of opportunities to educate families about the culture of the school—teachers can help increase the comfort level of parents and other family members.

Lustberg provides guidance for teachers when she goes to the heart of the issue for many families:

> Of all the types of involvement the one most parents want to know about is: How do I help my own child at home? Although this request is at the top of parents' wish lists, it is also the hardest to make happen because it requires teachers at all grade levels to continually communicate with families on how to assist learning at home. (1999)

Thus, the most obvious place for teachers to start their efforts to increase family involvement is at the family-child level. Caplan (1998) suggests teachers answer key questions the parents may have—such as, "Should I help my third-grader correct her math homework or should I leave the mistakes for her teacher to see?"—during back-to-school night programs or in newsletters. Teachers can ask parents to help them brainstorm a list of common questions and build on this list from year to year.

Finally, research has repeatedly demonstrated the strong link between family expectations and student achievement. When children know their families believe they can do well in school, they are likely to rise to these expectations (Thorkildsen & Scott-Stein, 1998). By communicating this simple but powerful concept to parents, teachers support students, their families, and the learning process.

In Summary

Although most schools—and especially teachers—put great effort into communicating and engaging parents in the educational process, frustration often remains among educators at the seeming low levels of involvement shown by many parents. However, a key may be stepping back and asking some crucial questions. For example, do we need to know more about how parents with whom we work view their role in education? Are we using what we know to design and implement approaches to serve the needs of families, their children, and the schools? The oft-used phrase "work smarter, not harder" aptly describes what may need to be done in many schools.

In Christenson's view, effective home-school collaboration begins with "an attitude, not an activity." It:

> occurs when parents and educators share common goals, are seen as equals, and both contribute to the process. It is sustained with a "want to" motivation rather than an "ought to" or "obliged to" orientation from all individuals…. Home-school collaboration is establishment of a mutual goal between educators and parents to create an ethos for learning. Home-school collaboration occurs when parents are seen as key resources who work to improve their own children's education and the education of all children. (n.d.)

Thus, the challenge for educators is to identify and build on already-existing family attitudes and behaviors that support student learning. While this does not mean, for example, abandoning efforts to increase participation in parent-teacher groups, it sometimes will require expanding our definition of "good" parenting and parent involvement.

References

American Association of School Administrators. (1998, Spring). Promoting parent involvement. *Leaders' Edge*, 2.

Boethel, M. (2003). *Diversity: School, family, & community connections*. Austin, TX: Southwest Educational Development Laboratory. Retrieved from http://www.sedl.org/connections/resources/diversity-synthesis.pdf

Caplan, J. (1998). *Critical issue: Constructing school partnerships with families and community groups*. Oak Brook, IL: North Central Regional Educational Laboratory. Retrieved from http://www.ncrel.org/sdrs/areas/issues/envrnmnt/famncomm/pa400.htm

Caplan, J. (2001). *Essentials for principals: Strengthening the connection between school and home*. Arlington, VA: Educational Research Service.

Center for Comprehensive School Reform and Improvement. (2005, August). *Meeting the challenge: Getting parents involved in schools*. Retrieved from http://www.centerforcsri.org

Christenson, S. L. (n.d.). *Home-school collaboration: Building effective parent-school partnerships*. Retrieved from http://www.cyfc.umn.edu/Learn/home.html

Cole, K. (n.d.). Study finds barriers to immigrants' involvement in their children's education. *George Street Journal*. Retrieved from http://www.brown.edu/Administration/News_Bureau/2000-01/00-124.html

Cotton, K., & Wikelund, K. R. (2001). Parent involvement in education. *School Improvement Research Series*. Retrieved from http://www.nwrel.org/scpd/sirs/3/cu6.html

EdSource. (2005). *Frequently asked questions about parent involvement*. Retrieved from http://www.edsource.org/pre_hrp05parent_faq.cfm

Epstein, J. L. (1995, May). School/family/community partnerships: Caring for the children we share. *Phi Delta Kappan*, 701-712.

Ferguson, C. (2008). *The family-school connection—Looking at the larger picture: A review of current literature*. Austin, TX: National Center for Family and Community Connections with Schools. Retrieved from http://www.sedl.org/connections/resources/sfclitrev.pdf

Funkhouser, J. E., & Gonzales, M. R. (1997). *Family involvement in children's education: Successful local approaches—An idea book*. Washington, DC: Office of Educational Research and Improvement. Retrieved from http://www.ed.gov/pubs/FamInvolve/index.html

Henderson, A. T., & Mapp, K. L. (2002). *A new wave of evidence: The impact of school, family, and community connections on student achievement*. Austin, TX: National Center for Family and Community Connections with Schools, Southwest Educational Development Laboratory. Retrieved from http://www.sedl.org/connections/research-syntheses.html

Hoover-Dempsey, K. V., Walker, J. M. T., Sandler, H. M., Whetsel, D., Green, C. L., Wilkins, A. S., et al. (2005, November). Why do parents become involved? Research findings and implications. *The Elementary School Journal*, *106*(2), 105-130. Retrieved from http://www.vanderbilt.edu/Peabody/family-school/papers/Hoover-Dempsey2005.pdf

KSA-Plus Communications. (2000). *Family and community involvement: Reaching out to diverse populations*. Austin, TX: Southwest Educational Development Laboratory.

Lopez, G. R. (2001, Fall). The value of hard work. *Harvard Educational Review*, 416-437.

Lopez, G. R., Scribner, J. D., & Mahitivanichcha, K. (2001, Summer). Redefining parental involvement: Lessons from high-performing migrant-impacted schools. *American Educational Research Journal*, 253-88.

Lustberg, M. (1999). *Partnering with parents to foster learning at home*. New York: ERIC Clearinghouse on Urban Education/Columbia Teachers College. Retrieved from http://www.eric.ed.gov/ERICDocs/data/ericdocs2sql/content_storage_01/0000019b/80/17/4a/b4.pdf

McCollum, P. (1996). *Immigrant education: Obstacles to immigrant participation in schools*. Retrieved from http://www.idra.org/Newslttr/1996/Nov/Pam.htm#Obstacles_to_Immigrant

National Opinion Research Center. (1997). *Study of opportunities for and barriers to family involvement in education*. Chicago: University of Chicago.

Northwest Regional Educational Laboratory. (2000). *Family involvement in children's education*. Retrieved from http://www2.ed.gov/pubs/FamInvolve/index.html

Perlman, C. L., & Redding, S. (2009). *Handbook on effective implementation of school improvement grants*. Lincoln, IL: Academic Development Institute.

Pinzur, M. I. (2005, August 7). Teachers' grade books will soon be a click away. *The Miami Herald*. Retrieved from http://www.miami.com/mld/miamiherald/living/education/1232082

Prichard Committee for Academic Excellence. (2002). *Summary of research on parent engagement*. Retrieved from http://www.fcps.net/fcs/docs/summary-research.pdf

Redding, S. (2000). *Parents and learning*. Brussels, Belgium: International Academy of Education. Retrieved from http://www.ibe.unesco.org/publications/EducationalPracticesSeriesPdf/prac02e.pdf

Thorkildsen, R., & Scott-Stein, M. R. (1998, December). Is parent involvement related to student achievement? Exploring the evidence. *Research Bulletin*. Retrieved from http://www.pdkintl.org/edres/resbul22.htm

U.S. Department of Education and U.S. Department of Health and Human Services. (1999). *A call to commitment: Fathers' involvement in children's learning*. Washington, DC: Author. Retrieved from http://www2.ed.gov/pubs/parents/calltocommit/index.html

Walberg, H. J., & Paik, S. J. (2004). Effective general practices. In G. Cawelti (Ed.), *Handbook of research on improving student achievement* (3rd ed.) (pp. 25-38). Arlington, VA: Educational Research Service.

Westat and Policy Studies Associates. (2001). *The longitudinal evaluation of school change and performance (LESCP) in Title I schools. Final report. Volume I: Executive summary*. Rockville, MD and Washington, DC: Authors.

Westmoreland, H., Rosenberg, H. M., Lopez, M. E., & Weiss, H. (2009). *Seeing is believing: Promising practices for how school districts promote family engagement*. Cambridge, MA: Harvard Family Research Project and Chicago, IL: National PTA. Retrieved from http://www.hfrp.org/content/download/3420/98238/file/SeeingIsBelieving.pdf

Implications for Our School: Questions for Discussion and Reflection

- How do we define family involvement? Do our practices actively encourage all these types of involvement?

- Are we collecting data—through conversations, surveys, etc.—on families' perceptions of our support for family involvement?

- Can we identify any practices that make it difficult for some families—for example, working parents or parents who don't speak English—to get involved?

- Are there any teachers in our school that have especially good relationships with families? What might we learn from them?

Follow-up and Action Items

_____

_____

_____

_____

_____

_____

_____

_____

_____

_____

_____

_____

_____

Chapter 20

A Proactive, Schoolwide Approach to Discipline

*Staff collaboration around developing and
implementing a schoolwide approach to discipline sends
a clear message to students and encourages the development
of an environment that supports learning.*

We have all walked into schools that feel qualitatively different. These are more than just "good" schools. Student-to-student and teacher-to-student interactions in the hallway are warm and positive. The buildings seem to hum with productive activity, and evidence of the high value placed on student work and learning is everywhere. In these schools, a critical connection has been made between students' academic needs and their need to feel safe, accepted, and valued.

By recognizing the power of the human being's basic needs for a sense of safety and security, self-worth, belonging, and closeness to others—and by addressing these needs every day—educators provide an environment in which students can focus on reaching their academic potential. Warm, supportive relationships make it easier for students to take the risks that are so critical to intellectual growth. One aspect of creating schools that students experience as safe and supportive is the development and maintenance of an approach to maintaining order—a positive approach to school discipline—that all students understand and that is applied consistently from classroom to classroom.

Rosenberg suggests that a problem with some schools' approaches to discipline is that a "piecemeal" approach to managing student behavior is taken. He suggests that a schoolwide approach to discipline is more effective since it

> promotes consistency by positively recognizing appropriate behaviors and acting upon inappropriate behaviors ... [and also] sets in motion a culture of recognition that reduces the risk of students slipping into situations where they misbehave to get attention." (in Brownell & Walther-Thomas, 1999, p. 109)

Students with emotional problems or those with some types of learning disabilities respond well to this type of schoolwide approach since consistency is even more critical for them than for most other students. If there is a common understanding and application of rules from classroom to classroom, it makes it simpler for them to internalize the expectations for behavior.

Experienced educators know that focused and proactive attention to discipline-related issues can help to minimize the time that school staff members need to spend reacting to inappropriate student behavior and so provide more time for teaching and learning. In part, these proactive approaches are successful because they make expectations clear and, thus, decrease the likelihood that students will "misbehave" simply because they misunderstood the boundaries between acceptable and unacceptable behavior. In addition, and because the general level of behavior is likely to be more positive, they make it easier for staff to focus on the needs of students with moderate to severe behavior problems.

Safe, Well-Managed Schools Are Characterized By:

- Commitment, on the part of all staff, to establish and maintain appropriate student behavior as an essential precondition of learning. Well-disciplined schools tend to be those in which there is a schoolwide emphasis on the importance of learning and intolerance of conditions that inhibit learning.

- High behavioral expectations. In contrast to poorly disciplined schools, staff in well-disciplined schools share and communicate high expectations for appropriate student behavior.

- Clear and broad-based rules. Rules, sanctions, and procedures are developed with input from students, are clearly specified, and are made known to everyone in the school. Researchers have found that student participation in developing and reviewing school discipline programs creates a sense of ownership and belonging. Widespread dissemination of clearly stated rules and procedures, moreover, assures that all students and staff understand what is and is not acceptable.

- A visible, supportive principal. Many poorly disciplined schools have principals who are visible only for "official" duties such as assemblies or when enforcing school discipline. In contrast, principals of well-disciplined schools tend to be very visible in hallways and classrooms, talking informally with teachers and students, speaking to them by name, and expressing interest in their activities.

- Delegation of discipline authority to teachers. Principals in well-disciplined schools take responsibility for dealing with serious infractions, but they hold teachers responsible for handling routine classroom discipline problems. They help teachers to improve their classroom management and discipline skills by arranging for staff development activities as needed.

- Close ties with communities. Researchers have generally found that well-disciplined schools are those that have a high level of communication and partnership with the communities they serve. These schools have a higher-than-average incidence of parent involvement in school functions, and communities are kept informed of school goals and activities (Cotton, 2001).

Taking a Proactive, Schoolwide Approach

Gaustad talks about why a proactive approach to discipline is important; it:

> goes beyond finding solutions to help and remediate the 5 percent or so [who chronically misbehave, and takes action] to encourage responsible behavior and to provide all students with a satisfying school experience as well as to discourage misconduct. (1992, p. 1)

After assessing discipline problems in 40 elementary and middle schools, Walker identified three "needs" that effective schoolwide programs address—prevention, efficient at-risk programs, and high-intensity interventions (in Horner, Sugai, & Horner, 2000). Horner, Sugai, and Horner have studied schools with effective disciplinary programs and have found similar "key practices"; these schools:

> invest in prevention of disruptive behavior; establish efficient systems for identifying and responding to at-risk youth early; build capacity for highly intense interventions with the small number of students with chronic behavior problems; and collect and use information about student behavior to guide ongoing improvement. (2000, p. 20)

Proactive efforts with an emphasis on prevention have proven to be key to improving discipline. Developing clearly stated expectations, understood by everyone in the school community, is the first step. The Learning First Alliance (2001) suggests that a simple message, such as "Be respectful, be safe, be kind" or "Respect yourself, respect others, respect property" should form the framework for more specific expectations. The Learning First Alliance also recommends the following:

- Rules should have a clear rationale with clear consequences for violations.

- Rules should be revisited and revised as needed.

- Staff members must also abide by school rules.

- Students and families should have significant input in determining school rules and how they are enforced.

- Students should be given the opportunity to practice effective decision making.

- Rules must be fairly and consistently enforced without regard to the class, race, gender, or other demographic characteristics of students (2001, pp. 14-15).

The Responsive Classroom approach described by Horsch, Chen, and Nelson also emphasizes the importance of rules that are understood by all and that have logical consequences for misbehavior:

> These classroom management tools are intended to instill "habits of goodness" in children and to promote and sustain community. Developed at the beginning of the school year, rules are *positive* statements that establish guidelines and expectations for classroom behavior;

they are the cornerstones of classroom life and are used to encourage conversation and problem solving related to ethical issues that arise at school. For example, first-grade rules include "Take care of friends and materials" and "Be a good listener and use your words to solve problems."

Logical consequences are nonpunitive responses to student wrongdoing. There are three categories of consequences: you break it, you fix it; loss of a privilege; and thinking time. All three are designed to be situation- and child-specific. Logical consequences are meant to support children as they learn to behave in socially responsible ways; they are also meant to help children learn how to make amends to their peers and soothe feelings when they've hurt someone. (1999, p. 224)

> *"Safe schools deal with disruptive behavior early, fairly, and effectively. To feel respected, students need to perceive discipline as being fair, consistent, and clear. Disciplinary policies . . . need to be age-appropriate, clear, and repeatedly communicated to students and parents." (Fager & Boss, 1999, p. 9)*

Developing a Differentiated Approach

Many schools are now implementing Response to Intervention, an approach that systematically identifies student instructional needs, matches interventions to these, and assesses the results of the interventions. A similar approach—Schoolwide Positive Behavioral Interventions and Supports (SWPBIS)—has been developed for use with monitoring student behavior and providing interventions intentionally selected to match a particular problem or behavior. The U.S. Department of Education Office of Special Education Programs (OSEP) Technical Assistance Center on Positive Behavioral Interventions and Supports describes key elements of SWPBIS and also the principles on which the system is based:

In general, SWPBIS emphasizes four integrated elements: (a) data for decision making, (b) measurable outcomes supported and evaluated by data, (c) practices with evidence that these outcomes are achievable, and (d) systems that efficiently and effectively support implementation of these practices.

These four elements are guided by six important principles:

- Develop a continuum of scientifically based behavior and academic interventions and supports

- Use data to make decisions and solve problems

- Arrange the environment to prevent the development and occurrence of problem behavior

- Teach and encourage prosocial skills and behaviors

- Implement evidence-based behavioral practices with fidelity and accountability

- Screen universally and monitor student performance and progress continuously (2009)

Continuum of Schoolwide Instructional and Positive Behavior

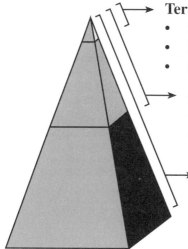

Tertiary Prevention:
- Specialized
- Individualized
- Systems for Students with High-Risk

Secondary Prevention:
- Specialized Group
- Systems for Students with At-Risk Behavior

Primary Prevention:
- School-/Classroomwide Systems for All Students, Staff, & Settings

Source: OSEP Technical Assistance Center on Positive Behavioral Interventions and Supports, 2009.

Schools implementing SWPBIS organize their interventions in a tier-like fashion, with all students "touched by" elements included as part of the primary prevention tier. "If the behavior of some students is not responsive, more intensive behavioral supports are provided, in the form of a group contingency (selected or secondary tier) or a highly individualized plan (intensive or tertiary tier)" (OSEP Technical Assistance Center on Positive Behavioral Interventions and Supports, 2009). Sandomierski, Kincaid, & Algozzine describe SWPBIS as a:

preventative approach to teaching academic and social behavior . . . the practice of teaching and reinforcing students for displaying the school wide expectations is considered to be a universal intervention, delivered to every student in every setting [Tier I]. By teaching and reinforcing expected behaviors, teachers and other professionals using [SWPBIS] increase the probability that the majority of students will act according to expectations, and acts as a proactive intervention for students with a history of problem behavior. (2009, p. 3)

> *"[It would be a] mistake to consider the creation of a safe and supportive school community as an add-on effort consisting of special programs to address specific topics such as bullying, character education, or dispute resolution. Unless the school has a clear sense of its vision and goals, along with a comprehensive plan to realize them, such programs will likely do little to positively affect the daily experiences of most students and staff." (Learning First Alliance, 2001, p. vii)*

Developing the Plan

Whether your school has serious discipline problems or is already a safe and emotionally supportive school that simply wants to get better, the starting point for its work should be developing a consensus—a vision—of what the school community would like to become. For example, a school might ask: "If we were successful, what would our school look like on a day to day basis?" After discussion, the staff would establish a few goals—such as, "students would show respect to staff and other students"—to focus their efforts.

Data from a recent survey of principals and teachers demonstrate why this type of discussion among school staff members may be particularly important. The survey found that:

> Most principals (96%) rate their school's discipline policy as excellent or good, whereas 71% of teachers rate the discipline policy as excellent or good. This is the largest gap in perception between teachers and principals for this MetLife Survey. (Markow & Cooper, 2008, p. 29)

This type of mismatch in perceptions between the principal and teachers, or perhaps among teachers, can lead to frustration as well as uneven application of school policies and procedures.

Miles (1999) suggests that schools interested in revising their approach to discipline focus their efforts with a "behavior audit." Staff, and, in some instances, students and parents are asked simple questions such as:

- How do we believe students should behave in our school?

- What are some of our problems related to behavior?

- What do we currently do to help students behave appropriately?

- What are some ways we need to improve?

A principal of a Louisiana school agrees and suggests that the first step should involve an identification of current behavior problems through staff discussion. In her view, the discussion itself is a key part of the process of moving toward a more unified approach to school discipline. For example, teachers with varying views on what constitutes a disruption in the hallways should attempt to come to consensus on the elements of acceptable vs. unacceptable behavior.

Reviewing data on past discipline problems can also be helpful. Specifically, are most of the problems occurring in the cafeteria, on the playground, or in particular hallways? Schools have also found that focusing on a few problems at first is often more effective and may also greatly improve the general atmosphere of the school fairly quickly. For example, one school identified decreasing problems in the cafeteria as a goal. The staff decided to make a simple change in procedures: Students were no longer permitted to walk to a table at the front of the room to pick up forks, napkins, etc., but, instead, raised their hands and received the needed items from a roving cafeteria aide. This one change quickly and significantly decreased instances of shoving and minor disagreements among students and greatly improved both the atmosphere in the cafeteria and students' attention in classes immediately following lunch.

Miles describes a process he has used with schools that have decided to implement a school-wide approach:

"We begin by developing positively stated schoolwide rules and procedures. These can be adapted for unique situations and operationalized for the different developmental levels of students.... Specifically, we talk about reasonable rules versus unreasonable rules. The team develops procedures, such as taking students to the lunchroom, lavatory, late entry, etc. Usually, we address procedures that have been identified by the team as contributing to student behavior problems.... We also develop consequences for rule compliance, noncompliance, and procedures for crisis.

We spend a significant amount of time developing consequences for compliance at the classroom level, team level, and schoolwide level and mechanisms as to how these consequences are to be delivered. It is the team's expectation that all teachers and staff will deliver positive feedback for following school rules and procedures such as coming prepared, using appropriate language and following directions.... [W]e encourage teams to think of ways to create a positive climate for students and faculty.

It may be hard to believe, but establishing positive consequences is the most difficult part of the planning process because many schools with high rates of behavior problems do not have a positive culture. Most often, educators tend to think of how we can punish bad behavior rather than promote appropriate behavior.

One silver lining in this situation is that the team has an easier time in the next step of the process, developing consequences of noncompliance. The team develops a hierarchy of consequences so that students know what to expect if they break rules. Developing a hierarchy of consequences requires that the team think of systematic and fair consequences for inappropriate behavior. This way teachers can avoid sending students to the office because they are "fed up" with their behavior, and administrators know that students were sent to the office for more serious behaviors and that they must respond consistently to those behaviors. Students do not get an office referral unless they have committed a certain offense.

In implementing the system of consequences, we encourage school personnel to present the consequences as the products of choices the students make. Students know if they engage in appropriate behavior they can earn certain positive rewards. On the other hand, if students choose to act inappropriately, they know what the negative consequences are. This way, students can choose to act appropriately or inappropriately. Helping students learn that consequences are the result of their behavior develops an internal locus of control that many students with cognitive and behavioral disabilities lack. Moreover, when teachers have a plan for dealing with behavior, they can move away from reactive responses to negative behavior and take a more proactive approach, reducing their stress."

Excerpted from Brownell & Walther-Thomas, 1999, pp. 110-111.

One middle school principal talked about how his school's approach to discipline decreased the number of referrals for intimidation or fighting from 1,332 to 402 in 1 year, with referrals for fighting after the change almost nonexistent. In his view, there are five simple keys to the success of his school's approach:

- "Consistency—Consequences are the same for everyone.

- Learning—Students are encouraged to make good choices both in and out of school.

- Parents, students, and community members—They play an important part in initiating, implementing, and evaluating the program, and their involvement has fostered universal buy-in.

- Real-life consequences—They involve law enforcement in and out of school.

- The focus is on the problem of inappropriate choice, not the student. Students, parents, teachers, and administrators are constantly reminded that good students make bad choices and there are logical consequences for inappropriate choices in school as well as outside school." (Malesich, 1994, pp. 39-40)

Lawrence and Olvey (1994) remind principals to set aside time to explain the school discipline plan to new teachers as well as to new students. Although this seems like "just good common sense," they had worked with school staffs that did not completely understand the school's plan and, thus, were enforcing rules inconsistently.

Gaustad highlights the importance of collaboration in all phases of the creation and maintenance of a policy:

> Written policies should be developed with input from everyone who will be affected by them. Teacher input is especially important because their support is crucial to a plan's success . . . as is parent and community involvement and input. Once developed, discipline policies must be communicated to staff, students, parents, and community. But a policy on paper is meaningless in itself. Ongoing administrative support, inservice training in new techniques, continued communication, and periodic evaluation and modification are needed to adapt a school discipline plan to the changing needs of the school community. (1992, p. 3)

Many schools, even those at the elementary level, are also working to include students in the development of schoolwide plans for three primary reasons. First, students who feel that their opinions have been considered may be more likely to behave in accordance with the rules. Second, discussions among students and staff while developing rules and consequences may help students to better understand them. Finally, it provides students with an opportunity to practice participation in a community, a skill that can be important to them through life. Schimmel (1997) provides two examples of the ways that schools involve students:

- In one middle school, all students participate during their first week in a structured process of rule-making that uses small group discussion, emphasizes responsibility and cooperation, identifies positive as well as negative consequences of student behavior, and culminates in a formal ceremony in which the teacher and each student sign their "Classroom Constitution."

Avoiding the "Traps"

Developing an effective approach to schoolwide discipline is a complex process. Horner, Sugai, and Horner identify what they describe as "traps" around which a school staff needs to navigate as they design an effective disciplinary system:

- Trap No. 1: Getting tough is enough. (In reality, it is simply not enough to get tough without a proactive system for teaching and supporting appropriate behavior.)

- Trap No. 2: Focusing on the difficult few. (Although an effective disciplinary system must address the small number of students who engage in chronic and intense disruptive behavior, procedures must be in place to build schoolwide social competence.)

- Trap No. 3: Looking for the quick fix. (Building effective schoolwide discipline takes time. A reasonable period to design and establish an effective disciplinary system is from 3 to 5 years.)

- Trap No 4: Finding one powerful trick. (Schoolwide discipline is not achieved through a single strategy. It must include components for defining and teaching behavioral expectations, rapid and low-effort support for students who continue to display disruptive behavior, and high-intensity support for students with high-intensity behavior problems.)

- Trap No. 5: Believing someone has the solution. (An effective system will be designed to meet a school's specific needs—identified through active self-assessment—and be continuously evaluated and changed to meet changing needs and goals.)

- Trap No. 6: Believing more is better. (Instead of accumulating more and sometimes inconsistent programs and approaches to deal with disciplinary problems, it is more effective to eliminate practices that are not working and very carefully match new practices to specific school needs).

Excerpted from Homer, Sugai, & Homer, 2000, pp. 22-23.

- In a Massachusetts elementary school, a principal uses community meetings that focus on the rights and responsibilities of members of the school community to establish rules at the beginning of the year and to develop the capacity to collaboratively solve school problems throughout the year.

The Relationship Between a Schoolwide Approach to Discipline and Instruction

Simply developing a system of rules and consequences is not enough. For example, elementary school children need to be instructed on classroom rules and procedures through modeling and practice. In Cotton's view:

> effective management, especially in the early grades, is more an instructional than a disciplinary enterprise. Effective managers socialize their students to the student role through instruction and modeling. It is important that these teachers be consistent in articulating

demands and monitoring compliance, but the most important thing is to make sure that students know what to do in the first place. (2001)

Kay and Ryan (2000) identify three elements that signal classroom-based support for a schoolwide approach to discipline:

- Teachers teach a social skills curriculum to help students understand and use expected behaviors.

- Teachers encourage suitable behavior by recognizing students when they behave appropriately. All classroom rules and consequences are clearly stated so that all students understand them.

- Options are available for children who learn core academic material at a different pace, or in a different way from the majority of their classmates.

Research has also identified links between effective classroom management, lower levels of disruptive behavior, and, importantly, higher levels of student learning. Included among the management strategies are elements of good teaching, including effective questioning/recitation strategies, learner accountability, smooth transitions, and teacher "with-it-ness" (Wang, Haertel, & Walberg, 1993/1994). The American Federation of Teachers agrees:

A teacher who has mastered classroom management skills keeps students constructively engaged and learning from the moment they enter the room. A good classroom manager carefully plans everything that occurs in the classroom, from the seating arrangement to instructions for children who finish planned activities early....

The heart of effective classroom management rests on ensuring that the instructional techniques, classroom arrangement, and classroom rules and procedures are all well thought out and supportive of the instructional program and students' learning. Instructional techniques will vary widely depending on the material being taught and the age and ability of the students.... While there may be limitations on the physical arrangement of a classroom, the most effective classroom managers have arranged their room to minimize disruptions and support instructional techniques. (n.d.)

The Role of the Principal

Leading by personal example and by effective policies, Gaustad sees the successful principal as a:

highly visible model...engaging in "management by walking around," greeting students and teachers and informally monitoring possible problem areas. (1992, p. 2)

Horner, Sugai, and Horner also emphasize the importance of effective leadership to developing and maintaining a schoolwide approach to discipline:

Supporting Appropriate Student Behavior in the Classroom

- *Holding and communicating high expectations for student learning and behavior.* Through the personal warmth and encouragement they express to students and the classroom requirements they establish, effective manager/teachers make sure that students know they are expected to learn well and behave appropriately.

- *Establishing and clearly teaching classroom rules and procedures.* Effective managers teach behavioral rules and classroom routines in much the same way as they teach instructional content, and they review these frequently at the beginning of the school year and periodically thereafter. Classroom rules are posted in elementary classrooms.

- *Specifying consequences and their relation to student behavior.* Effective managers are careful to explain the connection between students' misbehavior and teacher-imposed sanctions. This connection, too, is taught and reviewed as needed.

- *Enforcing classroom rules promptly, consistently, and equitably.* Effective managers respond quickly to misbehavior, respond in the same way at different times, and impose consistent sanctions regardless of the gender, race, or other personal characteristics of misbehaving students.

- *Sharing with students the responsibility for classroom management.* Effective managers work to foster in students a sense of belonging and self discipline, rather than viewing discipline as something imposed from the outside.

- *Maintaining a brisk pace for instruction and making smooth transitions between activities.* Effective managers keep things moving in their classrooms, which increases learning as well as reducing the likelihood of misbehavior.

- *Monitoring classroom activities and providing feedback and reinforcement.* Effective managers observe and comment on student behavior, and they reinforce appropriate behavior through the provision of verbal, symbolic, and tangible rewards.

Exerpted from Cotton, 2001.

We know schoolwide discipline requires the sustained use of effective classroom and behavior management practices by teachers, staff members, and families. However, we also know that workshops on classroom management procedures, anger management training, and crisis management strategies will produce minimal effects without clear, consistent leadership. (2000, p. 20)

In Summary

A schoolwide approach to discipline, with consistent expectations for behavior classroom to classroom, helps establish the environment needed for a productive focus on learning. Beginning with discussions about these expectations helps to ensure that everyone is "on the same page" and also provides a useful learning experience for students.

References

American Federation of Teachers. (n.d.). *Implement effective classroom management practices.* Washington, DC: Author. Retrieved from http://archive.aft.org/topics/discipline/techniques. htm

Brownell, M. T., & Walther-Thomas, C. (1999, November). An interview with Dr. Michael Rosenberg: Preventing school discipline problems schoolwide. *Intervention in School & Clinic, 35*(2), 108-112.

Cotton, K. (2001). Schoolwide and classroom discipline. *School Improvement Research Series.* Portland, OR: Northwest Regional Educational Laboratories. Retrieved from www.nwrel. org/scpd/sirs/5/cu9.html

Fager, J., & Boss, S. (1999). *Focused discussion…Peaceful schools.* Honolulu, HI: Pacific Resources for Education and Learning. Retrieved from http://www.eric.ed.gov/ERICDocs/data/ ericdocs2sql/content_storage_01/0000019b/80/16/07/8b.pdf

Gaustad, J. (1992). *School Discipline* [ERIC Digest]. Eugene, Oregon: ERIC Clearinghouse on Educational Management. Retrieved from http://www.ericdigests.org/1992-1/school.htm

Hartzell, G. N., & Petrie, T. A. (1992, July/August). The principal and discipline: Working with school structures, teachers, and students. *The Clearing House*, 376-380.

Horner, R. H., Sugai, G., & Horner, H. F. (2000, February). A schoolwide approach to student discipline. *The School Administrator*, 20-23.

Horsch, P., Chen, J., & Nelson, D. (1999, November). Rules and rituals: Tools for creating a respectful, caring learning community. *Phi Delta Kappan*, 223-227.

Kay, P., & Ryan, K. (2000, Winter). Prevention strategies for the elementary school classroom. *Behavioral interventions: Creating a safe environment in our schools.* Bethesda, MD: National Association of School Psychologists.

Lawrence, P. A., & Olvey, S. K. (1994, July). Discipline: A skill not a punishment. *The American School Board Journal*, 31-32.

Learning First Alliance. (2001). *Every child learning: Safe and supportive schools.* Baltimore: Author.

Malesich, R. F. (1994, February). Making schools safe for students. *Schools in the Middle*, 38-40.

Markow, D., & Cooper, M. (2008). *The MetLife Survey of the American teacher: A survey of teachers, principals, and students.* New York: MetLife, Inc.

Miles, B. H. (1999, May/June). Getting everybody on the same page: Conducting a behavior audit. *The High School Magazine*, 30-32.

OSEP Technical Assistance Center on Positive Behavioral Interventions and Supports. (2009). *What is School-Wide Positive Behavioral Interventions & Supports?* Retrieved from http://www. pbis.org/school/what_is_swpbs.aspx

Sandomierski, T., Kincaid, D., & Algozzine, B. (2009). *Response to Intervention and Positive Behavior Support: Brothers from different mothers or sisters from different misters?* Retrieved from http://flpbs.fmhi.usf.edu/FLPBS%20and%20RtI%20article.pdf

Schimmel, D. (1997, February). Traditional rule-making and the subversion of citizenship education. *Social Education*, 70-74.

Wang, M. C., Haertel, G. D., & Walberg, H. J. (1993/1994, December/January). What helps students learn? *Educational Leadership*, 74-79.

Implications for Our School: Questions for Discussion and Reflection

- Do we have a schoolwide plan for managing discipline? If so, is it effective or are any of the "traps" mentioned by Homer, Sugai, and Homer on p. 231 a problem for us?

- Do students experience consistent approaches to discipline across classrooms in our schools?

- Have we developed a differentiated approach to discipline such as that described in the Positive Behavioral Interventions and Supports (PBIS) model?

- Are there any persistent behavior problems in our school? For example, are there physical areas such as stairwells where a disproportionate share of behavior problems occur? What could we do about these?

Follow-up and Action Items

_____

_____

_____

_____

_____

_____

_____

_____

_____

_____

_____

_____

ERS ORDER FORM FOR RELATED RESOURCES

| Quantity | Item Number | Title | Price per Item | | | Total Price |
			Base Price	ERS Individual Subscriber Discount Price	ERS School District Subscriber Discount Price	
	0784	*The Principal's Playbook: Tackling School Improvement*	$30	$22.50	$15	
	0785	*Crucial Conversations About America's Schools*	$20	$15	$10	
	0538	*Handbook of Research on Improving Student Achievement, Third Edition*	$44	$33	$22	
		Shipping and Handling** (Add the greater of $4.50 or 10% of purchase price.)				
		Express Delivery** (Add $20 for second-business-day service.)				
	**Please double for international orders.				TOTAL PRICE:	

SATISFACTION GUARANTEED! If you are not satisfied with an ERS resource, return it in its original condition within 30 days of receipt and we will give you a full refund.

Visit us online at www.ers.org for a complete listing of resources!

Method of payment:

☐ Check enclosed (payable to ERS)   ☐ P.O. enclosed (Purchase order #_____)

☐ MasterCard   ☐ VISA   ☐ American Express

Name on Card: _____ Credit Card #:_____

Expiration Date: _____ Signature: _____

Ship to: (please print or type)   ☐ Dr.   ☐ Mr.   ☐ Mrs.   ☐ Ms.

Name: _____ Position: _____

School District or Agency: _____ ERS Subscriber ID#: _____

Street Address: _____

City, State, Zip: _____

Telephone: _____ Fax: _____

Email: _____

Return completed order form to:
Educational Research Service • 1001 North Fairfax Street, Suite 500 • Alexandria, VA 22314-1587
Phone: 703-243-2100 • Toll Free Phone: 800-791-9308 • Fax: 703-243-1985 • Toll Free Fax: 800-791-9309
Email: ers@ers.org • Web site: www.ers.org